Afro-*Eccentricity*

By the Same Author

Edward Said and the Religious Effects of Culture (2000)

Also Published by Palgrave Macmillan

Black Religion: Malcolm X, Julius Lester, and Jan Willis (2008)

Afro-*Eccentricity*

Beyond the Standard Narrative of Black Religion

William David Hart

palgrave
macmillan

AFRO-*ECCENTRICITY*

First published in 2011 by
PALGRAVE MACMILLAN®
in the United States—a division of St. Martin's Press LLC,
175 Fifth Avenue, New York, NY 10010.

Where this book is distributed in the UK, Europe and the rest of the world, this is by Palgrave Macmillan, a division of Macmillan Publishers Limited, registered in England, company number 785998, of Houndmills, Basingstoke, Hampshire RG21 6XS.

Palgrave Macmillan is the global academic imprint of the above companies and has companies and representatives throughout the world.

Palgrave® and Macmillan® are registered trademarks in the United States, the United Kingdom, Europe and other countries.

ISBN: 978–0–230–11157–8

Library of Congress Cataloging-in-Publication Data

Hart, William D., 1957–
Afro-eccentricity : beyond the standard narrative of black religion / William David Hart.
p. cm.
ISBN-13: 978–0–230–11157–8 (hardback)
ISBN-10: 0–230–11157–2 ()
1. African Americans—Religion. I. Title.

BL2525.H37 2011
200.89′96073—dc22 2010043077

A catalogue record of the book is available from the British Library.

Design by Newgen Imaging Systems (P) Ltd., Chennai, India.

First edition: April 2011

10 9 8 7 6 5 4 3 2 1

Printed and bound in Great Britain by
CPI Antony Rowe, Chippenham and Eastbourne

To all the generations: ascending and descending.

Contents

Preface

I regard the religious imagination as cultural artifact, which in turn is a distal product of evolution by natural selection, genetic drift, and related processes. Equipped with the capacity for highly symbolic language, humans developed intense forms of sociality that funded complex linguistically inflected cultures. A product of that culture, religion (religions and the religious) is the invention of *meaning-constructing mortals*. The order of explanation runs from that order of reality called the human imagination to artifacts such as g/God (God and the gods), the holy, William James' "more," the sacred, and the transcendent. In ontic terms, these "realities" are imaginary. God exceeds our concepts only because that very claim is our concept. We conceptualize god as ineffable and transcendent, advocate humility before a reality that exceeds our comprehension, and assert the arrogance of imagining that concepts can capture god. Thus we imagine god as a reality whom we cannot fully imagine. God is wholly our concept. Those who hold the opposing view subscribe to a religious version of the "myth of the given": the notion that religion is a response to the promptings of infra- and/or superstructural realities that are independent of the human imagination.[1] Though religion has no overarching transhistorical unity, underlying transcultural essence, or perennial identity, it does have discursive unities—objects, concepts, themes, and subject positions—that we recognize.[2] This discourse is primarily, though not exclusively, the creation of scholars of religion.[3] It is within the context of this discourse that scholars (and nonscholars) argue, agree, and disagree about the very nature of religion. As an interdisciplinary field of study, religion is a history of disagreement. But that disagreement occurs against the background of a remarkable amount of agreement.[4] It is precisely this discursivity that enables our agreement and disagreement.

In this light, my use of "God" is purposefully unconventional and inconsistent. Despite convention, I regard the English word God as a proper name for the Christian god and thus as a false generic. I take the generic and the proper name to be one and the same as a matter of practice. I signal my distrust of the convention by not capitalizing the word except where it is the first word in a sentence, when quoting others, or for emphasis. When referring to "God and the gods," I use the construction "g/God." Conversely, I capitalize "Black Religion" not to signify an underlying, nondiscursive "given" but to signal to the reader that this is my concept and I take responsibility for it.

A note on the genealogy of this book: originally, the material that it comprises was imagined as Part II of a longer book. However, readers suggested that each part had its own integrity and should be published separately. Part I of that imagined book was published as *Black Religion: Malcolm X, Julius Lester, and Jan Willis* (Palgrave 2008). The recommendation to publish separate books was good advice. Still, there are significant continuities between the two texts. The concept of Afro-*Eccentricity* is an important trope in both. The account of black religious narratives in the first text receives more extensive treatment in this text. In fact this material originally appeared as "Three Narratives of Black Religion" in the anthology *Companion to African American Studies* (2006), edited by Lewis and Jane Gordon.

Chapter 1

Afro-*Eccentricity*: An Introduction

Against the Standard Narrative

As I use the term, Black Religion is a discursive artifact that emerged from the tumult of the black freedom movement of the 1960s and early 1970s. As an academic term of art, a "covering term," I regard Black Religion as a proper name, hence the capitalization. Black Religion is part of a cultural shift in which people of African descent began referring to themselves as "black" and "Afro-American." This same shift produced the black arts movement in the mid-1960s and the black studies movement in the late 1960s.

While there are various ways of construing the academic discourse of Black Religion, I see three developmental moments of emergence, critique, and reconstruction. Though overlapping, especially the moments of emergence and critique, they are also temporally and, perhaps, ethically and politically discrepant. As there are no absolute beginnings, I take Joseph Washington's *Black Religion* (1964) as the "zero point" of emergence for the story I tell. However, I regard the intellectual movement leading to the founding of the Society for the Study of Black Religion in 1970 and C. Eric Lincoln's Series on Black Religion as the gestational events in the emergence of Black Religion as a distinctive and self-conscious discourse. Black Religion had a male-centered birth: dominated by masculine priorities and the ideological and practical subjection of women. These perspectives, to be sure, included an interest in black religious expression across genders, though they reveal a certain obliviousness about, if not leeriness of, a then emerging second-wave feminism. Two subjects of this study, Charles H. Long and William R. Jones, were founding members of this discourse; other subjects, Cornel West and Theophus Smith, are part of the "intellectual commonwealth" created by that (civil rights, black power, liberation-oriented) discursive conjuncture.

In this text, I explore the Standard Narrative of Black Religion *and*, under the term "Afro-*Eccentricity*," critical revisions and alternatives. The Standard Narrative is a common if not a commonsense way of constructing Black Religion. Within this narrative, Black Church and Black Religion are synonymous. Christianity in general and its institutional manifestation as church is the template for understanding what Black Religion is. When not mapped onto this template, other expressions of black religiosity are screened out of view. Black Church is a "terministic screen": it allows us to see certain things and prevents us from seeing others. Afro-*Eccentricity* is a tropological response to the Standard Narrative of Black Religion and the excluded field. As I remarked in *Black Religion: Malcolm X, Julius Lester, and Jan Willis* (Palgrave Macmillan, 2008): "Afro-*Eccentricity* is a critical pun and trope [a burlesque of the Afrocentric idea] that mimics, underscores, and reminds us of the difference within the same, the manifold within the apparent uniformity of American black people." Synonymous with difference, nonidentity, and the "nonconforming" black other, Afro-*Eccentricity* "...refers to ways of 'being black' that are off-center, 'off-color,' and outside the statistical if not 'the' axiological norm." On this view, the Afro-*Eccentric* other is neither confused, nor pretending, nor "passing" for black. Rather, s/he exemplifies the diversity of subject positions that a postmodern subject in a postindustrial world can (and does) occupy.[1]

The End of the Essential Black Subject

Afro-*Eccentricity* has much in common with Victor Anderson's "ontological blackness," which he defines as a tendency to reify race, making an objective, independent reality out of a historical contingency. "Ontological blackness is a covering term that connotes categorical, essentialist and representational languages depicting black life and experience."[2] Anderson tracks the role of ontological blackness in black identity formation, problematizes the representational role of such language in cultural studies, and criticizes the recapitulation of the European cult of heroic genius. If white supremacy ontologizes whiteness, making it a metaphysical category, then ontological blackness is the blackness that whiteness created.[3] Thus the cult of black heroic genius, where black people bask en masse in the reflected glory of talented black individuals or, on the flip side, feel shame in the presence of black Philistines, the proverbial black criminal, and ne'er-do-wells.[4] Anderson advocates going beyond ontological blackness because of its incompatibility with the dispersed, plural, and nonessentializable realities of postmodern black life. This reads a lot like Afro-*Eccentricity*. Anderson's analysis is particularly important since its target, like mine, is religious discourse. Finally, Anderson proposes the aesthetic category of "the grotesque" as better than the cult of black heroic genius for comprehending the internal ambiguities and complexities of black life.[5] In short, the aesthetic category of the grotesque exposes the untenability of romantic-essentialist conceptions of black identity, unity, and destiny.[6]

Anderson's analysis is part of a recent trend in black critical thought that anticipates and conditions my notion of Afro-*Eccentricity*. A highly influential current in this rethinking of black identity is found in the work of Stuart Hall, the Afro-British Marxist who famously proclaimed "the end of the innocent notion of the black essential subject."[7] Hall attributes this event to the encounter between black cultural politics and the Eurocentric discourses of poststructuralism and postmodernism. Even though he is writing specifically about the black British context, most interpreters take his account as equally applicable to Blackamericans. Hall remarks:

> What is at issue here is the recognition of the extraordinary diversity of subject positions, social experiences and cultural identities which compose the category 'black'; that is, the recognition that 'black' is essentially a politically and culturally *constructed* category, which cannot be grounded in a set of fixed trans-cultural or transcendental racial categories and which therefore has no guarantee in nature.[8]

In other words, essentialist notions of black identity associated with Afrocentricity and most forms of Black Nationalism are moribund if not dead. (There are some nonessentialist, " commonsense," critically self-conscious, and reflective forms that are not subject to this fate.) Equally dead is the belief that a particular politics, aesthetic sensibility, or religious orientation should follow from the affirmation of blackness. This emerging, plural, internally diverse black subjectivity that Hall began to identify in the 1980s undermines forms of cultural politics that are based on the notion that "all black people are good or indeed…the *same*."[9] A further consequence of this emergent plurivocal black subjectivity is that heteronormative masculinity is necessarily destabilized; it no longer norms, determines, and positions black subjects in a hierarchical and exclusive way. My notion of Afro-*Eccentricity* dovetails with Hall's account of the postcontemporary black subject.

Preceding Hall's work is the foundational work of black feminist and womanist critics who describe their experience in terms of the "simultaneity" and "interlocking nature of oppression" as a way of accenting the intersection of various currents in the formation of black female identity. Indeed, Kimberlé Crenshaw coined the term "intersectionality" to describe this phenomenon. Most of her work has dealt with the intersection of race and gender that arises in the "flesh and bone" of violence against women of color. Crenshaw argues that antiracist discourse is normatively male and that feminist discourse is normatively white, the consequence of which is the erasure of black women's experiences. It is precisely the intersecting nature of racism and sexism that the normative discourse cannot see. She remarks that:

> Among the most troubling political consequences of the failure of antiracist and feminist discourses to address the intersection of racism and patriarchy is the fact that, to the extent they forward the interest of people of color and "women," respectively, one analysis often implicitly denies the validity of the other. The failure of feminism to interrogate race means that the resistance strategies of feminism will often replicate and reinforce the subordination of people of color, and the failure of antiracism to interrogate patriarchy means that antiracism will frequently reproduce the subordination of women. These mutual elisions present a particularly difficult political dilemma for women of color. Adopting either analysis constitutes a denial of a fundamental dimension of our subordination and works to preclude the development of a political discourse that more fully empowers women of color.[10]

Though she gave it a name, Crenshaw did not invent intersectional analysis. Like most complex social practices, it does not have a singular or absolute beginning but in fact has many mothers, so to speak. Sojourner Truth, in her disputes with white female abolitionists and suffragettes and with black male leaders such as Frederick Douglass, engaged in what, retrospectively, we can call intersectional critique. Comparing Truth to her contemporary Francis Ellen Watkins Harper, Nell Irvin Painter claims that Harper was a "womanist" critic who engaged in a form of intersectional critique that was more explicit and pointed.[11] Recently, this form of analysis has been associated most closely with the work of Patricia Hill Collins, which accents "the intersection of multiple structures of domination" in the lives of black women.[12] Through their focus on "the interlocking nature of oppression," according to Collins, black feminists shift the target of investigation from race, gender, or class as discrete elements to "the links among these systems." Thus the investigation circumvents approaches that prioritize one form of oppression by assimilating and subordinating the others. The intersection itself and the creative, productive transactional novelty (superject) it encodes becomes the subject of interpretation.[13] In addition, this shift in focus also implies a different, "humanistic vision" of social order. Collins puts it this way: "Black feminists who see the simultaneity of oppression affecting Black women appear to be more sensitive to how these same oppressive systems affect Afro-American men, people of color, women, and the dominant group itself."[14] While this claim seems intuitively true, its truth is ultimately an empirical matter. In an updated and extended version of her theory, Collins refers to a "matrix of domination" in which race, gender, and class are axes while personal biography, community, and social institutions are levels of oppression and resistance. An intersectional analysis, she claims, which is attentive to the matrix of domination, rejects additive notions of oppression rooted in dichotomous, Eurocentric, and masculinist modes of thought.[15] As an inclusive model, intersectionality "provides the conceptual space needed for each individual to see that she or he is *both* a member of multiple dominant groups and a member of multiple subordinate groups."[16] On my view, this latter insight is the most important contribution.

With its focus on black identity formation at the conjunction of race, religion, and political orientation, one might think of Afro-*Eccentricity* as a riff on intersectionality. To be sure, the Afro-*Eccentric* narrators I explore in this text reproduce *some* aspects of the Standard Narrative of Black Religion as the Black Church. But they are Afro-*Eccentric* as well. To reiterate, Afro-*Eccentricity* is a trope for ways of being that deviate from the normativity of the Black Church narrative: a critical pun on the notion of Afrocentricity, a burlesque of the way that this notion reproduces the Standard Narrative under the figure of the "ancestor." These Afro-*Eccentric* narratives—which I extract and construct from the works of Charles H. Long, William R. Jones, Cornel West, and Theophus Smith—are at their best and go beyond the Standard Narrative when denying a normative relationship between Christianity and black identity.

Itinerary

Chapters 2 and 3 address overlapping versions of the Standard Narrative of Black Religion.[37] Chapter 2, "Three Narratives of Black Religion," provides a brief account of the interlocking nature of what I call the Church, the Soul, and the Ancestor narratives that compose the Standard Narrative of Black Religion. Though these narratives overlap in significant ways and are competitive, they are also discrepant in foci and emphasis. The Ancestor Narrative, which is the most discrepant of the three, has both Afrocentric and Afro-*Eccentric* versions. I regard the Afro-*Eccentric* version as an effort to break free of the Standard Narrative of which the Church, the Soul, and the Ancestor narratives are constitutive. In this light, chapter 3, "Art and the Ancestor Narrative," extends my analysis of the Afrocentric/Afro-*Eccentric* duality within the Ancestor Narrative through a reading of Paule Marshall's *Praisesong for the Widow*. I contend that this novel is the best artistic representation of the Ancestor Narrative ever written. I show how Marshall's artistry both reproduces and dislocates the Standard Narrative through its appeal to the traditions of African ancestors on both sides of the Atlantic.

Chapters 4 through 7 deal with figures who contest, with varying degrees of intentionality and success, the Standard Narrative of Black Religion as the Black Church. Chapter 4, "The Archaeologist," explores Charles H. Long's proposal for the study of Afro-American religion. Perhaps the most innovative thinker in black religious studies, Long counterpoises the metaphor of "opacity" to the Enlightenment metaphor of transparency. The lived realities of the "opaque ones"—slaves, the dispossessed, and the subjects of genocide—challenge the metaphor of transparency that relies too heavily on ocular metaphors of unencumbered vision. The reality of the opaque ones often lies in the blind spots of the Enlightenment spectator. Thus the tendency of enlightened moderns, with their transparent colonial gaze, to regard cultural translation as simple and unproblematic, as if we are all liberal subjects under the skin. Painful relationships of domination and subordination introduce forms of opaqueness that the enlightened spectator does not see. Thus the opacity of reality demands theories of knowledge and religion that are fine-tuned to the experiences of *suffering subjects*. As I interpret Long's argument, opacity is a necessary supplement to transparency.

Long's methodological proposal for the study of Afro-American religion, which presupposes the guiding metaphor of opacity, provides the template for my analysis in subsequent chapters. In chapter 5, "The Renegade," I explore William R. Jones' humanistic challenge to the Standard Narrative. Chapter 6, "The Prophet," assesses Cornel West's prophetic construction of black theology and religion. In chapter 7, "The Conjuror," I evaluate Theophus Smith's conjurational spirituality. While chapters 5 through 7 have distinctive themes, perspectives, foci, and methodologies and thus stand on their own, there are intertextual relations among them. Analyses in earlier chapters have a cumulative relation to later chapters. At the same time, there is a proleptical element: in analyzing Jones, I anticipate my analysis of West, and in assessing Smith, I look back to my analysis of Jones. In all cases, I refer to Long and his proposal for black religious studies.

Chapter 2

Three Narratives of Black Religion

Introduction

Blackamericans are truly American, omni-American.[1] They share America's virtues and vices, including the arrogance that comes with superpower status. As a consequence, Blackamericans construct the Black Atlantic —the world that the transatlantic slave trade made—in their own image. "African American" becomes a false generic for the Black Atlantic. I object to and strive to avoid this nationalist parochialism even though my account is about Black Religion in the United States of America. If black is a more expansive term than African American, then religion is a more expansive term than church. As the Black Atlantic cannot be reduced to the imagination of black natives of the United States, Black Religion cannot be isolated from African-derived forms of religiosity. The second reason for my preference of nomenclature is the danger of amnesia and nostalgia. The term "black" accents the irremediable wound of slavery, which constitutes us as black people. Our history as black people, as opposed to Yoruba, Kongo, Ibo, or hundreds of distinct nations, tribes, and ethnicities inhabiting the African continent, effectively begins with the horror, pain, and ugliness of the transatlantic slave trade. We are the descendants of enslaved people. Though this is a historical fact and not an ontological claim, accenting the agency of slave traffickers who enslaved Africans as if that did not result in an objective condition of slavery and everything that it entails is a kind of euphemism that makes slavery—a very bad situation, a condition of chronic violence, dishonor, and social death[2]—appear to be better than it was. Resistance to this fact is a form of amnesia (forgetfulness) and nostalgia (false memory) that undermines the prospects of Blackamericans in the only country that we know and dishonors the world that our slave ancestors made.[3]

Black Religion is a discursive artifact, a construction, a conceptual tool for categorizing a heterogeneous ensemble of cultural practices in the Black Atlantic. By discourse I mean loosely what Michel Foucault means: a complex relation between words and things that produces, disciplines, and normalizes subjects. I refer to the very dispositions, practices, and ways of living through which subjects come to be and their notions of normality are constructed. To avoid any confusion, I should emphasize my use of Foucault as a rough guide, useful for mapping the territory. Theories travel best when thoroughly digested and warped according to the specificity of one's need rather than followed slavishly. So I acknowledge the "conceptual violence" in my possibly "heterodox" usage. In this account, I provide a tropic and discursive analysis of several texts, many of which have played an important role in the construction of Black Religion, by analyzing them in relation to various narratives characteristic of the discourse. Thus I indentify three rival, interdependent, and discrepant narratives of Black Religion: the Soul of Black Folk, Black Church, and Ancestor Piety—the latter of which has Afrocentric and Afro-*Eccentric* versions.

Black Religion as the "Soul" of Black Folk

W. E. B. DuBois' "Of the Faith of the Fathers" is the prototype for studies of Black Religion. As chapter 10 of *The Souls of Black Folk*, it establishes the following conventions: that religion is the essence, genius, or soul of black folk; that this religion of African origin was transformed by slavery, Jim Crow, and Christianity; that "the Preacher, the Music, and the Frenzy" are the distinctive characteristics; that the church is the most important institution and social center in the black community; that the church teeters between resistance and submission to white supremacy, between "manliness" and "effeminacy" (accommodation and resistance). Much of this conventional wisdom is still evident in studies of Black Religion. Black Religion as the Soul of Black Folk prefigures—in both enabling and disabling ways—the Black Church and Ancestor Piety narratives.

DuBois' brief narrative provides a historical sociology, existential phenomenology, and metaphysics that continue to influence our understanding of Black Religion. The history of black religious studies, to a great extent, is a series of footnotes to "Of the Faith of the Fathers."

Metaphysically, within this interpretive tradition, Black Religion is the preeminent revelation of the character, "soul," or "inner ethical life," as DuBois puts it, of black people. Phenomenologically, Black Religion is distinguished by its theatricality, mesmerizing music, kinetic orality, passionate physicality, and combative spirituality.[4] As historical sociology, Black Religion is bifurcated geographically between north and south, dispositionally between militant church and submissive church, and politically between fashionable pursuits and hard questions. DuBois, who calls the Negro "a religious animal—a being of that deep emotional nature which turns instinctively toward the supernatural," provides a summary account of the historical-sociological foundations of Black Religion. I quote at length:

> [W]e must realize that no such institution as the Negro church could rear itself without definite historical foundations. These foundations we can find if we remember that the social history of the Negro did not start in America. He was brought from a definite social environment,—the polygamous clan life under the headship of the chief and the potent influence of the priest. His religion was nature-worship, with profound belief in invisible surrounding influences, good and bad, and his worship was through incantation and sacrifice. The first rude change in this life was the slave ship and the West Indian sugar-fields. The plantation organization replaced the clan and the tribe, and the white master replaced the chief with far greater and more despotic powers. Forced and long continued toil became the rule of life, the old ties of blood relationship and kinship disappeared, and instead of the family appeared a new polygamy and polyandry, which, in some cases, almost reached promiscuity. It was a terrific social revolution, and yet some traces were retained of the former group life, and the chief remaining institution was the priest or Medicine-man. He early appeared on the plantation and found his function as the healer of the sick, the interpreter of the Unknown, the comforter of the sorrowing, the supernatural avenger of wrong, and the one who rudely but picturesquely expressed the longing, disappointment, and resentment of a stolen and oppressed people. Thus, as bard, physician, judge, and priest, within the narrow limits allowed by the slave system, rose the Negro preacher, and under him the first Afro-American institution, the Negro church. This church was not at first by any means Christian nor definitely organized; rather it was an adaptation and mingling of heathen rites among the members of each plantation, and roughly designated as Voodooism. Associations with masters, missionary effort and motives of expediency gave these rites an early veneer of Christianity, and after the lapse of many generations the Negro church became Christian.[5]

The Souls of Black Folk was originally published in 1903. DuBois, quite understandably, was a product of the Victorian era and the racial and religious discourses of his time. Some of what he says and how he says it will no doubt offend contemporary sensibilities. While one might quibble here and supplement there, this is still the dominant narrative of Black Religion.

As Kwame Anthony Appiah has argued, DuBois' notion of racial identity is indebted to Herder's claim that each race has a *volksgeist*, a distinctive spirit irradiating all of its undertakings.[6] DuBois describes this spirit variously. In "The Sorrow Songs," he speaks of three gifts of black folk: "a gift of story and song," "the gift of sweat and brawn," and "a gift of the spirit." These gifts have a Herderian—hereditary and essentialist—sense. They express the racial character of black people no less than thorns and a pleasing aroma express the traits of roses. These "gifts of black folk" are the leaven, salt, and spice of American life. For, as DuBois asks rhetorically, "Would America have been America without her Negro people?" These gifts seem inextricably connected to the sorrow of the Sorrow Songs—spirituals, the antecedents of the blues. And yet, they transcend sorrow, expressing an undying, sweat-stained and blood-drenched hope.[7] They express black *religio* as both *relegere* (to bind) and *religare* (to retrace). *Relegere* is piety toward the ways of one's ancestors, those rites that gather black people together by retracing old ways. In this sense, *religio* is *traditio*. In contrast, *religare* refers to those rites of desire and fear that tie black people together by tying them to the gods.[8]

In these Sorrow Songs, where *religio* is both *relegere* and *religare*, the play of presence and absence is recorded. DuBois speaks of the presence of mother and child and the absence of father, the absence of "wooing and wedding" and of "deep successful love." Only a sorrow this great could have given rise to so great a hope. Such are the Sorrow Songs: "the most original and beautiful expression of human life and longing yet born on American soil."[9] According to Howard Thurman, "These songs were rightly called 'Sorrow Songs.' They were born of tears and suffering greater than any formula of expression. And yet the authentic note of triumph in God rings out trumpet-tongued!

> Oh, nobody knows de trouble I've seen;
> Glory hallelujah."

Thurman's theological skills enable him to supplement DuBois' account with important insights about the sources of the Sorrow

Songs. In addition to the *religious experience* of black people, these songs draw liberally from the Hebrew Scriptures (Old Testament) and from the portrayal of Jesus in the gospels, while assiduously avoiding the Pauline corpus. Thurman draws on personal experience to analyze this avoidance. A former slave to whom he regularly read the Bible, his grandmother disdained the letters of Paul because of their use by slave masters as a tool of slave management and social control: "Slaves be obedient to your masters..." She vowed, God willing, to "never read that part of the Bible!" were she ever freed and learned to read.[10] This anecdote is testimony to the intelligence and cunning of unlettered and illiterate slaves. It is characteristic of the vista that these songs provide into the souls of black folk. Indeed, Thurman discovers much about black folk in the spirituals, such as their ability to conjure freedom from bondage as revealed in the spiritual "The Blind Man." Thurman ponders a challenge to the very integrity of Blackamericans posed by the necessary deception—that is, the ethics of hypocrisy and compromise—that they, like all oppressed people, practice. This liberating deception and deceptive honesty is captured in songs such as "Heaven! Heaven!" In the spiritual "A Balm in Gilead," Thurman spies an ontological optimism: a basic trust in the ultimate goodness of things. In "Deep River," he discerns a certain universality and transcendence in the aspirations of black people.[11]

Like DuBois and Thurman, James Cone finds in the spirituals—and, unlike them, in the blues—the privileged vista on black character, soul, and life. "It is the spirituals that show us the essence of Black Religion, that is, the experience of trying to be free in the midst of a 'powerful lot of tribulation.'"[12] Cone describes the blues as "secular spirituals." He may well have added that the spirituals are "sacred blues," which would dovetail nicely with DuBois' description of spirituals as "Sorrow Songs." Within a perspective shared by DuBois, Thurman, Cone, and many others, which I call Black Religion as the Soul of Black Folk, music and dance are the privileged modality of black expressive culture, especially religion. The Sorrow Songs and the blues, the sacred and the profane, the art of sliding from sacred note to profane note, of always already "bluing," blurring, and fudging the difference between the two—is the substance of Cone's analysis. Where DuBois had primarily cast his analysis in historical and sociological terms that were decidedly nontheological, Cone brings to his analysis of the Sorrow Songs a disciplinary orientation and critical imagination that is self-consciously preoccupied with contemporary debates in Protestant theology. Even more than his great predecessor,

Howard Thurman, Cone discovers a full-fledged theology in the spirituals—doctrines of god and salvation, a Christology, theodicy, and eschatology.

The blues emerged from the same matrix that produced the spirituals and that inspire questions such as "What did I do to be so black and blue?" "Why do black folks catch so much hell?" "Is God a white racist?" These questions are generated by what theologians call the problem of evil, which arises in religious systems where the deity is conceived as singular, all-loving, knowing, and powerful. According to Cone, the meaning of the blues is inseparable from black suffering. "The blues mood means sorrow, frustration, despair, and black people's attempt to take these existential realities upon themselves and not lose their sanity." If spirituals offered a transcendent relief, then the blues often spoke of the body, food, and "sexual healing."[13] The spirituals and the blues help black people to transcend their "troubled minds" by representing, lyrically and musically, the sources of their suffering and the objects of their desire. Through the paradoxical juxtaposing of moods that are simultaneously beautiful and sublime, they capture the depths of black despair and the heights of black transcendence: "Wish I'd died when I was a baby, /O Lord rocka' jubilee, / Wish I'd died." Or: "Trouble in mind, I'm blue, / But I won't be always, For the sun goin' shine in my back door some-day. / Trouble in mind, that's true, / I've almost lost my mind; / Life ain't worth livin'—feel like I could die. /I'm gonna lay my head on some lonesome railroad line, /Let the two nineteen pacify my troubled mind."

Black Religion as the Black Church

It is hard to think of a place other than the church where more black people gather on a regular basis for nontrivial purposes. This must have occurred to DuBois. In the same year that he published *Souls*, DuBois published an edited volume, commissioned by Atlanta University, entitled *The Negro Church*. The first important study of its kind, it was followed by several studies that defined Black Religion as the Negro Church and later as the Black Church. The following is a highly selective list of Negro/Black Church studies that were chosen for the historical-social-scientific ambitions of the authors:

1. Carter Godwin Woodson's *The History of the Negro Church* (1921)
2. Benjamin E. Mays and Joseph W. Nicholson's *The Negro's Church* (1933)

3. Arthur Huff Fauset's *Black Gods of the Metropolis* (1944)
4. Ruby Funchess Johnston's *The Development of Negro Religion* (1954)
5. E. Franklin Frazier's *The Negro Church in America* (1964)
6. C. Eric Lincoln's *The Black Church since Frazier* (1974)
7. Hart Nelsen and Anne Kusener Nelsen's *Black Church in the Sixties* (1975)
8. Ida Rousseau Mukenge's *The Black Church in Urban America* (1983)
9. C. E. Lincoln and L. Mamiya's *The Black Church in the African American Experience* (1990)
10. Andrew Billingsley's *Mighty Like a River* (1999)

Woodson's *The History of the Negro Church* (1921) begins with an account of missionary activities among slaves and concludes with a contemporary account of the Negro Church. Following DuBois, it establishes, in detail, the Standard Narrative of the Negro/Black Church. The high points in this narrative are the emergence of the black preacher and the independent church movement, the catalytic effects of the Civil War and emancipation, and the tension between conservative and progressive forces within the church. It does not require much effort to see the ways in which Woodson's account follows a path that was canalized by DuBois. This path would be followed faithfully by subsequent commentators such as Benjamin E. Mays and Joseph W. Nicholson. In *The Negro's Church* (1933), they supplement and significantly extend Woodson's Negro Church narrative with a historical-sociological account. This allows them to provide a more detailed analysis of the social basis of the Negro Church—the process of urbanization, the way that different social classes bore different forms of religiosity—while commenting on a variety of demographic considerations such as church membership, finances, and leadership.

In their pursuit of accuracy, Mays and Nicholson do not shy away from the harsh conclusion that:

> the Negro church is in part the result of the failure of American Christianity in the realm of race-relations; that the church's program, except in rare instances, is static, non-progressive, and fails to challenge the loyalty of many of the most critically-minded Negroes; that the vast majority of its pastors are poorly trained academically, and more poorly trained theologically; that more than half of the sermons analyzed are abstract, other-worldly, and imbued with a magical

> conception of religion; that in the church school less than one-tenth of the teachers are college graduates; that there are too many Negro churches; that the percentage of Negro churches in debt is high; that for the most part the Negro church is little concerned with juvenile delinquency and other social problems in its environment; that less than half of the reported membership can be relied upon to finance the church regularly and consistently; and that the rural church suffers most because of the instability and poverty of the rural Negroes.[14]

Mays and Nicholson balance these harsh conclusions with an argument for the genius of the Negro Church. It reads like a DuBoisian litany: the Negro Church is the one institution that black people own; a school for common people, it is a place where black people can relax, away from the normalizing gaze of white supremacy. The Negro Church is a "commons" and a business park, a place of democratic fellowship where genuine interracial reciprocity is possible. Within the pulpit, Negro clergy have an expressive freedom that is unmatched and that white clergy should envy. Unlike the white church, the Negro Church is racially tolerant and accommodates white clergy.[15]

Arthur Fauset's *Black Gods of the Metropolis* (1944) and Ruby Funchess Johnston's *The Development of Negro Religion* (1954) provide a similar perspective. Both accounts underwrite the assumptions and priorities of the Protestant establishment, police "heterodoxy," and enforce an "orthodox" Christian narrative. Fauset defines black religious cults in terms of their deviance from the black Baptist and Methodist establishment. He finds nothing incongruous about including the Moorish Science Temple in his narrative of the Negro Church. The Moorish Science Temple and, for that matter, the Church of God (Black Jews), two of the cults that Fauset studies, are anomalous with respect to the Negro/Black Church narrative. To place them is to determine their degree of "deviance" from the Protestant Christian template. Johnston—whose language is more reminiscent of the crude, colonial, and evolutionary language of late nineteenth and early twentieth-century accounts of religion than of a presumably more enlightened, mid-twentieth-century, decolonizing discourse—is even more determined to cut Black Religion according to the Procrustean bed of the Protestant establishment. She remarks that "Religion signifies a system of beliefs centered around a supreme being and expressing itself in terms of regulatory principles of conduct and action, sometimes finding an outlet in physical, economic, political and social phases of life."[16] Thus Christianity provides the template for defining religion. And the Negro, Protestant establishment

(Baptist, Methodist, Pentecostal) becomes the template for understanding Black Religion.

Ten years after the publication of *The Development of Negro Religion,* E. Franklin Frazier's *The Negro Church in America* (1964) was (posthumously) published. And ten years after the publication of this text, C. Eric Lincoln published *The Black Church since Frazier* (1974). One of the merits of Frazier's book is the thorough summary he provides of his major claims. Frazier concludes that the peculiarities of their capture, transport, and enslavement in America has stripped black people of their African heritage; that "dancing, the most primitive form of religious expression," was the only African cultural trait that survived enslavement; that little progress was made in converting blacks to Christianity until the arrival of Baptist and Methodist missionaries; that a covert, "'invisible institution' of the Negro church," which developed under the noses of slave masters, was absorbed by an emergent, independent Black Church movement among free people of color after emancipation; that this integration produced class conflict and stylistic differences in the church; that the Black Church, nevertheless, became the center of black educational and political life while facilitating the emergence of a black business class; and that "the Negro church organizations became the most effective agencies of social control among Negroes in their relatively isolated social world." Though this is a highly condensed account of Frazier's view, I think it captures what is essential.

As a sociologist, Frazier is especially sensitive to issues of social structure, change, and stratification. So he accents processes of urbanization and class differentiation. The emergence of a black middle class is especially important. Frazier correlates middle-class religiosity with processes of secularization, racial marginalization, and the creation of a "make believe world." He correlates "lower" class religiosity with a paradoxical articulation: a "reactionary" return to primitive forms of Christianity *and* a turn toward "secular nationalistic aims." What vexes him most, however, is the authoritarian and anti-intellectual consequences of the Negro Church that "has left its imprint upon practically every aspect of Negro life." The "petty tyrant" style of the black preacher has stereotyped leadership in other spheres of black life. Therefore, blacks have been undereducated in the ways of democratic life, debate, and problem-solving. According to Frazier, "escape from the stifling domination of the church" is prerequisite to the intellectual and artistic development of Negroes. "This development is only being achieved on a broad scale to the extent that Negroes are being integrated into the institutions of the American community and as the social organization of the Negro community, in which the church is the dominant element, crumbles as the 'walls of segregation come tumbling down.'"[17]

The Black Church since Frazier was originally presented as the James Gray Lectures at Duke University in 1970. C. Eric Lincoln's chief claim is the following: "The 'Negro church' that Frazier wrote about no longer exists. It died an agonizing death" in the turmoil "of the 'Savage Sixties' as it confronted "the possibility that 'Negro' and 'Christian' were irreconcilable categories." From the ashes of the Negro Church the Black Church arose. This change in nomenclature signifies several things, not the least of which is the death of the servile and accommodating disposition of the Negro Church, whose peasant and working-class members consoled themselves through ecstatic liturgies, and whose middle-class members inhabited a "make believe world" of superficiality and conspicuous consumption famously described by Frazier in *Black Bourgeoisie* (1957).

Unlike Frazier, Lincoln is a "church sociologist." His sociology is driven by the theological priorities and normative assumptions of the Black Church. He has a vested interest in countering Frazier's dismal portraiture of the Negro/Black Church. Lincoln's defense has three foci: first, a description of its newfound militancy; second, an account of the "new black theology" as the intellectual face of that militancy; third, an effort to account for the Nation of Islam within the Black Church narrative.

The militant Black Church that Lincoln describes is really a small minority of black churches, specifically, those churches that actively participated in the civil rights and black power movements of the 1960s. It is unclear, Lincoln's claim notwithstanding, whether Frazier's assessment of the Black Church circa 1974 would have been all that different from his analysis of the Negro Church published in 1964. He would have to deal, as Lincoln suggests, with the phenomenon of Martin Luther King, Jr., and his leadership of the progressive wing of the Black Church. Though he died in 1962, Frazier was not unaware of King, the Montgomery Bus Boycott of 1955, and an emergent, church-led wing of the civil rights movement. This knowledge, however, does not figure in his account of the Negro Church. Given his leftist proclivities, interest in democratic forms of accountability, and attention to social differentiation and class conflict, Frazier is unlikely to have been as impressed by the post-1960s church as is Lincoln, who confounds the Black Church as such and the small, progressive, politically active wing of that church. That church, even its progressive wing, was still a domain of petty tyrants, if not an abode of anti-intellectualism.

Despite Frazier's unsparing critique of the Negro Church and Lincoln's apology for the Black Church, they share the narrative of Black Religion as the Negro/Black Church. Where Frazier folds an account of the Moorish Science Temple into his narrative of the Negro Church, Lincoln folds an account of the Nation of Islam into his narrative of the Black Church. Would Frazier have been impressed by new trends in black theology? It is hard to say. However, his claim that the "Moorish Science Temple represents the radical secularization of Negro religion or of the Negro church" may suggest the beginnings of an answer.[18] Frazier construes the Moors, a "heterodox" Islamic cult, as Christian deviants. He regards their Black Nationalist sensibilities as a radical form of secularism. Extrapolating from this analysis, we might well extend these conclusions to the advocates of the new black theology, especially the Reverend Albert Cleage, pastor of the Church of the Shrine of the Black Madonna in Detroit, Michigan, and to James Cone. Having said this, it is hard to discern Frazier's attitude toward secularization. He appears to share the ambivalence toward the process that is evident in the analyses of Weber. But where Weber saw the Protestant ethic as constitutive of the spirit of capitalism and of processes of bureaucratic rationalization and what he called "the disenchantment of the world," Frazier saw the Negro Church as a premodern relic and, therefore, an obstacle to the cultivation of democratic habits. For him, the Negro Church was the bane of critical intelligence.

Mukenge's *The Black Church in Urban America* (1983) is written in the tradition of Frazier's *The Negro Church in America* (1964). For analytical purposes, she distinguishes between Black Church and Black Religion. Black Church refers to the institution, Black Religion to the ideology that institution houses. This distinction allows her to reemphasize issues of social differentiation, class conflict, power, and social change that are muted in the Black Church studies of Lincoln (1974) and of Hart and Anne Nelsen (1975). Against their "church sociology," she self-consciously retrieves Frazier-style sociology of religion. Hence the following observation: "Organizational ideologies (and theologies), goals, or incentives, when used alone do not have explanatory capabilities; they can also be explained in terms of political economy."[19] This reads like a version of the old "base-superstructure" argument where ideology is merely a reflex of social structure. Whether Mukenge was aware of developments in social theory that undermine notions of a structural (economic) base and an ideological superstructure is unclear. When corrected in light of theoretical advances, her argument is a significant contribution to the sociology of the Black Church. This is especially evident in her analysis of the urbanization and transformation of the Black Church from a site of mass unity to one of class unity. She traces this process of class differentiation and stratification from the late nineteenth century through the third decade of the twentieth century. This development was inevitable, she argues, for many reasons, not the least of which was the decline of the church's monopoly as a service provider in the face of competition from secular philanthropic organizations. In addition, there was political competition from the secular offspring of the church such as the Afro-American League (formed in 1890), which "was the forerunner of the 1905 Niagara Movement, the immediate predecessor of the NAACP." Bureaucratic growing pains associated with the internal dynamics of the church, competition from new religions and new churches, and increases in government aid in the wake of the Great Depression also contributed to the transformation of the Black Church from a mass- to a class-oriented institution.[20] The Black Church ceased being the all-purpose site that DuBois describes in *The Souls of Black Folk*.

Mukenge's study appears to have had little influence on *The Black Church in the African American Experience* (1990), a massive if not definitive study. In this text, Lincoln and Mamiya provide a theoretically sophisticated account of the Black Church as Black Religion. Drawing on recent scholarship, they identify three components—religious, institutional, and dialectical—of a "sociology of black churches." The religious dimension refers to an underlying "black sacred cosmos" that emerged from the synergy of African traditional religions and Christianity under the conditions of slavery. The institutional dimension refers to processes of sphere differentiation between economy and society that is distinctive in the Black Church owing to its partial nature. The dialectical dimension refers to a variety of tensions within the Black Church: priestly/prophetic, worldly/otherworldly, communal/private, charismatic/bureaucratic, and resistance/accommodation to white supremacy.[21] This Dialectical Model of the Black Church is Lincoln and Mamiya's response to Hart and Anne Nelsen's *Black Church in the Sixties* (1975). I take Lincoln and Mamiya's model as attempting to summarize and elaborate the

Nelsens' typology of the social scientific scholarship on the Black Church. I quote Lincoln and Mamiya at length:

1. The Assimilation Model—The essence of this view is the belief in the necessity of the demise of the Black Church for the public good of blacks. The Black Church is seen as a stumbling block to assimilation in the American mainstream. The assimilation model also views the Black Church as anti-intellectual and authoritarian. This model is found in the views and studies of E. Franklin Frazier.
2. The Isolation Model—The Black Church is characterized by "involuntary isolation" which is due to predominately lower-class statuses in the black community. Isolation from civic affairs and mass apathy are the results of racial segregation in ghettos. Thus, black religion is viewed as being primarily lower class and otherworldly. The isolation model is found in the work of Anthony Orum and Charles Silberman.
3. The Compensatory Model—The Black Church's main attraction is to give large masses of people the opportunity for power, control, applause, and acclaim within the group which they do not receive in the larger society, as St. Clair Drake and Horace Cayton asserted in *Black Metropolis*. This view is also related to Gunnar Myrdal's perspective in *An American Dilemma* that the black community is essentially pathological and black culture is a "distorted development" of general American culture, so black people compensate for this lack of acclaim and access to mainstream society in their own institutions.
4. The Nelsens' fourth alternative (developed by themselves) is the 'ethnic community-prophetic' model which gives a more positive interpretation of the Black Church. This model emphasizes the significance of the Black Church 'as a basis for building a sense of ethic identity and a community of interest among its members.' It also accentuates the potential of the Black Church or its minister as "prophet to a corrupt white Christian nation."[22]

Again, Lincoln and Mamiya's Dialectical Model takes itself as superseding this four-part typology by appropriating its insights and correcting its myopia. But in their corrected account, Black Religion is still the Black Church.

Black Religion as Ancestor Piety

Ancestor piety is not unique to peoples of African descent; it is found within Chinese and other cultures that modernist anthropologists call "traditional." There are many ways of venerating the ancestors.

In his magnificent study *Slave Religion: The "Invisible Institution" in the Antebellum South* (1978), Albert Raboteau does a marvelous job of placing the emergence of the Black Church within the Black Atlantic context. He turns Frazier's suggestive metaphor for the Black Church, "the invisible institution," into a careful and groundbreaking analysis that is more generous, sophisticated, and multilayered than most church histories. And he provides a nuanced account of the Frazier–Herskovits debate concerning the survival or death of African cultural traits ("Africanisms") among Blackamericans. Raboteau splits the differences between Frazier and Herskovits, moderates their excesses, and unifies their perspectives where such unification makes sense. Equally subtle is his reading of Frazier's and Cone's polar (otherworldly/this worldly) interpretations of spirituals. Frazier's compensatory, apolitical reading and Cone's liberationist reading are persuasively, if not elegantly, reconciled.

Raboteau strives to do justice to *all* the ancestors: pre- and post-European encounter. Sadly, Afrocentricity is derelict in this regard. Now a generic term, Afrocentricity is an intellectual and cultural movement that is most closely associated with the name of Molefi Kete Asante and five texts: *Afrocentricity: The Theory of Social Change* (1980), *The Afrocentric Idea* (1987), *Afrocentricity* (1988), *Kemet, Afrocentricity, Knowledge* (1990), and *The Painful Demise of Eurocentrism* (2000). On its face, Asante's definition of Afrocentricity—"which means, literally, placing African ideals at the center of any analysis that involves African culture and behavior"—is simple.[23] But like many simple ideas, it is not as simple as it seems. Who counts as African people? What is African culture and behavior? Are the Berbers and Arabs of North Africa African? If not, why not? What about white South Africans? After three hundred years on the continent, are they not African indigenes every bit as much as Blackamericans are American? If Asante is not making an unacknowledged appeal to an essentialist (biogenetic, biospiritual, or biometaphysical) conception of race, which he claims is a Eurocentric idea, then why distinguish between black and Arab Africa (what about the Berbers?) and imagine white South Africans into nonexistence? Why are areas that are geographically near if not contiguous with the African continent, such as the Arabian Peninsula and the Middle East, not Africa? Except for a hidden appeal to an essentialist notion of race, why should we imagine that the culture and behaviors that Asante calls African should obey lines on a map that was drawn by European cartographers? At this point I merely pose these questions.

But Asante's failure to address them forthrightly detracts from his argument.

In the spirit of these questions, I pose another. What are the contours of Asante's Afrocentric version of Black Religion as Ancestor Piety? Ironically, the initial answer is the Black Church. According to Asante, "The black church is the single most authoritative religious force within our community. It is, furthermore, our only continuous anchor to the *orishas*, *loas*, and ancestors of our past." The communal nature of the Black Church experience recalls an earlier "time when our ancestors called the *loas* and *orishas* with the polymetric beats of the drum." But Asante is quick to add that it is our ancestors and not the church that is the source of this "power and spirit." The spirit of the ancestors is simultaneously the spirit of the church and the night club, of spirituals, blues, and "all that jazz."[24]

Asante rides piggyback on the Black Church narrative in the way that a parasite rides its host. Thus he describes the day when the Black Church will emerge butterfly-beautiful from the ugly caterpillar of whiteness and Eurocentrism in which it has been forced to crawl for so long. He describes a Black Church stripped of its Eurocentric garb and reclothed in the garments of the Afrocentric idea. Black Madonnas that replaced white Madonnas during the transitional phase will "give way to new symbols arising out of the lives of Isis, Yaa Asantewaa, and Nzingha."[25] In short, African deities, symbols, and ritual forms will replace the rites, symbols, and g/God of whiteness. Hence the Afrocentric idea, Black Religion as Ancestor Piety, will eat its way to strength, liberation, and dominance from within the belly of the Black Church. Asante presents the details of this Afrocentric perspective on transcendence in a cluster of interrelated ideas. "[*N*]*ommo*, the generative quality of the spoken word," underwrites the *sudic* ideology of harmony and epistemic wholeness, expressed ideally in the philosophy of personalism, whose expressive modalities of possession and music evade the dichotomous Western logic of matter and spirit.[26] This, in perhaps too concise a manner, is the Afrocentric idea.

Afrocentricity has been severely criticized.[27] In a wickedly ironic phrase, Clarence Walker describes Afrocentrism as "Eurocentrism in blackface."[28] "This can be seen in the very categories Afrocentrism uses to define itself. Frequently used words such as 'classical' and 'African,' for example, have a Western etymology and are not African in origin." But this minstrelsy is not enough. "In focusing on ancient Egypt as a site of black achievement, Afrocentrists like Asante create an idealized mythic space that stands in opposition to the present grim reality of black inner-city America."[29] More important, however, than Afrocentrism's preoccupation with pharaohs and queens is the "trivialization of black American history, Africa, and the black Atlantic," which privileges a synchronic over a diachronic narrative.[30] So the history of black people is reduced to a static phenomenon (a gross misunderstanding) by ignoring the difference that slavery and the Black Atlantic experience made. But that is not all—"Afrocentrism sentimentalizes Africa by depicting it as a place where blacks lived in perfect harmony before the arrival of whites."[31] Africa is sensationalized as the birthplace of civilization and of mighty kings and queens, which serves the therapeutic end of getting "black Americans to appreciate the real unity of their history." Walker adds the following coda: "Finally, Afrocentrism is a ritualistic invocation of community as the site or origin of racial authenticity: black people are nothing if they do not identify with the community."[32] Afrocentrism is a form of conservative reaction reminiscent of Booker T. Washington's accommodationism (though less justified) and of Louis Farrakhan's Jewish-envy, anti-Semitism, and *ressentiment*. A "totalitarian" form of identity, it is shot through with heteronormativity and a gender politics that is conservative in its reaction. This critique is harsh. Is it fair? Only so far as Afrocentrism is a proper name for Asante and fellow travelers such as Maulana Karenga, John Henrik Clarke, and Leonard Jefferies.[33]

I want to supplement Walker's critique by emphasizing Afrocentricity's captivity to a modernist, European idea of culture as a bounded, internally homogeneous entity that tracks, mimics, or otherwise serves as a proxy for a biology and/or metaphysics of race that underwrites a rank-ordering of cultures. This Afrocentric "metaphysical biology" is essential to Asante's way of imagining the ancestors. I propose a different way. "Afro-*Eccentricity*" is a competing version of the Ancestor Piety Narrative. In this version, which I shall outline in broad strokes, the notion of culture that Asante relies on is as big a villain as the notion of race that he claims to reject. One is no less Eurocentric than the other. Culture is not the bounded, internally homogeneous, genetically encoded, and timeless phenomenon that Asante's argument requires it to be. Culture is fluid; borrowing is the norm. This fact is just as deadly for the Afrocentric idea as it is for any notion of Eurocentrism. Europe and Africa are mutually constitutive. If Europe is an African artifact, then Africa is a European idea. Genetic lines and cultural lines—genes and memes[34]—have always already been mixed. Our ancestors are those to whom we, *presumptively,* owe a debt of gratitude. According to the Afro-*Eccentric* version of ancestor piety that I see as emergent in black culture (and for which I am an evangelist), we pay that debt by remembering. However, we diverge from the traditional view of ancestor piety in one important respect. We acknowledge the ethical and political task of choosing whether to remember and how. Among the multitude of ancestors are countless surrogate, step, foster, and adopted kinfolk. We imagine our kinship with them, which has nothing to do with consanguinity, through the reverence of remembrance. Consanguinity—"blood," family, and kinship—is the wrong idea; it places the accent in the wrong place. If we owe the ancestors anything, it is a kind of *natural piety*—that is, acknowledgment of our dependence on them and a *certain* gratitude for the choices they made even though their choices may constrain us in harmful ways. Though constrained by the choices they made, we choose our ancestors as much as we are chosen. Granted, we are thrown into families, kinship networks, and races. In this sense, ancestry and inheritance are given. In another and profound sense, however, ancestry and inheritance are also a choice, a product of appropriation and appreciation. Thus the claims of "biogenetic" and cultural ancestors must compete with the ancestors that we choose. And, above all else, that choice is ethical and political.

Where Afrocentricity would erect a "Great Wall of Africa" designed to maintain its alleged purity and cultural homogeneity, Afro-*Eccentricity* throws open the gates, welcoming cultural exchange, the stranger, strange ideas and practices. We Afro-*Eccentrics* remember our ancestors by remembering their traditions and gods but not necessarily as they would have us remember. There is no piety with impiety; we revere ancestors enough to disagree. As "cosmology busters," we invoke the names of Olorun, Damballah, Allah, Jesus, and Yahweh in the same breath. Is there any "god"— the Great Rainbow Serpent, Krishna, the Cosmic Buddha—whose name our ancestors have not called? So we refuse to choose between those ancestors who invoked the gods of Africa and those who invoked other gods. Indeed, we revere those who cursed the gods; or, like Countee Cullen's Blasphemer in "The Black Christ," trivialized God as a toy that should be put away[35]; or, conversely, who invoked no gods at all, for whom the existence or nonexistence of g/God (God and the gods) is irrelevant to how they lived; who, as *apatheists,* were indifferent. Thus, on one reading of this view, g/God is neither alive nor dead but a metaphor without a referent.[36] As religious dissidents, these ancestors disrupted false and oppressive forms of community by questioning nasty and unjust aspects of their societies in light of minor, alternative, scandalous, and "abnormal" currents within their tradition or through insights acquired from other traditions. They endured the ridicule of their compatriots who regarded them as culturally inauthentic: like a black person who cannot dance, whose expressive mode is solemn rather than festive, or who is otherwise different. Skeptical of uncritical celebration, these ancestors were willing to be ostracized and even exiled. Considering the example of these dissident ancestors, we honor all the ancestors best by remembering, criticizing, and revising what they have given us, by refusing—like a good jazz musician—to purify and mummify the tradition. Reverence requires "yea saying" and "nay saying," conservation and innovation.

Conclusion

The narratives of Black Religion that I have identified are dominated respectively by the Soul, Church, and Ancestor tropes. Each trope is part of an ensemble. Race, culture, and essence are analogies of the Soul trope and do its work by extending its scope. The Church trope is part of the discourse of economy and society, of institutionalization and differentiation. The Ancestor trope is the fulcrum around which a discourse of fiduciary responsibility—of debts incurred, rescheduled, or canceled—move. Accordingly, I offer the following typology of Black Religion narratives with their inferences and associations:

1. *Soul* = Race = Culture = Essence = The Eternal Same, which always reappears in the apparently different.
2. *Church* = Society = Institutionalization/Differentiation = The Changing Same, where the kernel remains the same even as the husk changes through time.
3. *Ancestor* = Fiduciary = Rescheduled/Canceled Debt = Emergence, Difference, and Novelty: descendants are not merely trustees of ancestral wealth; they are also the judge of what is wealth versus a burden to be cast aside.

The relationship among narratives is not perfectly linear. But there is a relationship of accumulation among them. Black Religion as the Soul of Black Folk is constitutive of Black Religion as the Black Church, and both are constitutive of Black Religion as Ancestor Piety, even if their relation to the Afro-*Eccentric* version is critically mediated. Each narrative is unimaginable without the reality of a white-supremacist, male-dominated, heteronormative social order whose brutal process of capital formation began with the "primitive accumulation" of black subject/bodies for purposes of chattel slavery. This accumulated wealth in black people, underwritten by the chronic violence and dishonor to which they were subjected, was simultaneously their material impoverishment. Thus the subject of Black Religion, though resilient, is anxious and insecure.

While there is no absolute difference in the ways that the subjects of these narratives respond to an oppressive social order, each trope—Soul, Church, and Ancestor—signals an important difference. The proponents of the Soul Narrative seek refuge in the *volksgeist* of black people, which soars majestically above or creeps stealthily beneath the veil of a white-supremacist social order. They seek refuge—that is, in a Platonic form, an ideal in the mind of god, an essence that is beyond the reach of white supremacy. In contrast, the proponents of the Church Narrative acknowledge if not embrace notions of social change in light of which the soul of black folk may be little more than an index of their historical experiences. But there is a powerful nostalgia in this narrative for the same *volksgeist* that animates the Soul Narrative: a principle of black identity, unity, and essence that traverses space-time and yet somehow remains the same. The Ancestor Narrative is both old and new. In its old, Black Nationalist/Afrocentric version, black people owe a debt to the ancestors that must be paid. This debt is paid through reverence and remembrance, through *religio* as *traditio*. When accurate, this form of *religio* is a slavish form of mimesis—of *relegere* that retraces the ways of the ancestors without question. When inaccurate, which is often the case, this form of reverence and remembrance is sheer fantasy, made in America. As should be evident, the proponents of this older Afrocentric version of Black Religion as Ancestor Piety are indebted to the essentialism of the Soul Narrative and the nostalgia of the Church Narrative.

Afro-*Eccentricity*, which is an emergent, if not an idealized reality, is made possible, in part, by three contemporary developments: (1) the globalization of culture, capital, and labor markets; (2) the "disestablishment" of authoritarian institutions and authorities, if not outright processes of deinstitutionalization, and the emergence of diverse forms of spirituality/piety; and (3) the emergence of a radical democratic and egalitarian spirit to which even God must submit. The claims of g/God and the ancestors must conform to our ethical-political standards. The proponents of the Afro-*Eccentric* version of

Black Religion as Ancestor Piety, therefore, have a different notion of indebtedness. In this view, it is imperative that we make our ancestors better than they were by judging them, insofar as they are entitled to our reverence, by our standards. Though they may be epistemically non-blameworthy, the ancestors may have engaged in behavior and held ideas that we, in light of our current judgments, should abhor. Sometimes the spirits of the dead weigh on us like a nightmare. When they do—when the traditions of our ancestors, to channel Marx, inhibit our ability to imagine something better, something new, to say "no" as well as "yes" to our inheritance—then we need an exorcist. The spirits of all the dead generations conjured by fear of the future and by retreat from the demands of the present must be allowed to die. As "ghostbusters," it is our duty to put to rest, reschedule, and even cancel our debts to these spirits. We must refuse to pay what we owe. To paraphrase Nietzsche, we must know when to remember the ancestors and when to forget them. Or as Kenneth Burke would put it, we need to know when to be pious and when to be impious. Sometimes—and this oxymoron is appropriate—the best way to remember the ancestors, those who prepared the way, is to forget them. To forget at the very least those aspects of our inheritance that do not address our contemporary needs or meet our ethical-political standards. As a dialectical ("yes" and "no") version of ancestor piety, Afro-*Eccentricity* exhibits the logic of *nepantla* (an Aztec word I use to reimage the paradox of black indebtedness and freedom), of being torn between competing goods, of negotiating the in-between space of competing cosmologies, bound by traditional obligations and breaking away. Afro-*Eccentricity* is inspired *bricolage:* the trial-and-error of experimental living where human intelligence, however inadequate and subject to deformation, is the best resource that we mortals have.[37]

Chapter 3

Art and the Ancestor Narrative

[T]he mutual gaze between Africans and African Americans, multidirectional travel and migration between the two hemispheres, the movement of publications, commerce, and so forth have shaped African and African American cultures in tandem, over time, and at the same time.... cultural artifacts, images, and practices do not simply "survive" or endure through "memory"; they are, rather, interpreted and reproduced for diverse contemporary purposes by actors with culturally diverse repertories, diverse interests, and diverse degrees of power to assert them. As if in a literal dialogue, such interpretations and reproductions can also be silenced, articulated obliquely, paraphrased, exaggerated, quoted mockingly, or treated as antitypes of the legitimate self.

—*J. Lorand Matory,* Black Atlantic Religion[1]

Introduction

Informed by the perspective articulated in Matory's observation, this chapter offers an extended meditation on Black Religion as the Ancestor Narrative through a reading of Paule Marshall's novel *Praisesong for the Widow*. Though I employ techniques of literary criticism and theory, my primary goal is to assess the Black Religion as Ancestor Narrative as represented in this novel. In this regard, the interests, approaches, and perspectives of the critical theory of religion are central. Of particular importance for me is the location of this novel with respect to the Afrocentric and Afro-*Eccentric* versions of the Ancestor Narrative. My exploration seeks to answer the question: does *Praisesong for the Widow* rest comfortably within one version of the Ancestor Narrative, split the difference between them, or displace the Afrocentric and Afro-*Eccentric* options altogether? The insights regarding migration, cultural reproduction, displacement, and self-creation in the Afro-Atlantic world as described in the introductory epigraph inform my analysis.

Despite powerful examples such as Octavia Butler's *Kindred* (1979) and Toni Morrison's *Beloved* (1987), *Praisesong* is the best literary account of the Ancestor Narrative ever written. Set in Grenada, South Carolina, Harlem and North White Plains, New York, *Praisesong* moves seamlessly between present and past and between real time and dreamtime. We encounter Avey Johnson, a sixty-four-year-old widow: troubled by an uncomfortable sensation in her stomach, haunted by memories long repressed, if not forgotten, by visions that unhinge and disorient her. Avey's hyper-bourgeois, highly disciplined life is falling apart. Her comfortable lifestyle—the "fruit" of the "Protestant ethic and the spirit of capitalism" that she and her late husband Jerome (Jay) Johnson had embraced during a thirty-year climb from the Harlem ghetto of Halsey Street to the middle-class community of North White Plains—has become a source of discomfort. Now she informs her travel companions, seventy-one-year-old Thomasina Moore and fifty-eight-year-old Clarice, that she is abandoning their Caribbean cruise and returning home. Home is North White Plains, whose very name symbolizes the cultural distance she has traveled since her and Jay's nearly fatal altercation in the winter of 1947. In response to the fight, Jay did not abandon her; rather, he transformed in the twinkling of an eye from a big-hearted, fun-loving man who took her into his arms and danced around the living-room floor as if they were at the Savory into a tightfisted, unsympathetic Puritan. This was Jay's response to Avey who, half crazed with pregnancy-induced jealousy, had falsely accused him of cheating with white girls at work. Four years after his death in 1973, this metamorphosis continued to haunt Avey in the form of Jay's face with the "pale outline of another face superimposed on his, as in a double exposure," complete with a joyless look and a mirthless, triumphant laugh. His laughter seemed to suggest that their life together post-1947 had been a joke. The Protestant work ethic had robbed them of joy—sending him to an early grave, leaving her an uptight widow.

Preparing for her return to New York, Avey is sidetracked by several events and finds herself in the rum shop of an elderly man with a mercurial personality and one leg shorter than the other. His name: Lebert Joseph. Lebert *tricks* her into taking an excursion from the main island of the nation of Grenada to the outer island of Carriacou. Avey becomes ill and vomits overboard, defecates, and sinks into semiconsciousness. In a scene reminiscent of "church mothers" at Mt. Olivet Baptist, her mother's childhood church, white-clad women rush to help Avey. They take her to the boat's deckhouse where, still in her soiled clothes, she recovers—in the dreamlike presence, it appears, of anonymous Africans in the fetid hold of a slave ship; ancestors caught up in the horrors of the Middle Passage, bathed in urine and feces. On Carriacou, Avey is escorted to the home of Lebert's daughter Rosalie Parvey where she spends the night. Assisted by her maid, Rosalie bathes and anoints Avey the following morning. That evening Avey participates in a simple yet elaborate ceremony called the "Big Drum" during which she has a *religious experience.* Transformed through a spiritual metamorphosis and rebirth, she discovers important things about herself, the transatlantic connections among people of African descent, and the importance of remembering.

Middle-Class Success as Spiritual Degeneration

It is 1947 and Avey Johnson is fat with child. Like many pregnant women, she feels a little insecure. Surely Jay must find her unattractive now. How could his eyes and desire not wander and run elsewhere? What about the young, slim, white salesgirls at work? Are they not always in his face, trying to get his attention and seduce him? Avey is convinced that Jay has given in to their desires, if not his own. Now she angrily confronts him "on a Tuesday evening in the winter of '47," accusing him of infidelity and threatening to leave—"*Goddamn you, nigger, I'll take my babies and go!*"[2] The miseries of her pregnancy, Jay's long hours at work, and her loneliness in a cold, drafty apartment have driven Avey to the edge of insanity. Jay resists the urge to run, to join the long list of black men who abandoned their families. He stands up to the assault: to a wife whose behavior reminds him of their neighbor's "low class," "ghetto" manner when her ne'er-do-well husband spends most of his check getting drunk and fails to come home, having spent the night, she suspects, with "some stinking 'ho"[3]: In a pathetic ritual, this wife walks the streets early Saturday mornings, barely dressed and unkempt, calling for her husband or retrieving him from some smoke-filled dive. Waking the neighbors, she loudly ushers her drunken, broke, and recalcitrant husband home. Her hard-knock life is tied tightly to this "do wrong man," as they do an undignified dance—one partner drunk, the other sober and sad—down Halsey Street.

Avey's undignified display horrifies Jay, reminding him of their unfortunate neighbor. Before he realizes what he is doing, Jay decides to control this "ghetto chaos," to exorcise the demons that have driven Avey and him to the edge of a steep cliff. They might live in the ghetto, but the ghetto will not be permitted to live in them. To prevent the chaos from seeping into their lives and making them a spectacle—objects of amused contempt like their neighbors—Jay adopts a regime of Puritan discipline, thrift, and respectability.

In portraying Jay and Avey, Marshall channels E. Franklin Frazier's analysis in *Black Bourgeoisie* (1957). Subtitled *the rise of a new middle class,* Frazier explores the historical sociology of this class—its roots in endeavors by free black people before the Civil War to acquire wealth, efforts that did not find fertile soil until the post-Emancipation period when the modern spirit of business enterprise emerged among a small elite. They began to play an important role within black communities during the 1930s. The black bourgeoisie derived its income chiefly from white-collar services provided to a segregated black market.[4] This is the same market that Jay in his post-1947 life attempts to exploit. In one important respect Jay does not conform to Frazier's account: he is a shipping clerk in a racially integrated department store.

Long hours, a new marriage, pregnancy, and financial stress precipitated the near catastrophe whose climatic scene Marshall describes:

> As he stood there straining to make his escape, another force equally as strong held him in place and even seemed to be trying to nudge him toward them. His anguished face, his eyes under the hat with the melted snow on the crown and brim reflected the struggle.
>
> It appeared finally that the street had won. All of a sudden, in the interminable silence, there could be heard the faint scraping of his shoe on the floor, and one foot could now actually be seen moving back. One foot and then the other and he would have taken the first (and she was convinced) irrevocable step toward the door.
>
> Before the step could be completed, he stopped short with a kind of violence, the other current asserting its hold on him.
>
> He drew himself up, tensing every muscle of his body to the point where it was clearly painful and he was trembling. Having steeled both his body and his will, he stepped forward, Jay stepped forward and the sound of his tears as he held her and Sis, the strangeness of it in

> the small rooms, brought Annawilda's shrill cry to a startled halt for a moment.[5]

After several years of Herculean effort, Jay manages to pull self and family up from the ghetto by their proverbial bootstraps. He writes his own Horatio Alger story as the family goes from "ghetto rags" to "middle class riches." Jay recreates himself in line with bourgeois virtues. Educated in schools founded by northern missionaries, Frazier remarks, the black bourgeoisie was shaped by Puritan moral ideas of piety, thrift, and respectability. They were taught to refrain from amusements that profaned the Sabbath: to shun worldly activities such as dancing, smoking, and playing cards, to exercise restraint in their emotional and bodily expressivity. No raucous displays, not even light frivolity—quietness, if not silence, it appears, was close to godliness. Chastity was a basic expectation, the violation of which meant severe sanction. In this gendered world structured by male supremacy, women students found guilty of "sexual immorality" were expelled from school. Only piety could restrain desire. Piety demanded that one attend chapel at least once a day. Frazier remarks that "In the pious environment of the colleges the students were taught to be industrious and thrifty, wasting neither time nor money."[6] Under a new regime of Negro administrators, the grip of white missionary piety loosened; respectability as conspicuous consumption (new capitalism) displaced respectability as manners and morals (old capitalism). Noting the historical amnesia of black college students in the 1940s, Frazier remarks, "As they ride to school in their automobiles, they prefer to think of the money which they will earn as professional and business men. For they have been taught that money will bring them justice and equality in American life, and they propose to get money."[7]

Like the students in Frazier's study, Jay Johnson buys the gospel of wealth. His twelve-year struggle to acquire enough wealth to move his family from the ghetto succeeds in 1957 when he moves the family to North White Plains. If Halsey Street in Harlem is a metaphor for the ghetto, then Fulton Street in North White Plains signifies middle-class life. The price he pays for this achievement, however, is a thoroughgoing, even maniacal commitment to the rat-race of economic rewards. Marshall describes the severe regime to which Jay subjects self and family as "a long and punishing marathon."[8] Chasing the dollar, Jay becomes a workaholic, working two and sometimes three jobs (as the generalization, if not stereotype, of West Indians would have it). Simultaneously, he pursues a business-oriented education through correspondence courses, reading himself to sleep at night and taking up his study manuals first thing in the morning. Eventually, he enrolls in night school at Long Island University and attains a degree in accounting. His bourgeois make-over is nearly complete. A respectable professional man, he trims his life as carefully as he trims his once-bushy mustache. A stern resolve squeezes the lightheartedness from his life. His appearance becomes somber. Joking and casual conversation become rare. The spontaneity and sensuality that long characterized his life with Avey disappear. They no longer dance in gay abandon across the living-room floor. Traditional sources of spiritual renewal die from disuse: sacrificed to money-making, to controlling the ghetto chaos, a frightening glimpse of which Jay had caught on a winter evening in 1947.

Jay's relentless pursuit of wealth, driven by his obsessive desire for "success," leads to spiritual impoverishment, communal alienation, and a kind of social death. Marshall describes Jay and Avey's spiritual wealth prior to the "near-fatal day"; their habit of dancing spontaneously, usually on Jay's initiative, as they spoke to each other with their bodies. The sensuality of the dance, usually accompanied by the transcendence of the blues and jazz, often culminated in the more intense dance of love-making where spirit and transcendence emerged from the sensuality of touch and the union of bodies. The dancing, music, and sex were sacred rituals, habits that they cultivated religiously. Then his mustache was dramatic, arching to his nostrils, above a mouth that smiled easily and was quick with some wisecrack or a risqué suggestion. In those halcyon days they were materially poor but spiritually rich. Marshall suggests that material poverty was a necessary condition of their spiritual wealth. I will say more about this later. Note, however, that this correlation of material poverty and spiritual wealth—a kind of ethical preference for the poor—is a common motif in the Bible. Marshall appears to accept this view when she distinguishes invidiously between the warmth of Halsey Street and the cold sterility of North White Plains.

Marshall associates the pursuit of material wealth with communal alienation and cultural deracination. She has Avey from her perspective as an elderly widow reflect on the spiritual transformation that resulted from Jay's relentless pursuit of wealth, the displacement of his generous concern for the well-being of ordinary black people by an "unsparing, puritanical tone"—

> "That's the trouble with half the Negroes you see out here. Always looking for the white man to give them something instead of getting out and doing for themselves..."

Or:

> "Just look at 'em! Not a thing on their minds but cutting up and having a good time."

And again:

> "If it was left to me I'd close down every dancehall in Harlem and burn every drum! That's the only way these Negroes out here'll begin making any progress!"[9]

Marshall suggests that Jay had learned the wrong lesson: that economic prosperity and traditional black culture are incompatible; that success demanded labor discipline, as there was no time for the languid pace of "CP" (colored people) time or for any pre-capitalist form of time-keeping. Time was money. If you could not keep strict capitalist time, then you could not make money. Black people needed to keep their eyes on the *real* prize. Money, not civil rights demonstrations and marches, not black power–inspired arson, was the key to the kingdom of liberty and justice. Further, Jay had learned that traditional black culture—dancing, singing, praying, and partying—was a vice, and even a vice grip that held black people in thrall. It was time that black people *finally,* if belatedly, *cast down their buckets* where they were.

Marshall's conclusion—that material prosperity equals communal alienation—is rooted in popular experiences as old as the differentiation of human societies into country and city. In *Black Bourgeoisie,* Frazier identifies the break with traditional black culture as a defining characteristic of middle-class success. Its deepest significance, he argues, lies in the abandonment of traditional forms of Black Religion. In the lives of the new black bourgeoisie, "Religion has become secular and practical in the sense that it is no longer concerned with the mystery and meaning of life and that it has become divorced from any real religious sentiment."[10] Marshall's characterization of Avey as a nostalgic widow, reflecting on what she and Jay had lost, comports with Frazier's analysis. Avey recalled the small rituals that bound her and Jay's spirits together (*religio* as *traditio),* which enabled them to transcend their material impoverishment and experience joy: "Two grown people holding a pretend dance in their living room! And spending their Sunday mornings listening to gospels and reciting fragments of old poems while eating coffee cake! A ride on a Jim Crow bus each summer to visit the site of an unrecorded, uncanonized miracle!"[11]

There are two issues catalogued in Marshall and Frazier's remarks: the labor discipline that success in a competitive capitalist society demands, and the conflict between bourgeois values and popular values of "sub" bourgeois classes. In their prodigious effort to escape the ghetto, Jay and Avey sloughed off habits they perceived as getting in the way. The shift "from production to consumption as the fulcrum of capitalism"[12] that occurred during the twentieth century is evident in their lives. The shift occurs on a micro-scale from Jay's workaholic productivity to Avey's obesity-producing consumption. Both production and consumption-oriented capitalisms posed threats to traditional black culture. Though well aware of the problem, Marshall is uncharitable in her account of the dilemma of pursuing economic mobility within a competitive capitalist economy and the disembedding of traditional culture that inevitably results. Though otherwise brilliant, her art is inadequate to the ideological burden it assumes when she has Avey pose the following questions to herself: would it have been possible to achieve economic success "while preserving, safeguarding, treasuring those things that have come down to them over the generations"—the most valuable and life-giving part of themselves?[13] This is a good question. Though Marshall poses the question very well, her answer skirts how truly difficult the dilemma is.

Jay and Avey experienced both the beauty and the ugliness of traditional black culture—the rituals of spiritual wealth and the material poverty that produced forms of spiritual sickness, with social manifestations such as alcoholism and irresponsibility, including male immaturity, what some call the "baby boy" phenomenon—that characterized the lives of their unfortunate neighbors on Halsey Street. Here the Ancestor Narrative as the valorization of traditional culture (sacred and profane) first becomes evident. Meanwhile, without providing an explicit argument, Frazier claims that the break with traditional black culture leads to feelings of inferiority among the black bourgeoisie, who compensate by creating a world of make-believe:

> In escaping into a world of make-believe, middle-class Negroes have rejected both identification with the Negro and his traditional culture. Through delusions of wealth and power they have sought identification with the white America that continues to reject them. But this delusion frustrates them because they are unable to escape from the emptiness and futility of their existence.... The black bourgeoisie suffers from "nothingness" because when Negroes attain middle-class status, their lives generally lose both content and significance.[14]

While this language is compelling in its broad strokes (the details of this account are another matter and require a skeptical analysis), Frazier fails to tackle the more important issue of whether these value-transformations are avoidable.

Consumer Spirituality and its Discontents

Jay's behavior reflects the mores of an older bourgeoisie whose members pursued their soul's salvation through their vocation, accumulating wealth while avoiding ostentation. Accumulated wealth (saving) was a sign of salvation. Avey represents the newer bourgeoisie obsessed with ostentatious displays of wealth, where conspicuous consumption (spending) signifies divine favor. Avey is obsessed with appearance and social status. The Caribbean cruise was a display of wealth, as was her cavalier decision to abandon what she had purchased at a dear price. Avey's girlfriends regarded her decision to abandon the cruise as obscenely extravagant.

If consumerism is the dominant form of spirituality in modernity/postmodernity, then Avey is exemplary. She has been captured by a materialist ethos where *to buy is to be*. Consumerism is her *being*. Addicted to consumption, Avey consumes novelty and stimulation like fuel. The pursuit of happiness, her very well-being, is inextricably tied to accumulating things. Happiness is property. There is certainly a deep wisdom in John Locke's analysis of property-ownership as a constituent of liberal freedom and in Thomas Jefferson's reconfiguration of property as happiness. The critical task is to preserve their genuine insights regarding the connections between property ownership and happiness without a wholesale identification of well-being with consumption. As a conspicuous consumer, Avey has not found a proper balance.

Avey and her cruise companions dine in the ship's Versailles Room. "Louis XIV décor and wealth of silver and crystal on the damask-covered tables" marks this dining option as the most formal. Etiquette requires that men wear dinner jackets and women wear gowns. The extravagant décor reflects the aspirations of cruisers who can imagine themselves as royalty for the duration of the cruise. To enter the room was to enter a gilded space that recreated a more recent American gilded age of extremes of wealth and poverty that rested in large measure on the dispossession of American Indians, an economic regime of neoslavery, imperial expansion, and banking, agricultural, and industrial polices that exploited the white peasantry and working class while encouraging them to view Blackamericans as the problem.

For thirty years Avey had constructed a bulwark against the ghetto chaos from whose physical confines she and Jay had succeeded in escaping less than twenty years ago. Paradoxically, she had cultivated the emotional reserve of the older bourgeoisie and the consumption habits of the new. A "control freak," she was well-groomed, tastefully dressed, properly deodorized and accessorized. Unknowingly, she had come to share Jay's contempt for "common Negroes." However, Avey's well-cultivated self-control broke down aboard the cruise ship. Her peace of mind was disturbed by troubling dreams, memories, and images she had long repressed—bizarre visions and recurrent "indigestion." As she ate a *sinfully rich* Peach Parfait à La Versailles, things fell apart. The parfait left her feeling bloated, with a nonspecific discomfort around her midsection. The symbolic weight of the parfait seems obvious. Marshall describes Avey's discomfort as "indigestion" and suggests that its cause is an *excessive* amount of calorie-*rich* food. Avey has consumed her own illness. Her illness is excess. She is sick because she eats too much. Obesity is its visible manifestation. Fat encases the heart, clogs coronary arteries, and causes myocardial infarction. Fat is associated with some forms of malignancy. Marshall describes Avey's symptoms as mimicking a heart attack, feeling like "a huge tumor," and as a "strange malaise." This malaise seems to emerge whenever she is engaged in an act of excessive consumption.[15]

"Indigestion" was only one indication that Avey's self-control had broken down. Stylishly dressed and age appropriate, the woman who stared at her from the huge gilt-framed mirror aboard the cruise ship, department store windows, even her bathroom mirror would never be confused with one of those uncouth, socially unacceptable Negroes. Avey no longer recognized herself. Her polish and certainly her lack of self-recognition, the doctor once told her, was a sure sign of money in the bank.[16] A kind of affluence-induced Alzheimer's had alienated Avey from herself. If Avey's affluence produced misrecognition, it also led her to acknowledge nightmare images she had long repressed: a white police officer beating a helpless black man into bloody submission on a rainy night. On second thought, the only thing raining that night on Halsey Street, many years ago, was the officer's billy club, as he pummeled the man. This nightmare kept company with day terrors, bizarre visions that seemed to threaten her sanity. Ordinary things assumed an extraordinary appearance; familiar things morphed in terrifying ways. And before all of this—the terrifying visions, the nightmare images, the lack of self-recognition, and the indigestion-inducing parfait—there was the recurrent dream of her long-deceased great-aunt Cuney.

Aunt Cuney is a wonderfully drawn character. Through her, Marshall confronts Avey with the consequences of the choices she has made, with, if I may be cute, her *forgetfulness of black being.* Aunt Cuney is a messenger from the divinities; or, perhaps, a manifestation, in the form of a woman, of Papa Legba himself: the gender-bending divine messenger, mediator between heaven and earth, and divinity of the crossroads. Avey was at a crossroads in her life. Before examining that crossroads, I will assess the kind of spirituality that had come to characterize Avey's life, after which we will be in a better position to consider the ways in which the symptoms of her disintegration might be viewed as harbingers of regeneration.

The excesses of Avey's bourgeois lifestyle—fattening food, fat bank account, pride, and the failure to remember and reverence the past, tradition, the ancestors—have literally made her sick. She is trapped in an "iron cage" that she and Jay built through their relentless effort to escape the ghetto. Her illness is the result of *The Protestant Ethic and the Spirit of Capitalism* that Weber analyzed in a book by that title. According to Weber, Protestantism influenced the capitalist lifestyle by turning its full ascetic force against "the spontaneous enjoyment of life and all it had to offer."[17] As I said earlier, this characterizes Jay's life post-1947. The spontaneity of his earlier life, the easy smile, sensuality, and sexuality virtually disappeared. When confronted with the possible chaos that his marital dispute with Avey portended, Jay sought salvation in Puritan asceticism where wealth was an external sign of worth and god's predestined favor. On this view, wealth was an ethical hazard only if it tempted one to a life of "idleness and sinful enjoyment." Otherwise, the accumulation of wealth was a moral obligation, evidence of fiduciary prudence. "The parable of the servant who was rejected because he did not increase the talent [money] which was entrusted to him seemed to say so directly. To wish to be poor was, it was often argued, the same as wishing to be unhealthy; it is objectionable as glorification of works and derogatory to the glory of God."[18] Or, as Jay put it, referring to the absence of the Protestant ethic among many black people—"If they'd just cut out all the good-timing and get down to some hard work, put their minds to something, they'd get somewhere."[19]

Though rooted in the religious sensibility that Weber describes, Jay and Avey had long since sloughed off the traditions associated with Calvinism. Perhaps they had never been Protestants in this sense at all. Their lives, nevertheless, were defined by consumerist spirituality. To reiterate an account that historians have challenged, the spirit of modern capitalism, with its accent on rational conduct based on the religious idea of a calling, emerged from the spirit of Protestant Christian asceticism. The consequences of this Protestant ethic leave Weber ambivalent. Puritans thought they were working out their "soul's salvation" by working diligently in their worldly occupation. Ordered by a capitalist labor discipline that was then new but is now old, they looked askance at spontaneous enjoyment and consumption. Inevitably, their anti-consumerism (self-denial) led to the accumulation of wealth and, eventually, to a disenchanted (bureaucratic and rationalized) world. They *chose* to order their lives this way, but we are forced do so. The unintended consequence of their ascetic choices is our lack of choice. They volunteered. We are conscripted. Their loosely fitting cloak constrains us like an iron cage.[20] One hears a note of melancholy in the following observation:

> To-day the spirit of religious asceticism...has escaped from the cage. But victorious capitalism since it rests on mechanical foundations needs its support no longer. The laughing blush of its rosy heir, the Enlightenment, seems also to be irretrievably fading, and the idea of duty in one's calling prowls about in our lives like the ghost of dead religious beliefs....In the field of its highest development, in the United States, the pursuit of wealth, stripped of its religious and ethical meaning, tends to become associated merely with mundane passions, which often actually give it the character of sport.[21]

This passage captures well the kind of spiritual road that Avey and especially Jay had traveled from Halsey Street to North White Plains. To paraphrase Weber's memorable phrase: Jay became a "specialist without spirit" and Avey, a "sensualist without heart."[22]

As I suggested earlier, Marshall's attempt to address this problem is artistically and ideologically inadequate. She concludes too easily that Avey and Jay could have protected the non-market aspects of their lives from market values: "It would have taken strength on their part, and the will and even the cunning to withstand the glitter and excess." She speaks of selective appropriation and critical distance.[23] Marshall is grappling with a very difficult historical and empirical question. I do not wish to be unduly critical. Whether Avey and Jay could have had it all—that is, the comfort and security of a middle-class life, without the diminution of spontaneous enjoyment and the tradition-destabilizing effects of capitalist labor discipline—is a "half open" question. I know of no national bourgeoisie that, having experienced the "all that's solid melts into air," tradition-disembedding effect of capitalist-driven social mobility, has not also suffered the loss of older traditions. The upwardly mobile bourgeoisie associate "folk" traditions with the authenticity of their group. Perhaps they wax nostalgically for their old home as did an older Avey when she thought about Halsey Street from her vantage in North White Plains. Avey thought about Tatem Island in South Carolina, where she was born, and the African-centered traditions she first learned there. However we answer the question regarding the conservation of old traditions within the dynamic anti-traditionalism of capitalist transformation, Marshall portrays Avey as a spiritually sick woman who suffers from various kinds of alienation—ancestral, cultural, and subjective.

Crossroads of Regeneration

In their popular hip-hop song "Crossroads," Bone Thugs-N-Harmony sing: "Tell me what ya gonna do/. . ./when judgment comes for you?/ See you at the crossroads."[24] Avey meets Lebert Joseph at a crossroads in her life. She had abandoned her cruise companions and was preparing to return home. But after much deception, the elderly proprietor of a local rum shop persuades her to delay her trip and attend the Excursion to the island of Carriacou. During the short trip from the main island of Grenada, Avey becomes violently ill, vomiting and defecating in her clothes. Her illness can be interpreted in many ways. A purely situational interpretation might attribute her illness to seasickness. After all, the boat did encounter a patch of rough water. It is not unusual for those unaccustomed to the sensation to become seasick. I interpret Avey's physical symptoms as signs of spiritual sickness. But to paraphrase Nietzsche, her sickness was like pregnancy. It harbored a new birth: the first stage in a process of regeneration. Before she could be regenerated she had to be purged of those things that had caused her degenerate condition in the first place. Avey literally vomits and defecates the consumer culture and lack of ancestral piety that had long made her spiritually sick—that manifested itself in haughtiness, obesity, and lack of self-recognition.

Within Christian traditions birth, death, and rebirth are prototypically construed in terms of creation, fall, and redemption. Avey Johnson has *fallen* away from her ancestral traditions. Avey has forgotten who she is, no longer knows her name, and has difficulty recognizing herself in the mirror. To put a Christian, though paradoxical, spin on the matter, Avey's sin is *lack of appropriate pride*. She forgot her ancestors. Her descent into the make-believe world of the black middle class, where she succumbed to the spirituality of consumerism with its gilded excesses and bourgeois haughtiness, blinded her to the spiritual wealth of her ancestral culture. Her material ascent left her culturally deracinated and obese. She *fell* from the grace, if not the paradise, of her earlier life. In the process of becoming the respectable matron Avey Johnson, the child and the ancestor within—the little girl Aunt Cuney called "Avatara"—died. Paradoxically, her death was not the absence of spirit. Rather, it was a form of demonic possession and possessiveness that deracinated her. This possession by a foreign spirit was Avey's *first death*. Death is the ultimate loss of control. Avey's loss of bodily control—her vomiting, defecating, and unconsciousness—represents the death of her deracinated, consumerist, and impious self. This *second death*, symbolized by the putrid waste that her life had become, is pregnant with spiritual rebirth. As she begins to regain consciousness, lying in her own waste—reborn, as it were, between her mother's urine and feces, exhausted by her singular experience of purgatory—Avey acquires a much-needed perspective on the "many thousands of thousands gone."

> She was alone in the deckhouse. That much she was certain of. Yet she had the impression as her mind flickered on briefly of other bodies lying crowded in with her in the hot, airless dark. A multitude it felt

like lay packed around her in the filth and stench of themselves, just as she was. Their moans, rising and falling with each rise and plunge of the schooner, enlarged upon the one filling her head. Their suffering—the depth of it, the weight of it in the cramped space—made hers of no consequence.[25]

Before her dreamtime encounter with ancestors in the belly of a slave ship, in her semi-conscious state of regression, Avey remembered an Easter sermon from her childhood. Where in real time, she was an adult woman soiled by the material manifestation of impiety and the forgetfulness of black being, in dreamtime she was a child in the hands of a preacher and his angry god. The preacher implores her to repent of her sin and take hold of salvation. The morning following this threshing-floor ordeal, Avey finds herself at the home of Lebert's daughter Rosalie Parvay who strips Avey of her dirty clothing and bathes her, methodically, from head to foot. As the filth is washed away, Avey reconnects with her body and experiences a long-repressed desire that has the intensity of an orgasm.[26] What she had submerged under the joyless ethic of work, economic mobility, and social status—the thrill of life, the lightness of being, the sensuality and joy—began to reemerge. Jay may have led the way. But Avey had consumed her own illness. The healing waters of the bath removed the literal filth (putrid fruit) of her excesses *and* the spiritual contamination as well. Under Rosalie's expert hands, Avey's body *sings* with pleasure and gratitude. She is rebaptized and initiated into the traditions of her ancestors.

The analogical imagination is powerful. We see analogies between the waters of Mother Earth, pregnant with life and the life-sustaining waters of the human womb. Regarding the prominence of aquatic symbolism in the religious history of humankind, Mircea Eliade remarks: "The waters symbolize the universal sum of virtualities; they are *fons et origo*, 'spring and origin,' the reservoir of all the possibilities of existence; they precede every form and *support* every creation."[27] Everything is present in water. *Emersion* symbolizes formation, and *immersion* symbolizes the dissolution of forms—water is a solvent. Birth and death: all life emerges from the waters of the earth, and water washes away life. It washes sin and leads to rebirth. The water needed for life to develop, whether from a seed, in an egg, or in a womb, is incorporated in the baptismal rites of various traditions.[28] The elemental waters that Eliade describes are evident in Avey's experience: sin and salvation, death and rebirth, impurity and purification, fragmentation (psychic, spiritual, physical) and reunification, exile and homecoming, spiritual blindness and insight. Avey's regeneration is achieved through the ritualistic reenactment of birth. As universality in potentiality, her bath water equals baptismal water equals amniotic fluid. When she climbed aboard the schooner to Carriacou and defecated like a distressed fetus in utero, Avey, in effect, re-entered the birth canal of her spiritual mother. In the hands of Rosalie Parvay, under the watchful guidance of Lebert Joseph, and with the inspiration of Aunt Cuney, Avey is coaxed from the womb a second time. She reemerges: washed, cleaned, and redeemed. Avatara Johnson is reborn. The ceremonial dances of the ancestors consummate her initiation.

The Black Atlantic Sacred Cosmos

Several scholars, Raboteau (1978), Sobel (1979), and Thompson (1984), among others, have distinguished aspects of West African religious worldviews (sacred cosmoi) that were recreated and transformed in America. An important aspect of these cosmoi is an all-pervasive *force* that emanates from the supreme spirit, irradiating divinities, humans, animals, and the non-animal world. The Yoruba concept of *àshe* is an example. This ontological force enables communication between the living and the dead.[29] In his account of the West African sacred cosmos, Raboteau identifies six elements: (1) high god (spiritual force), (2) lesser gods, (3) ancestral spirits,[30] (4) sacrifice and offering, (5) spirit possession, (6) magic and witchcraft.[31] These accounts inform my analysis of Avey Johnson's experiences on the island of Carriacou.

Carriacou

Carriacou is a resort island on which many Americans vacation. Like many an island paradise, it is a place to get away, let your hair down, and recreate. Tourist industries on such islands cater to the fantasies of Westerners, inviting them to *re-create* themselves in an exotic locale. Surely Avey and her girlfriends had come to Grenada to do as much. Yet, the behavior of the islanders both repulsed and attracted her. They were overly familiar, treating her as if she were one of them, as if they recognized something about her that she did not. Their language—"Patois," creole, or pidgin English—struck her as strange yet familiar. It liberated suppressed memories of the Black

English spoken on Halsey Street: the relaxed, graceful way of life in Tatem, South Carolina, her great Aunt Cuney, and a story about Ibo Landing.

Avey discovered that the well-dressed islanders she saw boarding rickety schooners, which offended her bourgeois sensibilities as did a disconcerting mixture of party-like fun and funeral-like solemnity, were on their way to the outer island of Carriacou. These "Out-islanders," she was told, were part of the Carriacou Excursion, an annual "family reunion" during which residents of the main island returned to Carriacou for both fun—Lebert described it as rum, women, and song—and the serious business of showing reverence and respect to the ancestors.[32]

Carriacou is a cipher for the Black Atlantic Sacred Cosmos and the powers of spiritual regeneration that reside in ancestral traditions. The Out-islanders reintroduced Avey to a sacred cosmos in which she was immersed as a child but had long left behind. This cosmos encompassed ideal types such as the Black Church in the United States and "New World Yoruba" traditions throughout the Black Atlantic. *New World Yoruba* refers to the recombination of Yoruba and other African traditions (Dahomean, Fon, Ewe, Ibo, and Kongo, etc.) and their ongoing exchanges and transformations. In Carriacou, Avey is reimmersed in this cosmos and discovers continuities in the spiritual culture of music (blues and jazz), dance (ring shout and nation), language (Black English and Patois), and the politics of pan-Africanism.

Lebert Joseph

"He had lied, deceived and tricked her into going on the excursion. Yet to her amazement she found herself all the more fond of him for having done so."[33] This is Marshall describing Avey's assessment of Lebert after he convinced her to go to Carriacou: after her illness, the humiliation of her sinful fall, her recovery through regenerative purging and ritual baptism, and initiation into a community that remembered and revered its ancestors. That Lebert is not above deception is one of several hints regarding his identity that Marshall drops like bread crumbs along the way. This moody, mercurial old man is a figuration of Eshu-Elegba, the Yoruba-Dahomean deity, orisha, and vodun. Like mercury, this shape-shifting deity is a trickster, messenger, and mediator. A divinity of the "crossroads," he mediates between the visible and the invisible world, life and death. Often depicted with a limp, "his legs are of different lengths because he keeps one anchored in the realm of the gods while the other rests in this, our human world."[34] Though disoriented, Avey notices Lebert's uneven legs when she first encounters him in a Grenadian rum shop on a hot tropical day. But she is unaware of their significance. As Eshu-Elegba, the misshapen one, Lebert is Proteus: a shape-shifting figure, symbolizing age, gender, and sexual indeterminacy. He embodies the polarities of loyalty and betrayal, chaos and community, creation and destruction. Later, Avey recalled with wonder Lebert's physical and dispositional transformations as he metamorphosed on several occasions before her eyes.[35]

As one scholar remarks, "Eshu came to the New World in the slave trade and appears as Exú in Brazil, Echu-Elegua in Cuba, Papa Legba in Haiti, and Papa La Bas in the United States."[36] This divinity of the crossroads did not travel alone. His companions included major orishas of the Yoruba pantheon: Orunmila/Ifá (divination), Osanyin (herbal medicine), Ogún (fire, iron, politics, and war), Oshoosi (hunting), Obaluaiye (healing and hurting), Nana Bukúu (mother of Obaluaiye), Yemoja (water), Oshun (love and the "dark arts"), and Shàngó, divinity of thunder.[37] A master of inversion, Eshu's trademark is the reversal of fortune.[38] Avey's fortunes are reversed when she encounters Lebert. But long before that encounter, Marshall invokes various deities to describe the sacred character of Avey and Jay Johnson's love-making:

> He would lie with her like a man who had suddenly found himself inside a temple of some kind, and hangs back, overcome by the magnificence of the place, and sensing around him the invisible forms of deities who reside there: Erzulie with her jewels and gossamer veils; Yemoja to whom the rivers and seas are sacred; Oya, first wife of the thunder god and herself in charge of winds and rain...Jay might have found himself surrounded by a pantheon of the most ancient deities who had made their temple the tunneled darkness of his wife's flesh.[39]

Erzulie is the Dahomean-derived New World Yoruba goddess of love. But whoever the orishas might be, Eshu-Elegba is the gateway to them. Prayer, offerings, and sacrifice are made to him first. He is the gatekeeper to *àshe,* to "the-power-to-make-things-happen." *Àshe* is the basic cosmological idea in the Yoruba tradition. Olorun (God almighty) and the orishas (divine spirits and avatars of Olorun) are embodiments of *àshe* or "ultimate reality." *Àshe* is movement, flow, dance, the dance of the spirits.[40] With Lebert as gatekeeper, trickster, teacher, and guide, Avey learns the purpose of the Carriacou Excursion:

> "Is the Old Parents, oui," he said solemnly. "The Long-time People. Each year this time they does look for us to come and give them their remembrance.
>
> "I tell you, you best remember them!" he cried, fixing Avey Johnson with a gaze that was slowly turning inward. "If not they'll get vex and cause you nothing but trouble. They can turn your life around in a minute, you know."[41]
>
> "...The Old Parents! The Long-time People!" There was both fondness and dread in his voice. "We must give them their remembrance."[42]

One shows respect to the Old Parents, the Long-time People—the ancestors—by dancing the dance of one's "nation," the dance associated with one's African-derived ethnic tradition. According to Sobel, "Africans had traditions of ecstatic dancing and singing, often 'working up the spirit' until a medium would go into a trance, be mounted by a divinity, and transmit the divinity's commands or advice. Ecstatic dancing and singing were brought into North America."[43]

Aunt Cuney

Like Lebert Joseph, Aunt Cuney embodies reverence for the ancestors. She pays respect to the ancestors by passing on the tradition of the ring shout to her great-niece, Avey Johnson.[44] Aunt Cuney schools Avey in the tradition regarding Ibo Landing, and she haunts Avey like a deceased ancestor whom the living have failed to remember and reverence. From age five, Avey had spent each August with Aunt Cuney "on Tatem Island, just across from Beaufort, on the South Carolina Tidewater." Avey recalls her great-aunt's righteous indignation when Cuney was accused of the venial sin of crossing her feet during a ring shout and thus profaning a sacred ceremony. Crossing one's feet was considered a dance step. In this austere Protestant milieu, dancing was a frivolous activity, if not a sin. Ordered out of the sacred circle, Aunt Cuney angrily refused, denied her guilt, and offered a competing interpretation of her behavior before acceding to the demands of her fellow shouters and leaving.

Spirituals and work songs are particular genres of slave song; the shout is a particular kind of spiritual. Often called "running sperichils," Raboteau remarks that they were not only sung but shouted:

"that is, danced in the ring shout," acted out and dramatized by a "band of shouters."[45] Consider the following lyrics from "Shout all over God's Heaven":

> I got a robe, you got a robe,
> All God's children got a robe.
> When I get to heaven,
> I'm going to put on that robe—
> I'm going to shout all over God's heaven!

A prominent form of Afro-Atlantic worship, the shout is a ritualized form of ecstasy, an embodied form of spirituality. There is no mind-body dualism. God is experienced, so to speak, in the unity of body and mind through dancing, singing, hand clapping, and foot tapping. The "ring shout" is a form of reverence and remembrance, a way of paying homage to the ancestors, of memorializing their suffering, perseverance, and resistance to white domination. The ring shout affirms identity. With the help of Raboteau and Sterling Stuckey, we can identify what Avey came to realize: that the "nation dances" and the ring shout are variations of common Afro-Atlantic traditions.[46] Such traditions "share basic similarities: (1) the song is 'danced' with the whole body, with hands, feet, belly, and hips; (2) the worship is basically a dancing-singing phenomenon; (3) the dancers always move counter-clockwise around the ring."[47] Counterclockwise movement is the signature of African-derived dancing.[48] Sung in antiphonal (leader–chorus form), the song lasts for an extended duration, building to an ecstatic climax.

Convinced that an injustice had been perpetrated against her, Aunt Cuney never performed the ring shout again. Like a hunger never satisfied, her nostalgia for the ceremonial power of the ring shout never disappeared. But she never broke faith with her ancestors; rather, her allegiance turned toward another ancestral tradition—the story of Ibo Landing. As the narrator remarks, she "made the Landing her religion." Marshall describes the considerable effort that Aunt Cuney, with a young Avey in tow, made to get to the legendary location. There she announced: "It was here that they brought 'em." So began her annual narration of a story full of marvels and wonders about enslaved Ibo ancestors. Upon reaching the American shore, they foresaw all the terrible things that would befall them in America. Uttering a collective "No!" they turned and began walking on water back to Africa, even though shackled in heavy iron—ankles, wrists, and necks. To be sure, this was a miraculous event. A curious, if not incredulous, ten-year-old Avey asks, "But how come they didn't drown, Aunt Cuney?" Clearly vexed, Aunt Cuney sounds a "quietly dangerous note":

> "Did it say that Jesus drowned when he went walking on the water in that Sunday School book your momma always sends with you?"
> "No, ma'am."
> "I din' think so. You got any more questions?"[49]

Like the inquisitive child in Sunday school, Avey has not learned that "common sense," conventions, and "regimes of truth" place certain questions out of bounds. Aunt Cuney is the adult who knows that Ibos walking on water is no more absurd than Jesus doing so. The point of the episode—an incipient interreligious controversy between child and adult regarding the miraculous notwithstanding—is that ancestors should be remembered and revered. Her effort to teach this lesson to a young Avey Avatara Johnson reveals the depth of Aunt Cuney's ancestor piety.

The third episode illustrating Aunt Cuney's role in Avey's regeneration is a dream. Aunt Cuney haunts Avey's dreams. Dreams are illogical, incongruous affairs. Consider the following: though dressed for a fancy luncheon at the Statler Hotel in New York sponsored by Jerome (Jay) Johnson's fraternal lodge, Avey finds herself on the road to Ibo Landing. Before her stands her long-deceased Aunt Cuney, silently beckoning. Avey resists the invitation. Changing tactics, the "old woman" gently urges Avey forward as one would a baby just learning to walk. Avey digs in her heels. More impassioned: "she was pleading with her now to join her, silently exhorting her, transformed into a preacher in a Holiness church imploring the sinners and backsliders to come forward to the mercy seat. '*Come/O will you come . . . ?*' "[50] When this tactic fails, Aunt Cuney charges her great-niece, grabs her by the wrist, and tries to drag her toward Ibo Landing. (This symbolism is dramatic and brilliantly obvious.) Eventually, their tug-of-war degenerates into "a bruising fist fight" that leaves Avey's "fur stole like her hard-won life of the past thirty years" trampled and dirty. To Avey's shame, they fought like cats. In this enclave of bourgeois respectability, they were a quite a spectacle before curious onlookers, before the normalizing gaze of her predominately white neighbors in North White Plains.[51]

These episodes involving Aunt Cuney accent the claims that Avey's ancestral traditions made on her. As Joyce Pettis puts it, Aunt Cuney was the first person to awaken Avey from her bourgeois-inspired, "racially inauthentic," and culturally deracinated sleepwalking.[52]

The Prodigal Daughter

In the biblical story of the "Prodigal Son," a wealthy young man demands his inheritance, then travels to a foreign land where he spends that wealth in a profligate fashion and sinks to a piggish level of poverty before begging his father to allow him to come home. The father welcomes back his son without recrimination and restores him to his previous status. Avey Johnson is a prodigal daughter who abandoned the wealth (traditions) of her father, his great aunt, and his aunt's grandmother only to return humiliated and humble, but with renewed respect.

Marshall divides her narrative into four sections that provide a running commentary and parallel narrative, recapitulating, as it were, the metamoves she makes throughout the main narrative. Section I is entitled "Runagate." The title comes from Robert Hayden's poem "Runagate Runagate"[53] and Marshall introduces the section by quoting Hayden and Amiri Baraka. Hayden: "...and the night cold and the night long and the river/to cross..." Speaking of his mother's college experience in the late 1920s as she contemplated the Blackamerican future, Baraka remarks, "there were black angels straining above her head, carrying life from the ancestors..." This life-giving bequest from the ancestors is full of knowledge, strong with "nigger" feeling.[54] The subjects of Hayden's poem are abolitionists—fugitive slaves and anti-slavery freedom fighters. The runagate is a renegade from the slave regime. In a sense, Avey becomes a runagate, a *renegade* from the prevailing class and cultural regime. Before that act of rebelling, she was a runagate in another sense. Runagate has several meanings: to wander off, to lose one's authentic self, or to become a renegade, apostate, or backslider from law, social conventions, religion, or ancestral traditions. Avey is a runagate from her traditional culture. Contemptuous of the "black folk," a contempt she now shares with her deceased Puritan of a husband, she no longer knows her real name and suffers from the "sin" of amnesia and irreverence—that is, ancestral impiety.

Section II is entitled "Sleeper's Wake." It's a metaphor for spiritual awakening, self-examination, and repentance, the resolve to become a different person and repair what you have broken. It is a double entendre implying, simultaneously, a person over whose corpse others are holding a vigil. In a sense, Avey had been sleepwalking for nearly thirty years. Ever since that fateful night in the winter of 1947 when her behavior provoked a reaction in her husband that turned their lives inside out, dissipating their spiritual wealth while sucking in toxins of consumerism and deracination against which it had protected them.

Section III is entitled “Lavé Tête.” Marshall begins with introductory quotations from a Haitian Vodun Introit and the poet Randall Jarrell. In Haiti, devotees offer prayer and sacrifice to Papa Legba (Eshu), the mediator between humans and divinities, in the hope that he will open the gate to the other loa (divinities) and to Bondye—god. The Introit remarks: “Papa Legba, ouvri barrière pou’ mwê”—Papa Legba, open the gates for me. From Jarrell’s poem “The Woman at the Washington Zoo,” Marshall quotes the following: “Oh, Bars of my...body, open, open!”[55] The poem’s narrator is a woman who I will assume is black. A buttoned-down professional, she compares her life invidiously to animals in a zoo. Observers find them interesting, while she, a fellow member of the human species, is invisible. Like the anonymous protagonist in Ralph Ellison’s *Invisible Man* (1952), the white observer cannot see humanity in her blackness. She is less remarkable than a zoo animal. Trapped in the sterility of her middle-class professional life, she longs for a kind of freedom beyond cages, prisons, and slavery. She imagines herself as a “wild brother” before whom “white wolves fawn” and a great lioness purrs. Addressing a vulture that shadows her and knows that she is dying, if not already spiritually dead, she remarks: “You know what I was, / You see what I am: change me, change me!”[56] Her condition reminds us of Avey: a trapped and dying animal, imprisoned in body (by obesity) and mind (by cultural-spiritual deracination), groping for a way out of her iron cage, begging Papa Legba—whom she encounters at a crossroads in her life—*open the gate for me.*

Lavé Tête, which literally means *washing the head*, is a “ritual baptism, to facilitate by way of water or any other liquid, the entrance of the loas ‘into the head’ of the new initiate, water being the pathway of the loas.”[57] To be reborn as a new person, a metamorphosis through which Lebert Joseph skillfully guided her, Avey had to regress, psychodynamically, to the newness and helplessness of an infant. She had to be soiled by her own vomit and feces—humiliated, humbled, and brought low—before she would acknowledge the spirits (Ibos, Aunt

Cuney, and the "many thousands gone") by allowing her head to be washed.

Section IV is entitled "The Beg Pardon." Marshall introduces it by quoting the cultural critic Susan Sontag: "Ultimately, the only response is to hold the event in mind; to remember it."[58] Drawn from "Reflections on *The Deputy*" in her great text, *Against Interpretation* (1966), Sontag asserts that some events defy rational understanding. Marshall suggests that the "Big Drum" and the transformations it produced in Avey's life is such an event. The Big Drum began when Lebert Joseph assumed a prayer position in the center of a clearing and begged the Old Parents, the Long-time People, for forgiveness. Those who joined him asked that their kin throughout the Afro-Atlantic be pardoned for failing to adequately honor the ancestors. This was the "Beg Pardon," the opening ritual in the ceremony of the Big Drum. The prayer was followed by a round of dancing whose pattern Avey was able to discern:

> First, from round the yard would come the lone voice—cracked, atonal, old, yet with the carrying power of a field holler or a call. Quickly, to bear it up, came the response: other voices and the keg drums. And the one or two or sometimes three old souls whose nation it was would sing their way into the circle and there dance to the extent of their strength. Saluting their nations. Summoning the Old Parents. Inviting them to join them in the circle. And invariably they came.[59]

It occurred to Avey that these dances, their names often mispronounced, and the African nations they were supposed to represent were the fragments and shadows of much older dances and songs. Along with the rum-keg drums, they were "the bare bones" and "the burnt-out ends" of traditions to which the participants in the ceremony clung like a lifesaver. The fidelity of these islanders to half-remembered traditions, the way they clung to them inspired in her a desire to do the same. "Thoughts—new thoughts—vague and half-formed slowly beginning to fill the emptiness."[60] The cultural-spiritual void that her life had become began to fill with new *and* old content in the sacred ceremonial space of the Big Drum. Eshu, Papa Legba in the person of Lebert Joseph, had opened the gates, striking down the "bars of her own body." Following his lead, Avey danced into a new life. In the midst of the music that had gone from sober to festive, she heard as if it were "the distillation of a thousand sorrow songs," about which DuBois, Thurman, and Cone have written so powerfully, a "single, dark, plangent note":

> The theme of separation and loss the note embodied, the unacknowledged longing it conveyed summed up feelings that were beyond words, feelings and a host of subliminal memories that over the years had proven more durable and trustworthy than the history with its trauma and pain out of which they had come. After centuries of forgetfulness and even denial, they refused to go away. The note was a lamentation that could hardly have come from the rum keg of a drum. Its source had to be the heart, the bruised still-bleeding innermost chamber of the collective heart.[61]

By the ceremony's end, Avey had *gone through the storm.* "She had finally after all these decades made it across." Accenting Black Atlantic continuities, Marshall melds the elderly ring shouters of Avey's youth with the "nation" and "creole" dancers at the Big Drum who joyously welcome Avey into their confraternity.[62] And when she rose and began to dance the dance of her ancestors—of Aunt Cuney, the ring shouters, and the many thousands gone across the Afro-Atlantic—the attendees of the Big Drum, beginning with Lebert, bowed to her in great reverence. They now recognized who she was—Avatara. Honoring her grandmother (a woman of deep spiritual insight) who had visited her in a dream, Aunt Cuney gave Avey the name, Avatara. As the great-great-great-great-granddaughter of Aunt Cuney's grandmother, Avey Avatara Johnson was a special emissary to a forgetful generation from a long-dead ancestor.[63] *Avatars* such as Rama are "incarnations," manifestations of Vishnu, the high god in the Hindu pantheon. By analogy, Avatara embodies divinity and the cosmological force *àshe*. Her embodiment is so powerful that the oldest participants in the ceremony, even Lebert, the figuration of Eshu, genuflect to her. As the end of the novel suggests, Avatara is a messianic or, at the very least, an evangelical figure. As an *avatar*—manifestation of *àshe*/divinity—Avatara left Carriacou to spread the *good news* regarding the salvation she found in the Afro-Atlantic traditions she had encountered.

Art and Ideology

In the introductory epigraph to this chapter, J. Lorand Matory describes an Afro-Atlantic cultural commonwealth rooted in the transatlantic slave trade. It underwrites an ongoing process of multidirectional travel, migration, and mutual self-creation among Africans and African Americans. Avey's life is a reenactment on a microcosmic level of this Afro-Atlantic experience of enslavement, emancipation, and migration. Marshall's fictional narrative has a normative view of that reenactment as necessary and good. Like all art, the narrative has ideological implications. The best ideology is artful; it tells a good story. *Praisesong for the Widow* is a very good story. I am less interested in whose ideology is expressed (Marshall's or her characters') than the ideology itself, which I see as more Afrocentric than Afro-*Eccentric.*

As the "prodigal daughter" of this Black Atlantic commonwealth, Avey rediscovers who she is. On a rickety boat, she vomits up her spiritual sickness: the consumerism and extravagance symbolized by the bloated mass in her stomach. Her purgation recalls John's experience on the threshing floor in James Baldwin's *Go Tell It on the Mountain* (1953). In recent literature, there is much talk of the Middle Passage in reverse.[64] It appears that such a reversal was a precondition for Avey's spiritual emancipation. She had to literally fall into a "shit hole" before she could be free. Like Sethe in Morrison's *Beloved* who was soiled by her slave experience and whom Baby Suggs bathed into spiritual health, Avey is bathed by Rosalie. In this ceremonial act of purification and regeneration, water is homologous with amniotic fluid, baptismal water, and holy water, with the purifying blood of the lamb of God (now that is an oxymoron!). Other homologues with these fluids are evident, such as the libations of Jack Iron rum used to consecrate the grounds of the Big Drum (after, of course, the solemn revelers had fed the orishas with roasted corn on a plate, lying on a cloth runner, starch white, under candlelight. Oh so simple, yet elegant).

Marshall's artful story invites us to think about the nature of identity among people of African descent: about cultural memory, authenticity, fidelity, and obligation. Despite a beautiful and captivating narrative, I have two skeptical questions: In what sense do we have an obligation to remember? Does memory demand fidelity to what we remember? Let's consider again Sontag's meditation on memory, especially what she says after the passage that Marshall quotes. Sontag acknowledges the moral function of remembering and the way it cuts across knowledge, action, and art. Drawing on Kant's analysis of the tripartite structure of knowledge, we may construe these as the theoretical, practical, and imaginary/judicial dimensions of human knowing. Yes, remembering has a practical (moral) function. But there is a caveat: "This capacity to assume the burden of memory is not always practical [here she means prudential]. Sometimes remembering alleviates grief or guilt; sometimes it makes it worse. Often, it may not do any good to remember. But we may feel that it is *right*, or fitting, or proper."[65] *Praisesong* poses this very question. Insofar as a fictional narrative provides answers (I am not suggesting that it must), *Praisesong* does not adequately consider the trade-offs among remembering, forgetting, and obligation. Whether construed as respectability/authenticity (the class question), roots/routes (the cultural question), or being/becoming (the ontological question)—trade-offs are irremediable.

Praisesong is an artful allegory of the Ancestor Narrative. It splits the difference between Afrocentric and Afro-*Eccentric* versions but is closer to the former than to the latter. Among the most important manifestations of the Afrocentric version of the Ancestor Narrative is the mystification of class among black people. This mystification occurs when social and cultural transformations, which are primarily economic phenomena associated with mobility within a dynamic capitalist environment, are construed in racial terms. The doxa among left-leaning critical thinkers is that race is "articulated" through class and vice versa. While this is undoubtedly true, it does not change the fact that race and class have their own specificity. We ignore that specificity and flatten the many relations between race and class to our own analytic peril. I see this mystification in several interpretations[66] of *Praisesong for the Widow;* this mystification may also be a fair characterization of Marshall's view.

Although extremely insightful, Eugenica DeLamotte provides an interpretation that mystifies: she attributes Avey's materialism to the violence of a "racist economy."[67] This claim ignores the extent to which racism is an artifact of modern capitalist class relations, the fact that capitalism generates consumerist sensibilities independently of racist strategies. Though often articulated in racial terms, consumerist spirituality has a nonracial specificity. DeLamotte repeats this reductive, racializing interpretive move throughout her analysis: the white, snowy, barren, plain, sterile, wasteland imagery associated with Jay Johnson's quest for upward mobility. In effect, those striving for bourgeois status are "acting white." In this interpretation, the upwardly mobile are a racially suspect class: guilty of racial betrayal until proven innocent; until they demonstrate that their quest for status and comfort has not detached them from a proper relationship to the "black folk." This is my interpretation of DeLamotte's reference to the "white stranger" who had taken up residence in Jay.

Though Marshall does not refer to this ghostly presence as white, DeLamotte's description seems like a fair interpretation of her view. DeLamotte juxtaposes the ghostly (white) stranger to black cultural icons (familiars) that have disappeared from Jay's life: Mr. B., Big Bill Broonzy, Ida Cox, Lady Day, Paul Laurence Dunbar, Ella, Lil Green, Langston Hughes, James Weldon Johnson, Ma Rainey, and Mamie Smith.[68]

DeLamotte conflates white identity and middle-class status when she interprets transformations in Jay and Avey's appearance, the fact that they appeared to be twins, as the reshaping effects of "white culture."[69] There are at least two major problems with this interpretation. First, it homogenizes "white culture" as bourgeois culture. There is a diversity of white cultures: peasant, working class, bourgeois, bohemian, old money, new money, super rich, and so on. By homogenizing white culture, DeLamotte can ignore the specificity of class: how Avey and Jay's transformations are typical of bourgeoisie culture regardless of race. The second problem: DeLamotte seems to have a normative conception of black identity associated with certain cultural markers. This reductive view ignores the multifarious, internally contradictory, and contested character of black culture. These reductive notions support a homogenized, Afrocentric narrative that construes sociocultural change strictly in terms of race (biologically, culturally, and geographically construed) while ignoring class and other kinds of difference among black people. Where such differences are acknowledged they are attributed to the adoption of white norms. While there are other examples in DeLamotte's account, these are sufficient to make my point.

If the Afrocentric narrative wishes to make class conflict among black people—that is, the struggle for economic resources, the desire for distinction, and the quest for social distance—disappear, then it also tends to mummify tradition. Tradition is everything; innovation is bad. Authority resides in the sacred times of the ancestors: hence the desire to re-trace the ways—religious, ethical, political, cosmological, and epistemological—of the ancestors. This reenactment must show a high level of fidelity; no deviations allowed. On this view, we have a duty to remember the ancestors *as they would wish to be remembered* and to orient our lives according to the traditions that ordered their lives. I have several questions. Is this Afrocentric perspective evident in *Praisesong for the Widow?* Does memory and reverence mean an undeviating retracing of ancestral traditions? Or can one remember and revere the ancestors while saying "no" to their claims? Is piety present only in obedience, or can we be piously disobedient? When do knowledge, justice, and judgment, *as we understand them*, demand the "pious impiety" of forgetting?

For my analytic purposes, I assume that Marshall and the narrator are the same. As such, she makes three interrelated claims. First, the ancestors are entitled to reverence; their descendants have a duty to remember them. Fail to remember the ancestors, to reenact their ways of life and to re-create the sacred times, spaces, and rhythms of their traditions, and you might lose your way like a sailor without a compass, set adrift on a turbulent sea of whiteness. Second, fail to value what the ancestors valued and you just might become ill: self-destructive, alienated, unable to recognize yourself, unhealthy in body and mind, and profoundly unhappy. Third, genuine reverence demands that descendants reenact ancestral traditions. To such memory (reverence as recapitulation, *religio* as *traditio*), the mental, spiritual and, as Avey's obesity proves, the physical health of black people is irremediably tied.

These sentiments capture well the point I made regarding the Afrocentric narrative in chapter 2:

> Asante rides piggyback on the Black Church Narrative in the way that a parasite rides its host. Thus he describes the day when the Black Church will emerge butterfly-beautiful from the ugly caterpillar of whiteness in which it has been forced to crawl for so long. He describes a Black Church stripped of its Eurocentric garb and reclothed in the garments of the Afrocentric idea. Black Madonnas that replaced white Madonnas during the transitional phase will "give way to new symbols arising out of the lives of Isis, Yaa Asantewaa, and Nzingha."[70] In short, African deities, symbols, and ritual forms will replace the rites, symbols, and g/God of whiteness. Hence the Afrocentric idea, Black Religion as Ancestor Piety, will eat its way to strength, liberation, and dominance from within the belly of the Black Church.

Applying this view to *Praisesong* and the ring shout of Avey's American childhood points backward in sacred time and authenticity to the nation dances, which in turn index the supreme authenticity of the dances of Africa. But when we consider the Black Atlantic sensibilities of her characters, the extent to which they are at home and not strangers in a strange land, the synchronicity of Afrocentrism and Marshall's narrative breaks down. Wittingly or not, the Afrocentric idea recreates an important colonialist trope—Africa as a land of *contemporary primitives* whose time is out of joint with the temporality of modernity. On this view, Africa is not contemporary with the West nor with that part of the West called Afro-America. Africa is Afro-America's past. Indeed, the real, "authentic" Africa is not contemporary with Afro-America or with contemporary Africans. She resides, rather, in the past, in the museums, timepieces, and imagination of the Afrocentric idea. As I read *Praisesong*, this radically nostalgic perspective does not come to mind. Avey Avatara Johnson has been dislocated, we might say, by the Afro-*Eccentric* idea. Therefore, she may not be the Afrocentric subject that Asante envisions but she does bear a strong family resemblance.

Chapter 4

The Archaeologist

The Challenge of Charles H. Long

In a 1971 essay entitled "Perspectives for a Study of Afro-American Religion," Charles H. Long threw down the scholarly gauntlet, challenging students of Black Religion to approach it systematically and programmatically. He issued this challenge in a context where popular and scholarly discourses equated Black Religion with Christianity and "reduced" it further to sociological or theological accounts. According to Long, a systematic study of Black Religion should not be equated with Christianity or any specific religion. Rather, as a proper object of study, Black Religion is an ensemble of images and meanings, a deep symbolic logic lying behind particular religions, experiences, and expressions. These symbolic images and meanings, he argues, double as methodological principles; that is, they should guide explorations of Black Religion. Long describes them as follows:

1. Africa as historical reality and religious image
2. The involuntary presence of the black community in America
3. The experience and symbol of God in the religious experience of blacks[1]

Regarding the first principle, Long notes what historians have long observed: the black slave was not a *tabula rasa*. He was an African in America. While the content of specific African cultures rarely survived enslavement intact, "a characteristic mode of orienting and perceiving reality" probably has.[2] We might call this Long's "bottom line" reading of the Frazier–Herskovits debate about the extent to which African cultures survived the brutalities of slavery. One thing is clear: Long regards Africa as a potent image. He attributes this power to the landlessness of black people, which gives the image of Africa a symbolic uniqueness in Black Religion. Obviously, the situation of blacks in America differed significantly from the situations of American Indians, who were dispossessed of their land, or from black South Africans and Zimbabweans, whose land was occupied by white settler colonialists. Even without these geographical, landed, and residential forms of authentication, Blackamericans attribute a religious meaning to Africa. "It thus emerges as an image that is always invested with historical and religious possibilities."[3] Long's essay was intended as a prospectus and a provocation for future research. As one might expect, he does not detail the religious meanings and possibilities to which he alludes. In the third section of this chapter, I provide an outline, a conjectural account of what these might mean in a cosmological context.

Long's account of the historical-existential horizon of black people in America, the second image-principle, should be understood in a similar light. "From the very beginning," he remarks, "the presence of slaves in the country has been involuntary; they were brought to America in chains, and this country has attempted to keep them in this condition in one way or another. Their very presence as *human beings* in the United States has always constituted a threat to the majority population."[4] On Long's view, this observation is obviously true, but there is a kind of hyperopia and astigmatism regarding the involuntary presence of black people in America and the historical image of Africa. Both are data whose religious meanings persist. With respect to them, we cannot see what is obvious, what is closest to us.

Consider the facts. Africans became slaves in the midst of the genocide of the native peoples of the western hemisphere. Slaves in the "land of the free," they became "black" in a land where nationality and citizenship were defined by white skin: a status that was legally codified by the 1790 Naturalization Act. They became idolaters, heathens, and fetish-worshipers in a Christian nation. From the greed of slave-trading Africans and Europeans to the horrors of the Middle Passage, the auction block, and a race-based chattel slavery to various forms of neoslavery (forced labor and peonage) enforced by various regimes of white terror, one discerns a phenomenology of darkness—the appearance of successive and overlapping forms of bondage, occurring under various regimes of capitalism. (Things have improved immensely, so much so that one almost forgets—and indeed many wish to forget—just how bad things were.) Bondage, in all of its phenomenological darkness—slavery, peonage, lynch mobs, racial cleansing, civic exclusion, and pathological animosity—is the middle term, the "vanishing mediator," between so-called traditional African religions and the methodical study of African American religion that Long advocates.

Oppugnancy is Long's term for the peculiar structure of the black religious consciousness, which he attributes to the incomprehensible animosity, cruelty, and barbarism that characterized involuntary servitude. Oppugnancy refers to the harsh conditions from which that consciousness emerged: the "hardness of life," the sense that reality was opaque and structured in opposition to enslaved Africans, the very presumption of which produces a willful opposition to that very reality.[5] "In the case of slaves, America presented a bizarre reality, not simply because of the novelty of a radical change of status and culture but equally because their presence as slaves pointed to a radical contradiction within the dominant culture itself."[6] Even though America was founded as a white republic where the equal humanity of black people was denied, their very presence contradicted the official creed of "life, liberty, and the pursuit of happiness." Most bizarre of all, black bondage was the very basis of white freedom. If America was the Promised Land for white people, then it was black people's Babylonian Captivity. Life abounds with contradictions and inconsistencies, none more jarring than slavery and freedom in the "land of the free." To cope with so massive a contradiction, the mind is forced to become a gymnast, to retreat into denial, or to engage in fantasy. If white people struggled to square this circle, so to speak, then black people had to do something much more difficult: they had to live within it.

Before they *became* black or even African, these people had been Ashanti, BaKongo, Coofa, Dahomean, Ewe, Fon, Hausa, Igbo, Kissi, Mande, Wolof, and Yoruba; too many to name, they were hundreds of ethnic-tribal, linguistic, and national groups.[7] The transatlantic slave trade transformed them into Africans or, one may prefer, into black people. The term "black" signifies the opacity this transformation wrought in the self-knowledge and traditional knowledges of African peoples. It was a "terrible transformation," a process of deracination as Africans were pulled up from the roots of their various lives in the most radical way imaginable, carried in the holds of slave ships across the Atlantic, and forced to labor for the benefit of a white, settler-colonialist population in the process of exterminating the native people and dispossessing them of their land. Unlike previous slave regimes, it was fed by a novel, potent, capital-driven, and protean discourse of racial identity structured by white supremacy. As Long puts it, "The slaves had to come to terms with the opaqueness of their condition and at the same time oppose it. They had to experience the truth of their negativity and at the same time create *an-other* reality."[8] Given constraints on "acting out," they acted within, innovating "on the level of the religious consciousness," creating a new inwardness. Expressed in new cultural forms that are indissolubly connected to the terrible transformation, to the creativity of slavery itself,[9] this inwardness is exemplified by the spiritual, the shout, and the blues, by black expressive culture as such.

Long is quick to dispute the charge of passivity: the claim that black people were resigned in the face of oppression and that their religion was opium.[10] In confronting a historical situation that appeared immutable and impenetrable, the black community did not become passive. Or to modify Long's claim, passivity was not the dominant response to the harsh realities of slavery. On the contrary, the furnace of slavery forged resistance in the form of "involuntary and transformative" modes of religious consciousness.[11] (This resistance, I might add, is an antitype of that oh-so-popular biblical prototype of the black slave experience: the story of the three Hebrew boys Shadrach, Meshach, and Abednego, King Nebuchadnezzar, and a fiery furnace.) When Long refers to the religious consciousness of Blackamericans, he speaks not merely of Christianity, much less of Protestantism or any notion of orthodoxy. Rather, he refers to the common background agreement in light of which differences are legible and meaningful, to the "involuntary structure or the opacity of the religious symbol." He refers to a trans-sectarian structure, an archaic religious consciousness, and tenacious eschatological hopes. Long remarks that "In both secular and religious groups, new expressions such as Moorish Temple, Black Jews, and Black Muslims retain an archaic structure in their religious consciousness and this structure is never quite settled, for it is there as a datum to be deciphered in the context of their present experience."[12] Thus we have the alpha and the omega, beginnings and endings of the black perspective.

If only Long had said more about this datum. What is its status? On the one hand, it appears to be a historical phenomenon—the involuntary presence of black people on American soil, oppugnancy, and the opacity of their experience that has left innumerable traces in folkways and mores—about which the inquirer can assemble an inventory of evidence and draw and support conclusions. On the other hand, it appears to be an ahistorical phenomenon, a Kantian thing-in-itself that persists across space-time and in the face of cultural transformations and that resists, if it is not immune to, the best efforts of the inquirer and demands for evidence. This construction of the datum is a problem that goes to an insuperable difficulty at the heart of the history of religions as Long practices it. Perhaps this is as it must be. Perhaps the paradoxical status of this datum is similar to the paradox of law where lawfulness presupposes an "outlaw," an enabling condition, act, or claim that is outside the law. If historical claims have ahistorical/metahistorical frames, something that cannot be historicized, brought fully under the regime of evidence and subjected to question, then perhaps the bedrock of every reasoned claim, where our ability to give reasons ends, is a groundless, unreasoned assumption.[13] Or, less charitably, perhaps Long subscribes to a version of the "religious given"—an archaic, primordial, or transcendent more that generates religious responses.

Of course, Long might push back against claims such as mine, which is precisely what he does in "Mircea Eliade and the Imagination of Matter." "[M]atter (nature) evokes modes of consciousness and experience (hierophanies); thus religious consciousness is an artifact of matter." In the following passage, Long is distinguishing Eliade's notion of religious consciousness (and his own) from the views of his more idealistic predecessors such as Rudolf Otto and Gerardus van der Leeuw:[14]

> [T]he specific intuition of human consciousness is always correlated with an *a priori* form of the world. It is the universality of matter itself in all of its several forms, rather than simply the inner working of the human consciousness epistemologically or psychologically which is the source of the religious consciousness. Mind and phenomena go together. The Kantian epistemology which has ruled out knowledge of "things-in-themselves" leaves us with the abstractions of consciousness proceeding from the vague intuitions and traces of the things-in-themselves, those things we can never know. For Eliade the very structure of the religious consciousness is predicated on a form of the world which is present as a concrete form of matter.[15]

I not sure that these remarks overcome my concerns about the role of a religious given in Long's account. So my critique of his notion of religious consciousness and his comments in this passage about the materiality of consciousness hangs in an unresolved, though not undecidable tension.

God as Symbol and Oppugnant Artifact

What distinguishes Long from theologians, church historians, and church sociologists is his database, which includes the folkloric sources of the sacred in the black experience, especially the experience of god. These sources include slave narratives, sermons, spirituals, blues, and black folklore—the stories of Brer Rabbit, High John the Conqueror, and others. He is further distinguished by his methodology: a comparative-phenomenological-morphological-history of religions approach that affirms "the sacred" as the object of religious studies; that g/God is one of many ways in which the sacred appears; that the study of religion is irremediably comparative; that religion is sui generis[16] and must be studied, in the last analysis, with a distinctively religious methodology; that *religionswissenschaft* embodies that methodology more faithfully than the reductive methodologies of theology and the diverse, non–religion specific disciplines that comprise the human sciences. Even if Long's methodological passion exceeds the arguments in support of its constitutive claims—such as the notion that religion is sui generis, Long's comparative-phenomenological-morphological methodology is still quite powerful. It distinguishes him among students of Black Religion.

Long uses this methodology in identifying and analyzing sources. What he derives from oral sources of the black experience are "religious meanings extending from the trickster-transformer hero to the High God."[17] His most important conclusion about representations of g/God in the black experience is that they exceed the constraints of Hebrew and Christian repertories. Trinitarian images are evident, to be sure, but so are non-Trinitarian images of Jesus as a "dema-deity," as co-sufferer with black people. (In this view, Jesus was lynched and black people are crucified.) There are images of god as one and images of god as many; solemn and moralistic images compete with festive, amoral, trickster images. In many Black Atlantic cultures, the trickster conflates "traditional" Christian distinctions between god and devil. According to Long, Blackamericans used Christian language and imagery because it was ready-at-hand. Christian imagery was part of a pragmatics of survival rather than a dogmatic investment for these New World *bricoleurs*. God was a symbol through which blacks imagined, elaborated, and performed a pragmatics of freedom. In short, the black imagination of g/God is a huge repertory of images used for transformative purposes.[18]

What are the historical conditions of this symbolism? The rudiments of an answer lie in the black experience in America. To speak of god is to speak about the meaning of America. "America is a hermeneutical situation."[19] Long argues that the meaning of America has to be interpreted. Her meaning has to be retrieved from multiple forms of obscurantism, beginning with misinterpretations of America herself, rooted in the unwillingness to think carefully about the presence of black people on this soil, to remember history, and to grapple with the ugly deed of slavery. On Long's view, Blackamericans embody the question "What is the meaning of America?" This question is posed with equal force by the massive absence and residual, if not ghostly, presence of the aboriginal occupants. Drawing on Doris Lessing, Long calls this failure to remember "the atrophy of imagination—the inability of the interpreter to come to terms with the reality of the obvious."[20] What would this reckoning amount to? The first answer is that it would lead us to reconfigure the subject of study: "the hegemony of Western Christian categories and thought models has to come to an end."[21] (This is Long's principal challenge to religious studies, African American religious studies included.) Native traditions and African traditions must be part of the story that we tell and not merely as coda or marginalia but a central strand. One expected outcome would be a better understanding of the expansive, fluid, and pragmatic meaning of the "God symbol" among Blackamericans. Second, the interpreter must come to terms with the ambiguities of American innocence: the claim to innocence is a massive form of denial, which is another way of saying an unwillingness to remember. Long describes this failure to remember as follows:

> The American has for one reason or another never taken the time to contemplate the ambiguity of act and value, the horror and the evil which is synonymous with the conquest of this new land. But this innocence of the American is not a natural innocence, that innocence which is prior to experience; rather, this innocence is gained only through an intense suppression of the deeper and more subtle dimension of American *experience*. Americans never had or took the time to contemplate the depth of their deeds.[22]

Long argues that Americans prefer nature to history. Perhaps this is related to the absence of national melancholy and even less a spirit of mourning. In their dominant unconscious mode, Americans imagine nature as the medium of the divine. "If Americans are not conscious of history," Long remarks, "it is not because they are innocent."[23] By spatializing rather than temporalizing they have been able to evade the work of remembering, mourning, and reparation; they have been able to preserve the myth of innocence, the tragedy-denying myth of paradise. But Long is suspicious of any turn from nature to history that does not acknowledge the ways that naturalization is complicit with historical amnesia, each providing cover for the malfeasance and deficiencies of the other. There is work of remembering, mourning, and reparation that must be done. Turn from nature too quickly and one loses sight of the multiple forms of destruction that have occurred under the sign of nature, the way that the conquest, destruction, enslavement, and death of the racial other is part of a larger ecological crisis. *Ecological devastation is a racial issue,* and the devastation of Blackamericans and American Indians is part of the ecology of white supremacy. In Long's own words: "It was precisely through theories of nature that the destruction of the Indian cultures took place, and a nation which at its inception proclaimed the equality of all human beings was able to continue the institution of slavery under the guise of nature."[24] One might contest Long's pejorative use of "nature" and "naturalize," which is a constitutive aspect of the larger phenomenological tradition of which he is part. Nature, naturalism, and acts of naturalizing need not be construed, as phenomenologists assume, as forms of naïveté and blindness. Their use of these terms does not correspond with their use in various American philosophies of pragmatism and process naturalism. While Long's point is clear enough, it is not clear that the history/nature distinction is the best way of making it. Despite this objection to Long's analysis, I think that he is right. The pragmatics of god in the Blackamerican experience relate directly to chronic violence, dishonor, and social death as exemplified by slavery.

If the involuntary presence of black people in America can be naturalized in harmful ways, then it can also be "historicized" in troubling ways. (Think: Hegel's *Lectures on the Philosophy of History.*) History is a reconstructed and highly disciplined form of memory. But with memory there is repression. Long is especially distressed by the forms of repression evident in the historiography of American religion. The standard narrative of American religious history begins with the Puritan "errand into the wilderness" and traces developments among European ethnic groups while consigning the native and African strands of American religious history to the margins if not rendering them invisible. This is true even of monumental studies such as Sydney Ahlstrom's *A Religious History of the American People* (1973). Long calls this a "European-dominated historical method."[25] Given the tripartite founding reality of "red," white, and black people, why this *white mythology* regarding American religious history? Isn't this narrative an assertion of (white) American innocence and a repression of the founding traumas of Native American genocide and African enslavement? The following passages dramatize Long's claim. The first passage comes from Ralph Ellison's novel *Invisible Man*. I shall reproduce Long's quotation in its entirety:

> I am an invisible man. No, I am not a spook like those who haunt Edgar Allen Poe; nor am I one of your Hollywood-movie ectoplasms. I am a man of substance, of flesh and bone, fiber, and liquids—and I might even be said to possess a mind. I am invisible, understand, simply because people refuse to see me. Like the bodiless heads you sometimes see in circus side-shows, it is as though I have been surrounded by mirrors of hard distorting glass. When they approach me they see only my surroundings, themselves, or figments of their imaginations—indeed, everything and anything except me.
>
> Nor is my invisibility exactly a matter of a biochemical accident of my epidermis. That inevitability to which I refer occurs because of a peculiar disposition of the eyes of those with whom I come in contact. A matter of construction of the inner eyes, those eyes with which they look through their physical eyes upon reality... You wonder whether you aren't simply a phantom in other people's minds.[26]

The second passage is a commentary on the trauma-induced evasions in the scholarship on American religious history, evident in its very language, which embodies a hermeneutics of conquest and suppression:

> It is a cultural language that conceals the inner depths, the archaic dimensions of the dominant peoples in the country, while at the same time it renders invisible all those who fail to partake of this language and its underlying cultural experience. The religion of the American people centers around the telling and re-telling of the mighty deeds of the white conquerors. This story hides the true experience of Americans from their very eyes. The invisibility of Indians and blacks is matched by a void or a deeper invisibility within the consciousness of white Americans. The inordinate fear they have of minorities is an expression of the fear they have when they contemplate the possibility of seeing themselves as they really are.[27]

Dispossession, genocide, and slavery are the founding traumas of the American nation. Long argues that the "old interpretive schema" of American religious history built on the repression of this trauma must be abandoned.[28] The upshot of Long's analysis (he prefers Eliade's language to the Freudian language I have used) is that we need a new myth of origins that places the fateful encounter between native people, Africans, and Europeans at the center of American religious history.

Implicit in Long's critique is the issue of how religion and race are co-theorized. Theories of religion emerged from two contexts: the "Europeanization" of the world and the critical orientation of the Enlightenment. Conquest and Enlightenment: in both instances Europeans encountered and constructed religion and non-Europeans (especially Africans and Native Americans) as *empirically other.* Long defines empirical otherness as "a cultural phenomenon in which the extraordinariness and uniqueness of a person or culture is first recognized negatively."[29] Some Europeans regarded black skin (and other differences in gross morphology such as nappy hair, broad noses, and thick lips) as symptoms of disease. European scientists spent considerable time looking for an explanation or cure.[30] The empirical otherness of religion has two manifestations: "Either religion was authentic to the extent that it constituted the past of Western culture or human culture at large or it was relegated to the peripheries of human existence."[31] On the European end of the spectrum, peripheral people included deficient classes and genders (the poor and white women) within Western societies. On the far end of the spectrum were the so-called "primitive" peoples, racial and cultural others whose technologies were inferior. During the Enlightenment, in all its national varieties, there was an attempt to displace religion as the source of normativity in modern society. Bayle, Spinoza, Hume, Voltaire, and Kant, among others, exemplify this intellectual disposition. Simultaneously, Long observes, the structure of Enlightenment discourse provided competing categories such as "evolutionary thinking, racial theories, and forms of color symbolism that made the economic and military conquest of various cultures and peoples justifiable and defensible. In this movement both religion and cultures and peoples throughout the world were created anew through academic disciplinary orientations—*they were signified.*"[32] Playing on the similarities and differences between "signifying" as a category in contemporary linguistic theory and as a term for black verbal artistry, Long claims that there is a complex relationship between the construction of religion as an object of academic study and "the peoples and cultures who were conquered and colonized during this same period."[33] This brings us back to the issue of race. Why the tradition of representing differences in racial terms, in terms of ideal morphological types? Long offers the following observation:

> The authenticity of intellectual power is expressed through those categories and procedures which strive for the clarity of descriptions and in the search for those structures in the lived world of the others which are both common and different in the worlds of the signified and the signifier. However, the latency of power of the context itself, the situation of cultural contact, filters through the categorical and intellectual structures. The descriptive and analytical categories and taxonomies form the basis for an accusatory or compensational order of meaning. For example, on the descriptive level, one cannot deny that there are peoples and cultures of dark-skinned, kinky-haired human beings who do not wear clothing in the manner of the cultures of the investigators, and, in addition, they express very different meanings regarding their orientations in their worlds. While this may be true on the descriptive and analytic levels, the fact that these characteristics were noted as the basis for significant differences is often unexplored. In other words, what leads one to locate the differences within what is the common? More often than not, the differences that bring a culture or a people to the attention of the investigator are not simply formed from the point of view of the intellectual problematic; they are more often than not the nuances and latencies of that power which is part of the structure of the cultural contact itself manifesting itself as intellectual curiosity. In this manner the cultures of non-Western peoples were created as products of a complex signification.[34]

As a historian of religion, Long describes his project as a form of "archaic critique." To use Edward Said's language, he is interested in "beginnings" and their relation to intention and method. Archaic critique is Long's response to the dominant "methodology of pathology" that he encountered in the study of black people.[35] Archaic critique is an attempt to make manifest what is latent: forcing the ego, as Freud might say, to go where id is; to let what has been suppressed appear (Husserl); to remember, as Heidegger might say, what has been forgotten. Long describes archaic critique as "a kind of crawling back through the history that evoked these experiences" of *mysterium tremendum.*[36] Within the history of religions school, this term refers to the basic phenomenology of a subject encountering the sacred. This phenomenon is famously described by Rudolf Otto as an overwhelming, simultaneous sense of attraction and repulsion. Malcolm Diamond describes it as the desire to look and to look away.[37] According to Long, the religious experiences of black people in America have been radically other, having the quality of *mysterium tremendum,* both fascinating and repulsing the white observer.

The religious history of black people cannot be properly understood apart from the colonial-anthropological discourse of the primitive and the civilized. Long "crawls backwards" through the discourse, excavating various levels of meaning. Drawing on the work of Arthur O. Lovejoy and George Boas, he identifies two concepts of primitivism[38] —chronological and cultural. One is concerned with the temporal development or decline of value, the other expresses nostalgia for a simpler and more authentic way of life. Both are the negative other against which the civilized is defined. *Civilized* life expresses the self-consciousness of Western people. "By this term Western society seeks to describe what constitutes its special character and what it is proud of: the level of *its* technology, the nature of its manners, the development of *its* scientific knowledge or view of the world and much more."[39] The primitive/civilized binary draws its meaning from the colonial encounter between Europeans and people they deemed as empirically other; people and cultures whose "extraordinariness and uniqueness" Europeans "first recognized negatively." Long cites the discourse of hysteria, the concept of the wild man, and Foucault's account of "unreason" in the Age of Reason as exemplary forms of empirical otherness. However, the forms of primitivism that emerged coincident with the colonial encounter, unlike earlier forms rooted in ancient and medieval categories, proved deadly for the native peoples of Africa and the New World.[40] They were not merely imaginary others like Africa's legendary Christian King, Prester John, but flesh-and-blood, negatively perceived empirical others. From this analysis, I conclude that *empirical otherness is a threshold issue in the study of Black Religion.*

Africa, Grammars of Creation, and Beginnings

This brings us back to Africa, the historical and mythical beginning. Along with Edward Said and George Steiner, Long is a theorist of beginnings. In his magnificent study of creation in Western culture, *Grammars of Creation* (2001),[41] Steiner explores the multiple meanings of creation, the irremediable relationship between creation as the act of god and human creativity as imitation and reenactment, between creation as prototype and creation as antitype. Creation is the deep, common, generative grammar of theology, philosophy, art, and science.[42] Every act of Western creativity, he argues, signifies on god's creativity. This is true in visual and nonvisual, discursive and nondiscursive forms of art, especially music. Steiner extends this claim to technology and pure mathematics where it is particularly evident. Presumably, the signifying-inducing power of the divine model of creativity also applies to architecture—a hybrid of art, science, and technology. In any event, Steiner appears to agree with Alfred North Whitehead's claim that music and mathematics are the highest expressions of the human spirit.[43] Otherwise put, they are activities whose very originality and creativity make humans most like god. On Steiner's view, the Bible and the oral traditions from which it emerged are the *ur*-text (original, generative source) of the Western creative imagination.

Said's point of departure in *Beginnings* (1975) differs from Steiner's. With a focus on written texts, it is narrower than Steiner's concern with signifying practices across the arts and sciences. And, in striking contrast, he brackets the idea of divine creation. Neither ignorant nor insensitive, he is actively hostile to the idea. So where Steiner speaks of creation, Said speaks of beginnings. He argues that "Beginnings inaugurate a deliberately *other* production of meaning—a gentile (as opposed to a sacred) one. It is 'other,' because, in writing, this gentile production claims a status *alongside* other works: it is *another* work, rather than one in a line of descent from X or Y."[44] Said's use of terms such as "sacred" and "secular" is not always clear. But his desire to sever human creativity from a divine model is clear. The prospect of severing creativity from originality leaves Steiner cold. Said, on the other hand, is not chilled at all. Indeed, one must begin because things have already begun. Beginnings are paradoxical, both mythical and logical. One cannot begin because things have already begun; there are no absolute beginnings, yet one must begin. Beginnings are a necessary fiction, an intentional and methodical form of self-assertion, an act of originality under conditions—discourse, god, history, other, text, the unconscious—that make originality impossible before the fact.[45] To show that this hermeneutical circle is not vicious, Said distinguishes between different beginnings: transitive (temporal) and intransitive (conceptual); beginnings as events in space-time and beginnings in logical space, at the "threshold of language," so to speak. The first kind of beginning enables us to work, polemicize, and discover. The second kind haunts us, shadowing our minds with the knowledge that it is both necessary and wrong. Intentional and methodical rather than accidental, this kind of beginning is "wrong" because it transgresses divine originality.[46]

Before turning to Long's analysis and the relation between stories of creation and the creative role of Africa in the religious imaginary of black people, I note a lacuna in Said's account. I find it curious that he does not directly confront the divine model of creativity and originality that shadows his account. "Lacuna" may be too strong a word, given the place in his thinking about beginnings of Kierkegaard and Vico for whom the relationship between divine originality and human repetition is an important theme. Said strives to distinguish the religious from the secular aspects of their work: preferring Kierkegaard's aesthetic writings to the religious ones, and devoting considerable effort to explicating the difference between Vico's "sacred history" and "gentile history." Explication is crucial to the distinction that Said draws between creation as divine and dynastic—as an act of god, filial authority, and repetition—and beginnings as a gentile, secular production of something different. Beginnings are humans acts that create difference. In contrast to Said, it is precisely divine models of creation that are the subject of Long's *Alpha: The Myths of Creation* (1963). Whereas for Said and Steiner creation is a rich metaphor (problematic or not) that reveals what humans do by signifying on what the gods have done, Long is interested in creation, origins, originality, and beginnings as acts of the gods, even if their existence is limited solely to the human imagination. What models of creation do the gods iterate, and what is the purpose of these creation stories? According to Long:

> The creation myths express in symbolic manner what is most essential to human life and society by relating it to a primordial act of foundation recorded in the myth. In the most general sense we could say that the creation myth is an expression of man's[47] cosmic orientation. This orientation involves his apprehension of time and space, his participation in the world of animals and plants, his judgment concerning other men and the phenomena of the sky, the interrelationship of these dimensions, and finally the powers which have established and continue to maintain his being in the world.[48]

Long argues that creation myths persist in a scientific age because they articulate realities that evade the grasp of science. Undoubtedly there are such realities. But mythic and scientific thinking are fundamentally related. Science is irremediably metaphorical, and metaphors relentlessly transgress limits. This point bears a striking resemblance to Steiner's claims regarding the relations between scientific cosmology and creation myths:

> Cosmology and astrophysics are proposing models of the birth of our universe with a sweep and speculative flight far closer to ancient or "primitive" creation-myths than they are to mechanistic positivism. Just now, the hypothesis of "continuous creation," of the provenance of matter out of interstellar "dark matter" or nothingness, is out of favor. Some kind of "big bang" is thought to have detonated our cosmos around fifteen billion years ago. Background radiation and compaction of "lumps" into new galaxies are held to be spoors of this *incipit*. In a sovereign paradox, the further the horizon of radio-astronomy, of the observation of nebulae at the "edge of the universe," the deeper our descent into the temporal abyss, into the primordial past in which expansion began.[49]

Long and Steiner agree that some realities exceed the facts. We believe in such realities without supporting evidence; these beliefs are the groundless ground of the evidence-based claims we make. (Consider scientific beliefs in "big bang" versus "steady state" cosmologies before there was evidence supporting or refuting either—we know that we believe, we believe that we know.) Steiner cites the inhuman or other that inhabits every great philosophic insight or work of art. Long speaks of realities "more than human and more than natural" that inhabit creation myths. According to Steiner, creation myths answer the ontological question: "why is there not nothing?"[50] Long refers to ontology as the "sacred" and the "real," which are both immanent to the "natural environment" and transcendent. "Part of the job of the historian of religion," Long remarks, "is to interpret the human reality in relation to this type of symbolic expression."[51] This is Long's way of posing the ontological question—why is there something rather than nothing?

The ontological question quickly becomes a religious question, which is integrally connected to art. "A vital religious life will tend to express itself in artistic forms. Art thus seems to be a necessary dimension of religion. In art forms the relationship of man to his world is objectified and made concrete."[52] Here Long anticipates Steiner's view regarding the religious importance of art. Whether he shares Steiner's fear that artistic creativity might be diminished if the theological notion of creation is consigned to the dustbin of history is an open question.[53] Long's account of the relationship between cosmogonic myths and art, which draws him closer to Steiner's view, provides a counterpoint to Said's view of beginnings as secular acts, as repetitions that—far from recapitulating the acts of the gods—produce difference, thereby displacing and usurping the place of divine originality.

The art of Paleolithic, Neolithic, and modern cultures is part of the data set that Long uses in his analysis of creation myths. He explores notions of creation across time and culture. As a historian of religion, he draws on a wealth of anthropological data—from the Dogon and Mande of Africa, the Aboriginal peoples of Australia, Indians in southwestern North America, the Mayans in Mexico, and the peoples of Japan and Siberia and from cultures as ancient as Sumeria, Egypt, and Greece. He identifies five categories of creation stories: Myths of Emergence, World-Parent Myths, Creation from Chaos and the Cosmic Egg, Creation from Nothing, and Earth-Diver Myths. I suggest that we might better understand the significance that Long attributes to the image of Africa in Black Religion by considering the image of Africa in relation to these "alpha myths," or categories of creation.

1. *Africa is the Land of Emergence*—the Great Mother, the black earth from whose womb black people (indeed, all people) and Black Religion were born. It is a magical land, pregnant with potential and power.
2. *Africa is Mother and Father*—the aboriginal parents locked in an embrace of undifferentiated unity; the point where the regress of black genealogical inquiry, disrupted in unimaginable ways by the transatlantic slave trade, comes to an end.
3. *Africa is the Cosmic Egg* in whose nutritious yolk and albumen life germinated and from whose shell life emerged: the chaos that an emerging cosmos overcame, the prototype of creation and procreation, physiological and spiritual vitality, fertility and inspiration.
4. *Africa is the Creative Void*—the nothingness, darkness, and absence from which everything—plenitude, light, and presence—emerged.
5. *Africa is the First Born*—the place where dry land first emerged from the primordial waters. Aboriginal sacred land-place-space, it is the first piece of soil that the earth-diving animal ancestors retrieved from the primordial depths. From this soil the earth grew to its current magnitude, and from this soil the ancestors of all humankind migrated around the world. Africa is the umbilicus of the human family.

"What," sang the poet, "is Africa to me?" Africa is the place of beginnings: the site of memory, dreams, and imagination, a point of reference and nostalgia. Of course, my account of what Africa might mean within the religious imagination of black people is speculative, constructive, and hypothetical, since Long does not provide details. Though the image of Africa is evident to varying degrees in the Soul, the Black Church, and the Ancestor narratives that I described in chapters 2 and 3, it remains to be seen whether Long's account of that imagery is evident in the work of Jones (the Renegade), West (the Prophet), and Smith (the Conjuror). Do they attribute religious significance to Africa, do they share Long's concern with the hermeneutical implications of black peoples' involuntary presence in America, and does the black experience of the god symbol factor in their analyses of Black Religion? Is Long's methodological challenge a useful heuristic for evaluating their claims? Before pursuing these matters, I consider the contributions of two scholars to our understanding of Long.

The Imagination of Matter

James A. Noel describes *Black Religion and the Imagination of Matter in the Atlantic World* (2009) as "the first sustained discussion and application of Long's thought by a single author."[54] The organizing concept of Noel's study is the "imagination of matter" as that term is used by Long and other members of the *religionswissenschaft* school of religion study. "Broadly conceived," he remarks, "religion is not separate from matter. The gods were imagined through primary material forms."[55] In light of this claim, I take the following as a statement of Noel's thesis: "that the religious subject and the religious object make their phenomenological appearance simultaneously and the hermeneutical problem in the study of black religion is that of apprehending and describing their mutual appearance."[56] Other issues are secondary to this subject-object problem of reciprocal emergence. Noel supports his provocative thesis by exploring cultural contact and exchange across the Black Atlantic, the continuities they sustain, and the discontinuities they produce as the material context for the study of Black Religion.

The first three chapters are contextual, while the last six are case studies. Noel contextualizes his account with a brief analysis of the scholarship on "survivals," "retentions," and "Africanisms" in Blackamerican culture, the kind of discussion that was canalized by the Frazier–Herskovits debate. Accenting the role of materiality in Long's work, Noel's principal claim, which is integral to everything he writes in these contextual chapters, is the following: "Materiality includes the total process, products, and modalities constituting human exchanges—the entire matrix. We cannot grasp the notion of materiality without coordinating the term with two others: 'contact' and 'exchange.' "[57] This is a very important observation regarding Long's theorizing of Black Religion. Noel adds that contact and exchange always reveal a "surplus." This language reminds us of Marx's labor theory and notion of surplus value. But Noel appears to resist a Marxist reading, accenting instead Marcel Mauss' notion of gift exchange. While critical of the flat-footed treatment of the black experience by many theologians, Noel, unlike Long, offers an explicitly Christian (theological) interpretation of surplus value and meaning, which he identifies with Jesus' "salvific act on the cross."[58] Here a gap opens between Noel's account and Long's view. Long *explicitly* avoids a theological reduction of this surplus. His view has more in common with William James' nontheological notion of an ontological "more" that exceeds our concrete grasp.

Despite this interpretative gap, Noel accents a point frequently noted by other scholars: there is a reciprocal relation between black identity and the circumstances under which it emerged. An artifact of the cultural contact and exchanges that occurred in the Atlantic world of modernity, black identity was created in large part by the transatlantic slave trade. Blackness is an artifact of whiteness, and vice versa. It is the underside of whiteness and a surplus—that is, a difference within the blackness that whiteness made. On both sides of this contact and exchange (triangulated through contact with the native peoples of the New World), there is a surplus of value and meaning. This point is directly related to Noel's claim regarding the recreation of African divinities in the New World. On both sides of the Black Atlantic, it was a dynamic process. African religions were not pristine before their encounter with Europeans; enslaved Africans did not merely carry the old gods with them to the Americas, they recreated them under different cultural-linguistic and geopolitical circumstances. Nor did this transformation wait until their arrival in the New World; it started aboard slave ships. Noel remarks: "The appearance of African gods in the New World doesn't only represent a form of continuity. Their appearance is also a radical critique of the oppression Africans underwent and experienced as a form of discontinuity. Black religion exhibits a longing for what was lost, but it also exhibits an eschatological orientation toward something that will be attained in the future."[59] The Middle Passage and slavery, as I read Noel, is the birthplace of Black Religion. This last point comports well with Long's claim regarding the importance of domination, slavery, and the involuntary presence of black people in America, in any account of Black Religion.

Noel approaches the contacts and exchanges that created the Atlantic World system from two angles: sixteenth-century voyages of discovery *and conquest,* and a new form of political and economic organization whose emergence and principles Adam Smith described in *The Wealth of Nations* (1776). "The beginnings of the study of religion as an academic discipline," Noel writes, quoting Long, "must be seen in light of the beginnings of modern globalization and its origins in the formation of the Atlantic world."[60] Following the logic of Long's claim, Noel argues that we must think of the interrelations of several historical processes as the proper context for the study of religion: "(1) Roman Catholic Reform, the Protestant Reformation, and Counter Reformation in Europe; (2) European global expansion through the Atlantic Ocean; (3) decimation and colonization of indigenous Americans; and (4) the enslavement of Africans during the 'long sixteenth century.'"[61] This is an eminently sensible argument to me. Noel succeeds in thematizing and concretizing what many of us know abstractly, if not vaguely. The processes he identifies are also the immediate context for the emergence of a new political and economic order.

Noel is right to think through the imagination of matter in relation to political economy and Marx's critique of that very idea. Certainly Marx has done more than any other thinker to educate us regarding the constitutive relation between the way we produce our economic existence and the ideas we live by. Or, in his own words: "The mode of production of material life conditions the social, political and intellectual life process in general."[62] Marx exposes the materiality of ideas; or, to turn Long's phrase on its head—the materialization of the imagination, the facts of *matter* (food, clothing, shelter, and leisure) that produce, through their very production, our imagination. I suspect that Noel does not subscribe to Marx's view that that the ruling ideas are the ideas of the ruling class. It is a pity that he does not pursue this line of inquiry toward the light it might provide. Though he is mildly critical of Adam Smith's account of capitalist political economy and the *tolerable* inequalities it produces, Noel uses Weber, "the bourgeois Marx," to buffer himself from the full radicality of Marx's critique. Where he gives a generous reading of Weber's theory, he is not so generous toward Marx, whom he reads in light of those passages that encourage a reductive, base-superstructure account of his theory. The critic then, in this hermeneutically less generous mood, can dismiss Marx as blind to the power of ideas.

Drawing on the work of William Pietz, and following Long's use of him in recent work, Noel analyzes the central role of commodity fetishism in Marx's *Capital*. He notes the derivation of the very idea of fetishism from the history of religions, which itself is ensconced in a history of contacts and exchanges between Europeans (travelers, colonizers, and missionaries) and Africans. Based on their misunderstanding of the Africans they encountered along the west coast of Africa, Portuguese explorers concluded that Africans worshiped (fetishized) inanimate objects such as stones to which they attributed human-like qualities. As Noel rightly notes, Marx appropriates the term "fetishism" and the religious discourse associated with it to characterize the central dynamic of capitalism, the fetishizing of commodities.[63] This important line of inquiry might shed light on the way that black people were caught up in a modern European way of imaging matter. Unfortunately, Noel does not do much with this opportunity. He's more interested in the theological points that Marx's critique allows him to make than with the substance of the analysis. He gets caught up in Marx's rhetorical gestures and does not recognize its tropic character. Noel gives a non-ironic reading of an account that screams irony.

Noel cites those passages where Marx refers to "metaphysical subtleties and theological niceties" and to money as the real god of this world as if Marx was not a critic of religion but was merely making a different kind of theological argument. He mistakes the back of Marx's dismissive hand as a kind of compliment to theology. What Marx is actually saying is that in their relation to commodities, modern, "civilized," Europeans, Christian and non-Christian alike, behave like fetish worshippers. (They behaved the way European observers imagined Africans behaved.) Hence civilized Europeans attribute their own powers to commodities; people are "thingified," as they become commodities and commodities become gods. Ironically, Noel questions the adequacy of Marx's analysis with respect to race while using the very analytical scheme that Marx provides. Noel remarks: "the slave was reduced to the form of materiality of the commodity. The slave, therefore, is also one of modernity's fetishes. While devaluing human beings by reducing them to chattel Europeans created the category of 'race.'" Noel is absolutely right. Indeed, Eric Williams, whom he cites and Oliver C. Cox whom he does not cite, show how this happened.[64] Despite the inadequacy of Marx's race critique,

Noel's own language illustrates the illuminating power of the analysis. The real question is why didn't Noel do more with it? Repairing the defects of Marx's analysis may have exceeded Noel's purposes. So my question should not be read too negatively but rather as a wishful expression of what Noel's critique might have accomplished, and as a goad to the kind of work that the community of scholars should do. The most important question for my purposes, which is to explore Long's influence on the study of Black Religion, is whether Noel's interpretation is a reasonably accurate construction of Long's view. The answer to this question is not as clear as I would like.

As I remarked earlier, I divide Noel's text into "contextual" and "case study" chapters. In the case study part of his analysis, Noel applies Long's ideas to specific issues, figures, and expressive forms in Black Religion. There are two clusters of ideas in particular that I wish to explore: the first comes under the heading of "signifying silence," the second, under "opacity."

Signifying Silence

Noel appears to be invested in the idea that certain aspects of the black experience are ineffable, a view he claims is inspired by Long's reflections on "silence and signification."[65] When the claim is made that certain phenomena are ineffable, two distinct interpretations are possible. The speaker may be understood as saying that language is inadequate to that reality as media, representation, or inference. Or, the claim could be taken as normative: one should not attempt to capture certain realities in language; to do so is to minimize or otherwise distort the reality captured. Often the speaker vacillates between the first and the second possible meanings. "Unspeakable" is often merely a synonym for "really bad" or "so bad that I do not wish to speak about it." Here language is not so much inadequate as undesirable for a *certain* speaking subject. This is how Toni Morrison uses the concept in *Beloved* when in the final pages her narrator refers to a story that is not to be passed on. In light of this, it is not clear to me what Noel is claiming when, for example, he accents the ineffable character of the Middle Passage in the experience of black people in the Americas. Is it really the case that these experiences cannot be spoken? Or is the writer trying, through a particular kind of rhetorical performance, to create the reality he claims to discover? This is what I take Noel to be doing when he says that the experience of the Middle Passage eludes the grasp of language. Consider his account of

Olaudah Equiano's first-person description of the Middle Passage that Noel quotes extensively. He notes Equiano's use of adjectives such as "astonishment, fear, terror, and horror." Regarding the experience that Equiano *actually describes* Noel remarks: "The experience defies linguistic expression."[66] Captives such as Equiano, he claims, were "transported beyond the bounds of known or imagined sensibility."[67] Accordingly, they did not directly express their encounter with terror linguistically. This is an odd claim in light of Equiano's narrative. In contrast to Noel's account, Equiano does not give the reader the impression that his experience of the Middle Passage is ineffable, beyond his powers of articulate speech, a wordless and word-defying depth, an apophatic holy of holy.[68] Despite the weight of Equiano's own witness, his performative refutation of this claim before the fact, Noel asserts that Equiano's experience was ineffable; that whatever he did say about the Middle Passage, the most important thing about his experience could not be said. Thus the sublime (secret) heart of the Middle Passage eludes "linguistic capture." What I hear in Noel's account of Equiano's narrative is an articulation of "Middle Passage Piety."

Middle Passage Piety reminds me of Holocaust Piety, which is the notion of "chosenness" (divine election) in the form of the sublime. As Gillian Rose suggests, the Holocaust has become a form of piety in the face of the sublime—sublime piety. Holocaust Piety is the notion that the Shoah cannot truly be represented and that we ought to resist straightforward and comprehensive attempts to do so. On this view, the Holocaust is fundamentally ineffable; its truth cannot be spoken. It is a sublime mystery whose sublimity depends on its mysteriousness. Those who attempt to speak the truth of the Holocaust without acknowledging its impossibility are guilty of Holocaust Impiety. Rose retorts: "To argue for silence, prayer, the banishment equally of poetry and knowledge, in short, the witness of "ineffability', that is, non-representability, is *to mystify something we dare not understand*, because we fear that it may be all too understandable, all too continuous with what we are—human, all too human." Holocaust Impiety is what postmodernist and poststructuralist skeptics call the fascism of representation. Rose offers the following rejoinder:

> The demonstration that fascism and representation are inseparable does not lead to the conclusion, current in post-modern aesthetics, philosophy and political theory, that representation is or should be superseded. On the contrary, the argument for the overcoming of

> representation, in its aesthetic, philosophical and political versions, converges with *the inner tendency* of fascism itself. Only the persistence of always fallible and contestable representation opens the possibility for our acknowledgement of mutual implication in the fascism of our cultural rites and rituals.[69]

What Rose says regarding the Holocaust is equally true of the Middle Passage, whose horrors *can* be represented. Equiano performs this representation in his own narrative. To claim otherwise is *to mystify something that is human, all too human, something we dare not understand.* There is no virtue in pretending that the terror and horror inflicted on Africans during the Middle Passage cannot be understood. Chosenness in the form of the sublime—a perverse form of divine election, a pathetic bid for dignity under the conditions of extreme abjection—is too high a price to pay.

Speaking of abjection, Noel poses a provocative question: "What I am wondering is whether the near dehumanization of Africans and other Third World people through slavery and colonialism was somehow refracted in the reflections of Western Philosophy on the problem of Being."[70] Unfortunately, he does not pursue an answer. The question is overtaken by a confusing account of nonbeing in the black experience of enslavement and its aftermath. I call it confusing because Noel conflates the conventional notion of "being as presence" with Heidegger's reconstructed notion where being is nothingness, the absence of any kind of transcendental ground, onto-theology, metaphysics of substance or subject. On this Heideggerian view, the being of being(s) is nothing. In contrast, Noel conflates presence and being. He confuses a Thomistic notion of "being as plenitude" with Heidegger's being as nothing.[71] In short, he construes being as something rather than nothing. These distinctions are important because of the claim that Noel makes regarding the primal reality of Non-Being (his capitalization) in black identity formation and religion.

Noel confuses abjection and subjection with nonbeing. They are not the same. On the contrary, subjection of the most extreme, abject kind is a modality of being. His distinction between being and nonbeing is more Hegelian than Heideggerian. This conflation is related to his confusion of Heideggerian and Thomistic notions of being and his failure to distinguish Husserl's Cartesian-inflected phenomenology with its transcendental subject from the existential phenomenology of Heidegger, which overcomes the subject-object distinction at every turn. On Heidegger's view, we are always already "being-in-the-world" and "being-with-others" rather than subjects over against others and objects. Husserl is preoccupied with epistemology, a concern that Noel appears to share, while Heidegger's focus is ontology, where being (the "question") precedes knowing. In his account, Noel conflates at least three kinds of phenomenology (Hegelian, Husserlian, and Heideggerian) without explaining to the reader how this can be done. In his own phenomenological reflections, I think that Long is more careful in sorting out the complexities among the three.

Opacity

Noel uses Nat Turner to illustrate Long's concept of opacity and opacity to illuminate Turner's biblical hermeneutic. I find his effort disappointing in large part because he seems more interested in making a certain intervention regarding contemporary debates in biblical hermeneutics than he is in exploring the opacity that Turner purportedly represents. Though Noel presents an interesting discussion of hermeneutics, he does not show how it explicates Turner's act of insurrection. On a basic level, he never tells the reader what Long means by opacity—that is, he applies the concept without explicating it. Absent even a rudimentary definition, the reader can only assume that Noel's use of the term is "common" rather than "technical." It functions as mere rhetoric, producing a certain kind of effect, rather than substantively as a category of analysis. For Long, opacity is an anti-Enlightenment metaphor: a critique of epistemic certainty (Descartes' "I think, I am" and of the root metaphor of transparency regarding what we can know), of a presumed unencumbered vision of the—colonial, slave, primitive, idolatrous, or racial—"other." In contrast, Noel's clearest statement of what he means by Turner's opacity is the following:

> The meaning of his deed would be fulfilled and revealed in his execution. Turner's execution would, in turn, serve as a sign of indictment upon the system that provoked his rebellion. Therefore, whites would have to search their own souls to discover the meaning of Turner's rebellion. Turner's opacity is directly related to white's incapacity and unwillingness to encounter the Other through a radical self-critique.[72]

Noel focuses on the least opaque aspect of Turner's insurrection, namely, his biblical hermeneutic. For the biblically literate, Turner's apocalyptic hermeneutic is not particularly opaque. A variety of millenarian thinkers and movements subscribed to this kind of hermeneutic throughout the nineteenth century. I would argue that the grammar, if not the syntax and vocabulary of Turner's apocalyptic hermeneutic—white spirits, black spirits, conflict, blood, and disembodied voices—would have been accessible to his contemporaries across racial and cultural lines. The horror provoked by Turner's bloody insurrection was probably exacerbated by the *transparency* of the narrative in which it was embedded and the audacious bid for biblical sanction of his prophetic authority that it represented. When Turner responded—"Was not Christ crucified?"—to his interrogator's mocking suggestion that his prophetic vision was an illusion and the insurrection he led a terrible mistake, he appealed to a common (transparent) grammar.

I am not claiming that this hermeneutic would be transparently accessible without remainder; some aspects of Blackamerican life, forged under the conditions of chattel slavery, would probably remain opaque. Noel's argument is more persuasive when he focuses on the opacity of slavery in the "land of the free" and the celebration of "life, liberty, and the pursuit of happiness" in a society founded on the denial of such to "first nation" people through acts of dispossession and genocide. These are bizarre and opaque phenomena. Rather than accidental features, slavery and genocide were constitutive of white republican liberty. *Opacity lies in fundamentally irreconcilable notions of liberty: a concept of liberty that includes property rights in other people's lives, bodies, labor, and possessions versus a concept of liberty that denies such rights.* This is an ambiguity and a darkness in liberal theory that cannot be resolved noncontroversially. This bizarre reality, as Long describes it, produced forms of opacity that still characterize different constructions of meaning across and within identity constructions.

Noel's study is a valuable contribution to scholarship. There is much in the book that I will not address in detail but from which the reader can benefit. He provides an interesting account of creolization as the process through which black people experienced an emerging modernity with a brief synthesis of recent scholarship on the emergence of *race*. Noel organizes the creative response to modernity by African-descended people under the category of the salsa/jazz/blues idiom, which is a product of the very emphasis on cultural contact and exchange that he derives from Long. This analysis relates thematically to his account of the mulatto as a site of contact and exchange (interracial sex) in the Atlantic World. If creolization is primarily a site of cultural exchange, then the mulatto is a bio-cultural site, an exchange of sex, intimacy, and genes. Both creolization and the mulatto emerge within the brutal exchange (commodification) of black people in the Atlantic World. Concluding his account of the salsa/jazz/blues idiom, Noel quotes Robert Gooding-Williams:

> The distinction between being a black person and being authentically a black person makes no sense in my view, since one becomes a black person by, and only by, acting under certain descriptions...I postulate no black personhood apart from a black person's actions. I do not suppose that, prior to the performance of discursively shaped actions, there exist black selves or persons that such actions could authentically express.[73]

On Gooding-Williams' point about the nonontological status of black people, which resonates with my concept of Afro-*Eccentricity,* I suspect that Long would agree.

Theology and Opacity

In his fascinating text, *Race: A Theological Account,* J. Kameron Carter raises important questions about Long's perspective, particularly his concept of opacity. Though he finds the concept illuminating in many respects, Carter does not believe that it surpasses theological discourse in illuminating black religious life. This claim represents a direct challenge to my claim that Long provides the most sophisticated set of tools for understanding Black Religion. If Carter is right, then I must abandon or modify my claim. I begin with a summary account of Carter's critique and then comment on what I think he is doing, why, and whether he hits his mark.

Carter charges Long with abstracting from the forms of concreteness that characterize the religious lives of black people, with privileging *the religious as such* over specific forms of religious life such as Afro-Christianity. In short, he accuses Long of bleeding Afro-Christianity of it content and embalming it in the formaldehyde of "the religious." This is the second of two reservations that Carter articulates. His first reservation goes to the success or, as he claims, the failure of Long's theory of opacity to interrupt the reign of whiteness within interpretations of Black Religion. According to Carter, Long substitutes *opacity* for *transparency* (the Enlightenment idea), one ocular metaphor for another. Though he inverts their normative relationship, he remains a captive of the normalizing gaze of whiteness that relies on ocular metaphors. This reliance is constitutive, he contends, of Long's inability to satisfactorily account for encounters between the religious consciousness of black subjects and historical others. Long entertains no prospect of change and growth as a result of such encounters. There is no concrete encounter: religious consciousness is solipsistic; religious subjects, in the final analysis, are windowless monads or Cartesian subjects, contemplating their own minds, surveying their own interiority.

There is much here to unpack. We need to assess Carter's attributions and interpretation. Is it truly the case that Long's concept of opacity presupposes a solipsistic notion of the black religious subject, closed off from any real encounter with historical otherness, immune to the contingencies of history? Ironically, there is a certain ahistoricism in some traditions of *religionswissenschaft*. Recall the point I made earlier regarding Long:

> On the one hand, it [the black religious consciousness] appears to be a historical phenomenon—the involuntary presence of black people on American soil, oppugnancy, and the opacity of their experience, which has left innumerable traces in folkways and mores—about which the inquirer can assemble an inventory of evidence, draw and support conclusions. On the other hand, it appears to be an ahistorical phenomenon, a Kantian thing-in-itself that persists across space-time and in the face of cultural transformations and that resists, if it is not immune, to the best efforts of the inquirer and demands for evidence. This construction of the datum ["archaic structure" in the religious consciousness of black people] is a problem that goes to an insuperable difficulty at the heart of the history of religions as Long practices it.

On the issue of ahistoricism Carter's view and mine overlap but they are discrepant as well. I recognize the complexity of Long's view that Carter does not. To illustrate, I will analogize from Freud's view of the mind in which the ego (the conscious) is like the tip of an iceberg and the id (the unconscious) its submerged bulk. If we invert this model, then we have a picture of the religious consciousness as Long construes it. An artifact of historical contingencies, the religious conscious is largely visible. There is an ahistorical "kernel," however, that resists historical determination. Like the id, it is submerged—in this case, beneath the contingencies of history. Like any analogy, this one is not perfect but it provides a better account of Long's view than Carter's account. Contrary to Carter's claim, Long's notion of religious conscious is all about the *materiality* of historical encounters, cultural contact and exchange. It is precisely the encounter with European others within the context of an emergent Atlantic World system, driven primarily by the triangular slave trade, that characterizes the oppugnant and opaque reality that is the black religious conscious. Europeans literally "bumped" into Africans, who developed a hermeneutic for that encounter. Carter draws on Charles Peirce's phenomenological categories of "firstness," "secondness," and "thirdness" to criticize Long. Contrary to Carter's claim, this example of "Peircean thirdness"--where Europeans violently encountered Africans who creatively interpreted that encounter--is as basic as it gets.[74]

Carter does not like the way Long handles first-person accounts by ex-slaves of their conversion experiences. He claims that Long minimizes the Christian specificity of their prayers and the centrality of the Trinity for how they imagined the subject of those prayers; that he reads these testimonies as providing "further evidence that for black folks their confrontation or encounter with God is itself not historical."[75] Carter's construction ignores what Long explicitly says, as evident in this passage:

> These two narratives are illustrative of the inner dynamics of the conversion experience. The narratives combine and interweave the ordinary events with the transformation of the religious consciousness. *It is not merely a case of God acting in history, for the historical events are not the locus of the activity but then neither do we have a complete lack of concern for historical events in favor of a mystification of consciousness* [emphasis added]. It is the combination of these two structures that is distinctive in these narratives; clues such as these might help us to understand the specific nature of the black religious consciousness.[76]

Long's account of religious consciousness and the very idea of "the imagination of matter" is more complex than Carter's analysis. A simple analogy may help us to better understand the structuring role that the religious consciousness plays in Long's account. In Long's theory, there is "religious conscious" and there are specific historical encounters and forms of religion. If we construe "religious conscious" linguistically, then we can describe it as the irreducibly metahistorical component in every historical experience of g/God (including the Christian god) or the really real. Or to put this differently, there are no unmediated experiences. Whether this metahistorical component needs to be construed ahistorically is an entirely different matter. But

Carter is simply wrong when he claims that Long ignores the Christian specificity of the black religious subject he describes. He is equally wrong in claiming that Long's theory does not allow actual engagement with historical otherness, marked as such encounters must be by evidence of change and transformation. The real object of Carter's complaint is that Long denies unmediated encounters between the Christian god and the black religious subject and implicitly relativizes its importance. Like all other historical encounters, encounters with the Christian god are mediated by religious consciousness—and, in the case of the black subject, a religious consciousness forged dialogically within the oppugnant and opaqueness of the American context.

Regarding his second reservation, Carter is maladroit in applying the concept of "the blackness that whiteness created" to Long's notion of opacity. He appropriates this term from Victor Anderson's *Beyond Ontological Blackness* (1995). "The blackness that whiteness created" describes a situation in which the notion of black racial genius mirrors European notions, hence the concept of ontological blackness.[77] Carter's accusation is supported by reference to Cornel West's account of the normalizing gaze of white supremacy, which is indebted to Foucault and before him to Sartre. Also drawing on Rorty, West criticizes the excessive valorization of ocular metaphors within modern discourse. Wedding the analyses of Anderson and West, Carter claims that Long extends the reign of whiteness by rearticulating a version of "the blackness that whiteness created." While it may be fair to charge Long with ontologizing religious consciousness (unlike his fellow Historian of Religion, Jonathan Z. Smith, Long's notion of religion, religions, and the religious is not sufficiently historicist and constructivist for me), to accuse him of ontologizing blackness is gratuitous.

Carter's accusation encodes two errors. First, he confuses the logic of inversion/subversion with the logic of the mirror: opacity disrupts the (sometimes) disciplinary agenda of transparency; it does not mirror it. Stated otherwise, Long does not substitute a black normalizing gaze for the disciplinary work that panoptic whiteness has historically performed in its effort to make black subjects docile and useful. Second, Carter ignores Long's critique of this mirroring logic in liberation theology or, as he calls them, "theologies opaque." (Perhaps I should amend this point. Carter does acknowledge Long's critique of black theology but appears to ignore it when attributing the same malady to him—ontologizing blackness—that Long attributes to opaque theologians.) To grasp the error of that attribution, consider Long's question: "What is one to make of these theologies of redness, blackness, and blueness of deity and being?"[78] Long answers his own question as follows:

> If God is red, if black is beautiful, then this modality of the godhead has always been the case and there are those who have lived this testimony. The opacity of God forms a discontinuity with the bad faith of the other theological modes. There is a theology of accusation and opposition which is to the fore in the theologies opaque. But it is precisely at this point that these theologies should not move forward to possess the theological battlefield wrested from their foes. It is at this point that theologies opaque must be deconstructive theologies—that is to say, theologies that undertake the destruction of theology as a powerful mode of discourse.[79]

The real object of Carter's "opaque" analysis (pun intended) is Long's act of radically relativizing the status of theology within religious studies. Carter is especially vexed by the narrow space left for the postliberal/radical orthodox theological modality he prefers. Long's call for *the destruction of theology as a powerful mode of discourse* has little sympathy for a model of religion study that, in its desire to bring the universe into the biblical/postliberal/radical orthodox world, rearticulates and radicalizes the most noxious aspects of Barth's imperial "doctrine of other religions," that is, his distinction between Christianity as the revelation of god (and the abolition of religion) and religions as human, all too human.[80] Long's analysis levels this Christian/other distinction. Carter construes this act as "positivism."

Positivism has been a controversial idea in critical discourse for some time. Today it is hard to find a self-described positivist, which is a measure of just how unpopular the term is. Positivism has become a term of negative critique when it isn't merely a term of abuse. Carter accuses Long of several kinds of positivism, so my task is to determine if he uses the word as a legitimate form of negative critique or merely a term of abuse, a dismissive form of name-calling. One can use the term in a fairly precise and "rigorous" way: positivism as a dogmatic form of empiricism, a dismissive attitude toward religious and ethical forms of knowledge; where, properly speaking, they are not forms of knowledge at all but literally nonsense, noncognitive, emotive expressions. Loosely construed, positivism may mean nothing more than "I disagree with the subject of my critique." Carter's use is fairly loose. Rather than denigrating religious knowledge claims as such by construing them as merely emotive, he criticizes Long for not privileging a specific form of religious knowledge, namely, Christian theology and a particular version of it—Postliberal and Radical Orthodox.

To get a clear handle on what Carter means by positivism, I quote him extensively. The quotation is part of his critique of Long's purported lack of interest in the Christian specificity of the black religious subject, specifically, Long's mistreatment the black praying subject. Carter remarks:

> The first problem is what can be called a positivism of history, indeed, of the black experience of history in America. Such a positivist approach to history has the effect of establishing a sociopolitical positivism in which the horizon or upper limit of black existence becomes America itself. The deep structure of this historical positivism is the black religious consciousness as such, which itself has no history. The task of the historian (of religion) is to uncover the structures of black consciousness by archeologically uncovering their traces in the sands of history. Stated otherwise, history is but the analytic of consciousness, which itself does not dialogically unfold so as to move and grow, not simply *under* the provocation of encountering the other, but rather *in* the provocation itself such that there is no escaping the encounter. History so structured through the positivity of encounter itself is precisely what Long's notion of the opaque refuses: hence his philosophical positivism. For Long, history does not structure the religious consciousness as such, and because it does not, religious experiences and practices and, at the end of the day, culture itself, are only so many aesthetic accoutrements, at best, of a consciousness that always already, in a priori fashion, is intact. The paradoxical result is that there can be no history within this understanding of the opaque.[81]

Since I have already responded to most of the issues raised in this passage, Long's alleged positivism is the sole focus of my response. Carter construes Long's "methodological leveling" with respect to the status claims (to uniqueness, categorical difference, and superiority) made on behalf of the Christian god as positivism. However, he fails to establish his claim that Long is a positivist in any substantial, non-name-calling sense. In Carter's use of the term, positivism is virtually empty of analytic content. It is merely a term of abuse. He does not support his assertion that Long is a positivist and, therefore, is inappropriately critical of theological knowledge. Carter does not give the reader any reason to endorse his claim. One would expect him to consider basic questions such as: Is Long a proponent of Auguste Comte's evolutionary account where knowledge improves progressively from religious, to metaphysical, and finally to scientific forms? Does he posit a fact-value distinction where religious utterances are construed as nonsense? Does Long claim that all true knowledge is scientific (one wonders whether Carter confuses the *"wissenschaft"* in *religionswissenschaft* with scientism)? In which of these specific senses is Long a positivist? Carter drops terms such as *historical, sociopolitical*, and *philosophical positivism* as if they were self-explicating. This language is merely rhetorical. The terms have no analytic content. Carter's desire to support his claim for the categorical difference of Christianity and its transcendent relation to religious consciousness, which he construes as merely a human capacity for encountering otherness, explains his recourse to the charge of positivism and the confessional character of his critique. But these desires do not entitle him to the claims that he makes or to the endorsement of the reader.

On Carter's view, Long is ill-disposed toward theology. This poor disposition leads him into a positivistic reduction of Christianity, which prevents him from fairly assessing the Christian specificity (uniqueness and transcendence) of his subject matter, in this case the black Christian subject. On this issue and regarding the superiority of Christianity to other religions, in fact, its fundamentally "nonreligious" and, therefore, categorical difference, Carter remarks:

> God, in Christian terms, is not an-other either to history or to historically constituted beings in the way that oil is an-other to water. Long's notion of the opaque as a means of probing the significance of a deity or deities for the religious consciousness wants to fit the Trinitarian God of Israel into this Procrustean bed. But, as the religious experience and practice of prayer seems to suggest from Long's own examples, God relates to the world as its genuine other not because God is an-other to the creature but because God is first and foremost "non-other" (*non aliud,* as Nicholas of Cusa once put it) to the creature. As *non aliud,* the Trinitarian God of Israel disrupts all logics of creaturely other-ing. This is one of the most important claims of Trinitarian thinking, a claim driven from within the practices of Christian faith and spirituality, including, and perhaps supremely, the practice of prayer.[82]

So there you have it: postliberalism and neo-orthodoxy in all its glory. Lest Carter be let off too easily, I should note that it is not the so-called Procrustean bed of the history of religions to which Carter objects. He is quite willing to cast every god into that bed except the "Trinitarian God of Israel." I won't comment on the bizarre notion of the god of Israel as *Trinitarian* except to say that Carter's Christian imperialism knows no bounds: the god of Israel, through this blatant form of supersession, is "turned out." YHWH is forced to testify against "himself," to acknowledge that "he" has "associates" (Jesus and the Holy Spirit), to speak "Christian" rather than Hebrew. It is Long's refusal to accept Christian exceptionalism, his determination to place the Christian god in the same bed as other gods, that Carter cannot abide. Long refuses to be pulled into the normative vision—the world of the Patristic as interpreted by postliberalism and the neo-orthodoxy—that Carter prefers. (Throughout his critique, Carter vacillates between negative criticism and attempts to recruit Long to his postliberal, antimodern, anti-Enlightenment, Patristic-inflected approach. So Carter positions Long, temporarily, as an ally. As there are no permanent friends in theological politics but only permanent interests, the alliance extends only so far as it enables Carter's postliberal/radical orthodox aims. Long is useful where his critique of religious studies supports Carter's critique of theological liberalism—the *bête noire* of postliberalism and radical orthodoxy.) In disagreeing with Long, Carter writes as if his confessional claims are self-evident. He does not recognize the level on which his disagreement with Long must be argued, if in fact he thinks an argument regarding first principles is possible. The conflict between Long and Carter is that basic: a matter of how they prehend or intuit the very structure of reality, the very nature of things. This point merits emphasis. Carter fails to establish a genuine dialogue with Long, which would require that he carefully consider Long's presuppositions. Such a dialogue would have been even more substantial had Carter considered his own commitments in light of Long's presuppositions and thereby put his own claims at risk. His approach is imperial. The other is not someone to be engaged but a subject of conquest. There is no good reason to think that Carter would *or even should* abandon his views. But it would have made the dialogue real, if not really contentious, had he taken a risk. Taking such a risk is his obligation to Long and the reader. After all, he chose to engage Long.

Carter takes a particular Christian construction of human reality as basic. He seeks to absorb the universe into the biblical world as interpreted by theologians such as John Milbank (his mentor) and Stanley Hauerwas with Karl Barth in the near background. In contrast, Long's basic intuition is quite different. For him, the Christian account of human reality is merely one among many and is not entitled to special consideration. More basic than any particular religious tradition, including Christianity, is a human modality of encountering the world called "the religious" or the religious consciousness. Humans are *Homo religiosus*. On Long's view, this is the most important *truth* about religious studies. One might question, as I do, the neo-Kantian and Schleiermacher-esque resonance of this notion without accepting, as I do not, Carter's alternative. Carter tries to "do" for black religious studies what Milbank does with secular academic disciplines, which is to subject them to the imperial vision ("dominion theology" with a difference) of postliberalism/radical orthodoxy; to construe them as an inadequate, if not failed, effort to do what these theologies do better, construing them as obtuse if not unfaithful offspring. His effort, as I hope my analysis has shown, is no more convincing than Milbank's neo-Augustinian construction of secular academic knowledges as the *privation* of the Christian theological good.

Having considered Carter's critique, I reassert my initial claim: Charles H. Long, Archaeologist of the black religious experience, provides the most sophisticated set of tools for understanding Black Religion. Long digs his way out of the Standard Narrative of Black Religion by exploring a distinctive set of comparative, morphological, and phenomenological questions.

Chapter 5

The Renegade

The Problem of Divine Racism

In this chapter, I provide a constructive analysis of William R. Jones' critique of black theology in light of Long's threefold challenge regarding the study of Afro-American religion. Specifically, I shall support the argument that Jones' analysis raises the stakes regarding "the experience and symbol of God in the religious experience of blacks." Just as Eshu-Elegba stands at the crossroads in the Afro-Atlantic religious imagination, there is an unacknowledged, threshold question for black theologians: "Is God a white racist?" Jones anticipates and responds to the objection that his inquiry is either nonserious or driven by motives that are inimical to the interests of black people.[1] He remarks: "Think not as you read these pages that they were conceived in certainty and ease. Fear and trembling confusion and doubt gave them birth. And if my words bespeak an irreverent iconoclasm and profane dissent for the sake of notoriety, they contradict my conscious motives."[2] Echoing Long's challenge, Jones intends to call black theologians to account for the images of god they have constructed.

Evidence, Arguments, and "the" Question

Jones' analysis is bookended by a prologue that pivots on the poignant question regarding the suffering of black people that DuBois addresses to god—"What meaneth this?"—and an epilogue that calls for a debate among black theologians regarding the issue of divine racism. Jones contends that the conflict between the pro-liberation image of god in black theology and the status of black people makes the issue of divine racism unavoidable. Between prologue and epilogue, Jones provides an unparalleled analysis of the untoward consequences of this conflict and a proposal, organized under the concept of "humanocentric theism," for how they might be overcome.

Jones' basic thesis is the following: the inordinate suffering of black people combined with the conventional claim that god is benevolent generates the charge of divine racism, which is the unacknowledged threshold issue for black theology. Divine racism is an ensemble of analytical tools that Jones uses to evaluate the claims of black theologians. These tools include (1) the very idea of a malevolent god who wills the oppression of black people, (2) a tradition of black humanist thought that raises the possibility that god is a white racist, (3) a critique of quietism (where theodicy is a prop for oppression) in black theological constructions of god, and (4) a method of arguing from counter-evidence designed to make the quietistic implications of black liberation theodicy explicit, thus defeating its power.

Jones contends that the very enterprise of black theology presupposes a negative answer to the question of divine racism. The arguments of black theologians, however, do not support this negative answer. On the contrary, they give credence to the claim that god hates black people. Jones' purpose is not to make the case for god's racism. Rather, he wants to show how bad arguments within black theology make it possible to raise this question. That the question can be raised, and that it arises logically and consistently in the work of black theologians, is a theological weakness that is inimical to the well-being of black people. It undermines a liberating agency among the wretched of the earth. This is crucial because the "liberation" of black people, which is ostensibly the purpose of black theology, motivates Jones' critique.[3]

The concept of "divine racism" is a heuristic concept designed to test what Jones believes are the liberation-defeating qualities of black theology. This heuristic has two subconcepts: the "multievidentiality of suffering" and "God as the sum of his acts." The fact of suffering can support competing judgments regarding god's benevolence. For example, the meaning of the "cross" is not univocal, which is another way of saying that it is multievidential.[4] Is the cross evidence of god's love or evidence of perversity, cruelty, and bloodlust? Perhaps god is a demon, and not merely the demon who crept into Descartes' dreams, troubling his "clear and distinct ideas," but a bloodthirsty demon who hung Jesus on a cross and thousands of black men and women on trees. As Jones suggests, this interpretation of the evidence is most likely when god is viewed as the sum of his acts. If god is what god does, then god's character can only be inferred from what god has done or is currently doing. Character is a retrospective, inferential judgment.[5] Given the suffering of black people, what can the black theologian say in retrospect about god? If god is the sum of god's acts, then how can they evade the ugly evidence of black suffering? Can they evade such questions by looking to a liberation-deferring eschatology? Jones denies the plausibility of any future-oriented argument in the absence of an "exaltation event"—an event in the history of black people that radically transforms their suffering. Such an event would be "akin to the principle 'from last to first,' "[6] the replacement of suffering by its opposite. Jones cites the Exodus as the paradigmatic exaltation event in the Bible. However, the Exodus, which was a liberation event for the ancient Hebrews, cannot be cited as a liberation event for black people. It must be an event in the *actual* history of black people.[7]

Failure to identify the exaltation event leaves black theologians incapable of distinguishing positive suffering from negative suffering, between "the suffering servant and the rank sinner encountering his deserved punishment."[8] Deferring the exaltation event to the future makes it impossible to credibly regard black people as god's suffering servant: the collective embodiment of a form of innocent suffering that is redemptive. Black suffering loses any positive (redemptive) divine warrant. On the contrary, it appears to be negatively warranted. Negative suffering is nonredemptive and nonpedagogical. With no redeeming qualities, it does not promote the well-being of the sufferer. In the absence of a better argument, the enormity, disproportionality, chronic nature, and "ethnic" specificity of black suffering—the fact that god appears to hate and to harbor a racially specific animosity toward blacks—are prima facie evidence of divine racism. The multi-evidentiality of suffering and the principle that god is the sum of his acts only increases the possibility that god is a white racist.[9]

Jones is speaking of a suffering unto death (suffering without measure). The death of Blackamericans hangs shroud-like over his account. Though arcane, the issue is a matter of life and death. Black people are suffering and dying. Black theologians, therefore, should not offer sunny metaphors nor arguments that promote quietism, adding to misery by linking the actuality of suffering unto death to the possibility that god is a white racist. Their metaphors, concepts, and arguments should *break* the link. Jones is a secular humanist, which I take as meaning that he does not believe in "God" as a reality independent of the human imagination. However, he recognizes the power of the idea among most Blackamericans and wishes to establish criteria that will prevent that idea, as much, as possible from undermining black liberation. Thus his claim that we should get our concepts right is not a matter of defending the goodness of god. Divine goodness cannot be a theological axiom for black theology, an unquestioned starting point.[10] That black theologians get their ideas about god right is intimately related to preserving the lives of Blackamerican in their full bodily and psychic dimensions. The metaphysical desire to preserve the innocence of god must not supersede the requirements of liberation. If the well-being of black people requires the destruction of god, then so be it.

Jones is preoccupied with the suffering of black people and the causal relation between belief and action. Beliefs matter. They are habit-forming. If beliefs predispose us to act in certain ways, then beliefs that encourage Blackamericans to accept an anti-black order is a form of quietism; that is, conformity and passivity in the face of injustice. Theological quietism takes the form of theodicy, which Jones argues is a prop for oppression.[11] To counter this support of oppression, Jones suggests that black theology must be an *inverted* or *antitheodicy*. Since god is the sum of god's acts, *a posteriori*, evidence-driven conclusions should replace *a priori* assumptions about god's character. Claims regarding god's benevolence must be subjected to the evidentiary demands of a "black tribunal of critical judgment." To anticipate a possible objection, this empirical turn cannot be dismissed as "positivism" since it demands that black theologians make good on their explicit claims about god's liberating agency in history. Or that they acknowledge that such talk is merely rhetorical.

Informed by his antitheodicy, Jones identifies three ways that theodicy provides a prop for oppression: first, by declaring the status quo to be just and remediation unnecessary; second, by insisting that remediation is impossible; third, by claiming that remediation is inappropriate.[12] The initial examples of theodicies that Jones analyzes in relation to the work of black theologians come from two sermons Father Panaloux delivers in Camus' novel *The Plague* (1947). Jones describes them as "demonstrative" and "last resort" theodicies. The former regards suffering as punishment for prior sin. In the face of sufferers who are clearly innocent, the latter entails a leap of faith that goes against the evidence,[13] suggesting that "We'll understand it better by and by." If, as the theodicy of last resort suggests, the suffering of innocents is "beyond human comprehension," then its injustice will be resolved eschatologically. But, Jones remarks, eschatology is no resolution at all. It merely defers justification, and it begs the question regarding the benevolence of god, which is the very claim that requires an argument.[14] Such theodicies are acts of desperation.

A Note on Antitheodicy

To get a better handle on Jones' critique, consider the following comments regarding theodicy by Kenneth Surin:

> [I]n an identifiably Christian context, the 'problem of evil' arises (at least in part) when *particular* narratives of events of pain, dereliction, anguish, oppression, torture, humiliation, degradation, injustice, hunger, godforsakenness, and so on, come into collision with the Christian community's narratives, which are inextricably bound up with the redeeming reality of the triune God. These events...generate epistemological crises in which agents come to realize that the schemata of interpretation on which they have so far relied have broken down irretrievably, a realization which gives an impetus to the construction of more adequate narratives and forms of narrative.[15]

Surin describes the circumstances that produce theodic reasoning, an account that I take as describing why black theology got off the ground in the first place; that is, the evil of black suffering, which is *underdetermined*[16] by white supremacy. In this section, I use Surin's distinction between theoretically and practically oriented forms of theodicy and his critique of the former to explore Jones' claim that black theology *must* take the form of a theodicy. Among the more important claims that Surin makes, one that Jones anticipates in his critique, is about the relationship between theoretical claims and practical behavior:

> *[A]ll* philosophical and theological reflection, no matter how abstract such reflection may be, inevitably mediates a certain social and political praxis. All significant intellectual visions have socially-mediated purchase on reality. They thus have the capacity to determine the way(s) in which a certain segment of reality is either to be transformed or else maintained in its existing form. The philosopher and the theologian do not reflect and discourse *in vacuo:* it is their responsibility, therefore, to ask themselves, continually, what particular praxis their work mediates. For it is only by such self-scrutiny that they can avoid being implicated in a rarefied discourse which legitimizes and mystifies the social processes that block the transformation of life and reality.[17]

Surin distinguishes broadly between "theodicies with a 'theoretical' emphasis" and "theodicies with a 'practical' emphasis." He contends that the first kind is wrong and pernicious: wrong because it denies what the previous quotation affirms, namely, that ideas have practical implications; pernicious, because it justifies what cannot be justified, presumes that evil as such, which is inexplicable, can be explained, and thus insults those afflicted with pain and anguish.[18]

Like Jones, Surin derives insights from literary existentialism. He draws on the theistic tradition of Russian existentialism while Jones taps the French humanists such as Sartre and Camus. Where Jones relies on Father Panaloux, a character in *The Plague,* through whom Camus criticizes "the theodicy of last resort," Surin uses Ivan Karamazov, a character from Dostoevsky's *The Brothers Karamazov,* to support a "theodicy of the cross."[19] According to Surin, Ivan is a moral rather than an ontological or epistemic atheist: that is, knowledge of god or god's existence is not the issue for him. What he objects to, rather, is the monstrosity of worshipping a god ensconced in an eschatological vision where a higher final "harmony" is purchased with blood, on the "slaughter bench" of history, where the horrible suffering of innocent children is necessary to achieve god's "higher" purpose. The price of such harmony is more than Ivan is willing to pay. Such harmony is immoral, especially if god commands it. No moral being, he thinks, should be willing to pay. As Surin remarks:

> The person who thinks that Ivan's crisis can be resolved by constructing a more coherent, a more intuitively plausible, a more 'religiously adequate', a more personally moving *apologia* on behalf of the God who *'exists'* and who is *'good'*, has utterly misperceived the nature of Ivan's epistemological crisis. For Ivan is not pleading to be convinced that there is a God, and that this God is benevolent, etc. Rather, Ivan is obsessively convinced that the affirmation of such a God serves only to make the 'problem of evil' more—much more—intractable.... What Ivan is engaging in is best seen as a form of metalinguistic reflection: he is attending here to the *a priori* possibility of applying those concepts which purport to express the reality of such love and graciousness. (He is thus engaged, generally, in the activity which Kant designated as 'transcendental logic', Hegel as logic, and Wittgenstein 'grammar'.)[20]

Jones' critique of black theology goes to the logical and grammatical heart of its claims, to how black theologians conceive the "object" of their discourse. He poses difficult questions: How is it possible for black theologians to make the claims they do about the nature of god and the condition of black people? What is the grammar of these claims? Is preserving treasured assumptions about god's benevolence worth the price of quietism in the face of the chronic and inordinate suffering of black people? Under these circumstances, what does it even mean to say that god is good, is *for* the oppressed—for black people—and liberates them from oppression in history? Jones anticipates Surin's remarks regarding Ivan's twofold challenge to theodicy. The uptake of this challenge is the task of determining, first of all, whether in the nature of things "it is inconceivable for the person *in extremis* to be in a position to speak of God as benevolent and gracious." While Surin accents the subjectivity of the sufferer and makes a cautionary point about the limits of articulate language with respect to evil and suffering, which retain an irreducible element of explanation-defying mystery, it reminds us of Jones' analytical category where god is the sum of god's acts. Ivan's second challenge for us is whether "we" are positioned to imagine and strive for a way of living in which concepts such as divine love and providence might be activated. A theist at the time he wrote, Surin believes the latter to be possible within Christianity, especially as understood through a "theology of the cross." "What God reveals is that divinity itself, through the cross of the Son, endures the sufferings that afflict us."[21]

Drawing on Camus' interpretation of Golgotha, Jones' critique of black theology anticipates this turn to a theology of the cross. Camus' interpretation denies any relation between Calvary and salvation. To put it crudely, Calvary was a perverse "public relations gimmick" designed to improve god's image by mitigating god's responsibility for suffering. "By arguing that human suffering should be endured and accepted because God Himself suffered even more, the strategy is laid to keep man, particularly the oppressed, docile and reconciled to his suffering. *Accordingly, human suffering does not become a springboard for rebellion*" (emphasis added). In a perverse twist, god's supreme act of self-sacrificial love precludes our ability to create a more humane existence. In light of this inverted interpretation of Golgotha, Jones argues, an incarnational theology is inimical to the liberation of black people.[22] That Jones and Surin are on opposite sides regarding the cross illustrates Jones' point about the multievidentiality of Calvary.[23]

Here the theist and the secular humanist part company. They disagree about the *practical* role that a theology of the cross might play in addressing evil and suffering. Where Jones regards the meaning of the cross as ambiguous if not undecidable, Surin construes it as univocal if not stable. Let's consider another difference. Among the lessons Surin draws from the character Ivan Karamazov is that divine omnipotence, omniscience, and moral benevolence *and* their negation are irrelevant to the problem of evil. They offer no practical solution. "This 'problem', if it is to be overcome, must be situated in a theological context void of any apologetic intent."[24] Given his perspective, Jones would certainly agree that the mere affirmation or negation of such beliefs have no practical import when viewed in abstraction. Within the logic and grammar of black theology, however, such claims are not abstract. They bear directly and powerfully on the question of human agency. There is nothing abstract about Father Panaloux's question "Should a priest call a doctor?" In his case, it has everything to do with what he should do in the face of the plague. Should he prayerfully accept the plague as god's will or call a doctor? This question has everything to do with how we should act, and more importantly, how we are likely to act given our beliefs. The question is about agency and the role of beliefs in motivating our acts.

Surin assumes that an incarnational (Trinitarian) theology is free of the defects of a merely theoretical interest in evil and suffering and that it guides us toward a praxis that might transform a world in anguish through the revelation of a god who suffers with us. Drawing on Camus, Jones accents the multievidentiality of the cross: its ability to support both Surin's conclusion that god incarnate is our co-sufferer and its opposite where god is a cruel demon.[25] Surin might rightly retort that this is a matter of basic grammar, the point at which "we" hit Wittgensteinian bedrock and our spade is turned. Jones might retort that even our deepest logic and grammar, which normally go uninspected, are subject to archaeological excavation, critique, and revision. What we encounter as bedrock today may appear as sandstone, if not sand, after careful critique. Jones' critique goes to the bedrock of black theology. Given inordinate and chronic black suffering, which the liberation theologians Jones surveys deem unjust (with the distinctive exception of Albert Cleage), their liberation claims only intensify the question of why black people suffer in the first place, reasserting the threshold question of divine racism—"Is God a white racist?"

So, Jones contends, black theology must be an antitheodicy. God's benevolence cannot be a presupposition. Vindicating god cannot be its principal aim. Jones prefers a humanist rather than a theistic approach to black liberation. But insofar as black theology is a liberation *theology*, with its traditional notions of divine omnipotence and omniscience, as opposed to a *humanist philosophy* of liberation, black theologians must refute the charge of divine racism. They must do this negative work before they can make positive claims regarding god.

The Concept of Internal Critique

To remove the albatross of divine racism from the necks of Blackamericans, Jones argues, black theologians must employ a methodology of counterevidence, arguing from the existence of the devil, from the *reductio ad absurdum* argument that god is a white racist. As a tool of inverted theodicy, the methodology of counterevidence goes hand-in-glove with Jones' claim that black theology must employ "a *de novo* approach to theologizing."[26] This approach requires a radical, root-and-branch critique of all received theological traditions, including the presumption of god's goodness. A kind of *via negative,* the methodology of counterevidence and *de novo* theologizing tell us what god is not—a white racist—by considering evidence that god *is* a white racist. This has to be a real investigation. The outcome cannot be prejudged. If an honest investigation leads to the conclusion that god is a white racist, then "metaphysical rebellion" or a frank embrace of atheism that ruthlessly sweeps aside any residue of theism might be the best options available to Blackamericans. According to Jones, black theology does not merit the adjective "liberation" if it fails to meet this minimal requirement.

In summary, Jones remarks: "I conclude that the initial task of the black theologian is to liberate the black mind from the destructive ideas and submissive attitudes that checkmate any movement toward authentic emancipation. It is to effect what I term the gnosiological conversion of the black psyche."[27] In assessing the success of black theologians in this regard, Jones provides the following criteria for an internal critique of black theology: "(1) The key elements of the critical apparatus used to analyze the black theologians are present either explicitly or implicitly in the black theologians own materials. (2) Their own presuppositions and conclusions make the question 'is God a white racist?' and its refutation the necessary point of departure for the construction of their respective systems."[28]

Jones appears to employ two methods—the external methodology of counterevidence and internal critique. In actuality, however, the former is implicit in the latter. To show why that is the case, I will draw heavily on Antti Kauppinen's analysis of internal critique,[29] which appeals to the subject's own criteria whether explicit or implicit. Internal criticism is a reaction to the perceived failures of external critique whether universalistic (Platonic, Kantian, and utilitarian) or ethnocentric (Rorty). It is also a response to normative skepticism (Nietzsche and Foucault).[30] The basic move of the internal critic is to expose a contradiction between norms and practices or between explicit and implicit norms within a practice. An example of the former is the claim that god is pro–black people, acknowledges the reality of their chronic, enduring, and unjust suffering and liberates them from oppression in this life. To illustrate the latter, consider the example of a Taliban recruit who feels a vague sense of guilt after "beating a woman who is outside her home at the wrong time" even though he is absolutely convinced that the religious norms he genuinely believes in prescribe such a beating.[31] Setting aside any possibility that the Taliban recruit's guilt is pathological, how do we account for it? By showing how norms that are implicit in a practice and normally unacknowledged can produce such a reaction. The internal critic makes "explicit the normative expectations that his actions violate: the fundamentally gender non-specific reciprocal norms of respect for persons that are...found in some (however rudimentary and implicit) form in all human societies by anthropological necessity." By bringing the practice and implicit norm into sharp relief, the critic gives the recruit a reason implicit in his own social practices to question his explicit normative beliefs and, therefore, to stop what he now recognizes as abusive behavior. The contradiction exposed is within a practice rather than between theory and practice.[32]

Kauppinen calls the first approach that accents conflict between theory and practice "simple internal critique." The latter approach is "reconstructive internal critique." The simple kind is vulnerable to the fanatic who simply refuses to acknowledge a contradiction between norms and practices or who otherwise disregards what the ethics of his own belief might entail. That explicit norms are easy to revise, especially when the subject of critique wishes to avoid substantive change, is an additional vulnerability. It is more difficult to change implicit norms, which are often embedded in unarticulated emotions, informal sanctions, religious prohibitions, proverbs, or laws. Reconstructive internal critique is not subject to these vulnerabilities because it does not depend on the unreconstructed acknowledgment of the subject. Reconstructive internal critique is more difficult to evade.[33] Jones' critique of black theology is of the reconstructive variety where he makes implicit norms explicit—especially the norms that presuppose the goodness of god and that regard god as the sum of god's acts.

Jones' Internal Critique of Black Theology

In this section, I explore Jones' assessment of five black theologians in light of these criteria. The guiding frame for this inquiry is Charles H. Long's third methodological principle: the "God symbol" in the black religious experience. I contend that Jones provides the most sophisticated inquiry regarding god in black religious studies. Again, my purpose is not to establish relations of genealogical descent between Long and Jones. Rather, I hope to defamiliarize the familiar and provoke new thoughts about old material. Two questions guide Jones' critique: "What is the best way to desanctify oppression?" and "Should appeal be made to the sovereignty of a just god or to the functional ultimacy of humans?"

A quick preview: Jones associates Joseph Washington, James Cone, Albert Cleage, Major Jones, and J. Deotis Roberts with specific kinds of theodicy that fail to adequately address the threshold question "Is God a white racist?" Washington's and Cone's theodicies share a common assumption regarding divine election. Both regard Blackamericans as god's chosen people: god's suffering servant, according to Washington; the oppressed subjects of god's liberation, according to Cone. The theodicy of vicarious suffering and the theodicy of divine liberation are two sides of the same coin. They pivot on how divine election is construed. In contrast, Cleage's theology relies on the highly controversial theodicy of deserved punishment. Jones has difficulty identifying the theodicies of Major Jones and Roberts with the same simplicity and clarity as he does those of Washington, Cone, and Cleage. Nevertheless, he claims that Major Jones and Roberts fail to adequately refute the theodicy of deserved punishment. The very theodicy that Washington and Cone claim, implicitly or explicitly, to refute and that Cleage embraces forthrightly, William R. Jones attributes to Major Jones and Roberts by default. I now turn to the particulars of Jones' critique. Part of my task is to determine how well Jones holds to his reconstructive internal critique and whether the external criteria he identifies, the multievidentiality of suffering and god as the sum of his acts, are *in fact* implicit as consequential commitments in the normative assumptions of the black theologians he analyzes.

Joseph Washington

Jones construes Washington as an uncritical exponent of the suffering servant/chosen people theodicy. Washington's exposition is uncritical because he never addresses black theology's threshold question and, consequently, does not adequately refute the theodicy of deserved punishment. Further, he does not think through its implications for notions of human freedom and divine responsibility. Though he writes passionately about the superiority of black people as exemplars of the suffering servant idea within the context of white supremacist Christianity, he does not finish the argument. Or, as Jones might put it, he never stipulates the evidence of black people's chosen peoplehood, which minimally requires that he identify an event *specific* to the history of black people that overturned or reversed their oppressed status. As the reader should recall, Jones calls this an "exaltation-liberation event." The biblical paradigm for such an event is the Exodus of Israelites from Egyptian bondage. (Jones fails to consider the degree to which this exaltation-liberation event was a *genocidal event* for the Canaanites.[34] One thinks of the line from the song that Louis X wrote before he became Louis Farrakhan that articulates a similar view: "The white man's heaven is the black man's hell." To his demerit, like the black theologians he criticizes, Jones never considers the bitter irony of a liberation event that obliterates innocent third parties.) The inadequacy of the biblical model notwithstanding, Washington does not provide evidence that black people are in fact suffering servants/chosen people as opposed to miserable creatures in the hands of a just god—or, for that matter, a racist god.

His failure to provide such evidence in concert with the idea that black people suffer because they deserve it (Noah's curse, the mark of Cain, etc.) empowers the idea of divine racism. Under Jones' critique, Washington's argument is a snowball rapidly tumbling downhill. The speed of descent only increases when we consider the implications of Washington's theodicy for human freedom and divine responsibility. In sovereignty and freedom, god elects whom god wills. Humans have no choice in the matter: "He does not ask for volunteers as His suffering servant." As divine conscripts, black people must do what god wills; they must suffer so that white people can be saved from their racial idolatry. Given this construction of sovereignty and freedom, god is clearly responsible for black suffering. Citing Washington's own words, Jones concludes that blacks may very well suffer until the eschaton:

> On the basis of the evidence already marshaled, it is safe to say that the inevitability and perpetuity of black suffering, and God's responsibility for it, at least raise the issue of divine racism. And the reader should keep in mind that this is my primary concern: the charge of divine racism, because his own position makes it a threshold issue.[35]

Jones concludes that Washington's theodicy of vicarious suffering, suffering servant, and chosen peoplehood is the least desirable among the various options. To take this option seriously, the Blackamerican Christian should be willing to suffer and die for the racist other, as did god himself.

Albert Cleage

Jones summarizes his internal critique of Cleage's theology:

> Can Cleage's position serve as a refutation of divine racism? Does Cleage's viewpoint suggest that God is a black God for black people, a black Uncle Tom, or a paleface deity? If God himself is black and for blacks, and if redemptive suffering and eschatological compensation are rejected, continued and disproportionate black suffering remains inexplicable in Cleage's own terms. Maybe his insistence upon a black God should force a reconsideration of theological dualism. Maybe there are two Gods, one white, one black, and the black God, like His children, is impotent to liberate His worshipers, because He is opposed by His white counterpart. Maybe the earthly black-white confrontation is simply a reflection of a transcendent state of affairs. Maybe...[36]

As Jones acknowledges, the chief problem he encounters in assessing Cleage is the sermonic, nonacademic character of his theology or what Jones describes as its pragmatic as opposed to logical-argumentative intent. Nevertheless, he resolves to treat Cleage's collection of sermonic writings as if they were logical-argumentative in nature. Still, problems with Cleage's theology are obvious. Prefiguring a claim that James Cone would make two years later, though his version is less crude and literal, Cleage argued that god is black and that Jesus is the Black Messiah. Jones disputes Cleage's assumption that he has established the blackness of God. But Jones seems to think that were Cleage to successfully establish the "fact" of god's blackness he would have then, by definition, refuted the charge of divine racism. This clearly is not true. Racism need not be interracial. Blacks can be anti-black racists in the same way that women can engage in gender bigotry and discrimination against women. If this kind of othering within the self were not possible, then we could not make sense of the very notion of treachery. Contra Jones, god's blackness does not guarantee his "racial loyalty." This reservation notwithstanding, Jones identifies a major problem with Cleage's theology, a problem which is shared by Cone: Cleage cannot account for black suffering. Or he can do so only by resorting to a theodicy of deserved punishment, an option that other black theologians avoid like the plague. On this view, god is chastising black people with the rod of his "love" for cowardice in battle, for failing to faithfully resist white supremacy. Jones considers this inversion of the concept of deserved punishment a clever but illicit move on Cleage's part that is designed to evade a very real dilemma. First, the severity of god's correction (the suffering of black people) seems disproportionate to their alleged sin. Second, the persistent, noncatastrophic (i.e., chronic) nature of black suffering and the correlative prosperity of whites suggest that god is not black. Behind this dilemma lies a failure to adequately refute the charge of divine racism: the threshold question for black theology.

James Cone

I take the following as a concise statement of Jones' critique of Cone: "Strictly speaking, the real mystery of mysteries in Cone's system is the *origin* of black suffering. For if God is for blacks, if their suffering is neither vicarious nor merited punishment, whence their suffering in the first place?"[37] Cone's theology is a performative paradox. Supporting his claim, Jones teases out the consequences of Cone's refutation of defective theodicies—suffering servant and deserved punishment—embraced, respectively, by Washington and Cleage. As Jones suggests, in refuting defective theodicies, Cone is more systematic than the other subjects of critique. But he makes his argumentative task exceedingly difficult when he denies any appeal to traditional theodicies. Arguments from the inscrutability of god's will, or that construct suffering as a mystery beyond human comprehension, or promise an eschatological resolution of the problem have no place in Cone's system. When these denials are combined with Cone's affirmations regarding the nature of god—that god is pro–black people and against white oppressors; that god does not call black people to suffer vicariously for the white oppressor; that blacks do not suffer at the hands of white oppressors because of deserved punishment for prior sin; that god is not a white racist—Jones' perplexity regarding the mysterious origins of evil in Cone's system is accented.

In Jones' critique, Cone has created a logical prison from which he cannot extricate himself. He has deprived himself of options (like an eschatological resolution of black suffering, however unappetizing an argument) that might account for the logical disconnect between his portrait of a pro-black god and the absence of any evidence of god's liberating activity on behalf of Blackamericans. In the absence of such an option, the very notion of a god of the oppressed with the attributes of sovereignty that Cone attributes to god does not make sense. Cone fails to do, in his far more sophisticated theology, what theologians within the Nation of Islam succeeded in doing: providing an account of why black people "catch so much hell." The "Yacub myth" explains why Blackamericans, the "so-called" Negro, do not live in paradise, why evil exists and black people suffer. To make a long story short, black people suffer because of the pride and *racial treason* of a mad, "big-headed," and villainous black scientist named Dr. Yacub who genetically engineered a race of white oppressors.[38] We may smile indulgently at "Yacub's History" but it is no more incredible, implausible, or less believable than the myth of Adam, Eve, and the Serpent. More to the point, it succeeds precisely where Cone fails by providing an explanation for black suffering. The explanation may not satisfy but the challenge of providing one is met.

Cone provides an impassioned response to Jones' critique in *God of the Oppressed* (1975), wherein he remarks:

> I am thoroughly sympathetic with William Jones' attempt to make the problem of black suffering central in Black Theology. But he is absolutely wrong in his assessment of my perspective when viewed from the methodology of "internal critique." Anyone who reads my works can see that any theological problem (and especially suffering!) can and must be dealt with from the perspective of Jesus Christ. This may not be true so much for the other black theologians he treated; but for me, Jesus Christ is the essence of the meaning of liberation. Thus he is the decisive historical event beyond which no one needs to appeal. Of course Jones and others may not agree to the high place given to Jesus Christ in black religion generally and my theology in particular, but for Jones to ask about the "definitive event of black liberation" (p. 116, *Is God a White Racist?*) from the method of an *internal* critique, as if Jesus Christ is not a proper answer in my own perspective, is to

> misunderstand totally what he claims to be doing and thus to distort my perspective.[39]

Cone's response pivots on the question of whether Jones actually provides an internal critique. Unlike the other subjects of Jones' critique, as we shall see, Cone understands the presuppositions of the critique. He understands that the force of Jones' critique rises or falls, principally, in relation to its adequacy as an internal critique. As a methodological critique, he understands that it is empowered by what Jones regards as tensions between black suffering and theological claims regarding a liberating god. Cone responds by foregrounding Christology: arguing that his doctrine of god—indeed, all of his theological doctrines—must be viewed through a Christocentric perspective that nullifies the purported internal character of the critique. He removes the wedge that Jones drives between Jesus Christ as *the* liberation event and an exaltation-liberation event specific to black history:

> Therefore, to William Jones' question, What is the decisive event of liberation? we respond: Jesus Christ! He is our Alpha and Omega, the one who died on the cross and was resurrected that we might be free to struggle for the affirmation of black humanity. I know that this answer will not satisfy Jones or others who view black humanity from another vantage point than Jesus Christ. But for blacks during slavery and its aftermath, Jesus was not a clever theological device to escape difficulties inherent in suffering. He was the One who lived with them *in* suffering and thereby gave them the courage and strength to "hold out to the end."[40]

While acknowledging that Jones' critique has purchase as an external critique, Cone concludes that it is unfair insofar as it purports to be an internal critique of his perspective.[41] Is Cone's response adequate? Does the Christocentric character of his theology prevent the notion of divine racism from arising in a non-question-begging way?[42] Or does it merely shift the locus of critique, a shift that Jones anticipates and criticizes? One point that must be acknowledged upfront is that an internal critique is always potentially controversial. Controversy arises when the critic identifies implicit norms that the subject of critique does not acknowledge. Cone claims that his theology is normed by Jesus Christ: by the biblical and historical record that shows him identifying with the oppressed; by the status of Jesus within the first-order religious world of black people (from slavery to freedom) where the life, death, and resurrection of Jesus Christ is the paradigmatic liberation event in black history. Cone asserts that his position is misunderstood if the mutually constitutive normativity of Jesus Christ and black liberation is denied.

There is no noncontroversial way of resolving this disagreement. Even if we concede Cone's point and, in the spirit of generosity, conclude that this concession pulls other concessions in its wake—such as the notion that Blackamericans are oppressed, it does not save him from Jones' critique.[43] As Jones remarks:

> If for the sake of argument we should allow his theodicy a gratuitous validity, a troublesome question would still remain unanswered. Indeed the greater his success in establishing that black liberation is essential to God's nature, the more troublesome this question would become: Whence comes the suffering of the oppressed in the first place if God is for the oppressed?[44]

Cone's response does not address what Jones claims are the quietistic implications of his theology. Cone cannot, in good faith, refuse this challenge since his entire systematic theology is designed to contest traditional doctrines—God, Christ, revelation, church, and eschatology—that get in the way of black liberation. Jones shows why the invocation of Jesus Christ does not answer the question.

If we consider *Black Theology and Black Power* (1969), where his views are less Jesus-centered, if not Christocentric, then Cone agrees with Jones. Cone remarks that "We cannot solve ethical questions of the twentieth century by looking at what Jesus did in the first. Our choices are not the same as his." Our existential situation is such that we must act "without knowing what Jesus would do" in a similar situation.[45] Here Jesus is not the norm. But in the text that Jones subjects to critique, Cone remarks, emphatically, that "*The norm of all God-talk which seeks to be black talk is the manifestation of Jesus as the Black Christ who provides the necessary soul for black liberation.*"[46] Cone constructs his theological norm in such a way that black liberation is constitutive. In a chapter entitled "Jesus Christ in Black Theology," Cone remarks, "Christian theology begins and ends with Jesus Christ. He is the point of departure for everything said about God, humankind, and the world."[47]

What made Cone's *A Black Theology of Liberation* (1970) new, exciting, and attractive (or repulsive, as the case may be) is its radical elevation of black liberation above every theological doctrine as traditionally conceived. His Christology aside, the requirements of black liberation—the well-being of Blackamericans—are the controlling criteria. Or so it seems. In *God of the Oppressed,* Cone essentially repudiates these criteria.[48] Under the pressure of Jones' critique, I presume, Cone becomes a rather conventional theologian. The radical edge of his theology in the earlier text, which is precisely its exclusivity and Black Nationalist priorities, is blunted in the later text. Consider the following: "black theology refuses to accept a God who is not identified totally with the goals of the black community. If God is not for us, if God is not against white racists, then God is a murderer, and we had better kill God."[49] ... "The God of the oppressed is a God of revolution who breaks the chains of slavery."[50] Perhaps dulling the sharp edge of such claims is the price that Cone had to pay (and was willing to pay) in his failed effort to elude the sharp point of Jones' critique.

Major Jones

William R. Jones identifies a constitutive contradiction at the heart of Major Jones' theology. (To avoid confusion between William R. Jones and Major Jones, I will refer to the latter by his full name.) Major Jones embraces incompatible notions of god's sovereignty: the traditional model that construes god as omnipotent and the nontraditional view where god is powerless to intervene coercively in this world, weakness exemplifies divine agency, and god is humanity's co-sufferer. God can witness and "feel our pain" but cannot coerce the oppressive agents of that pain to stop. Here Jesus crucified is the guiding image of divine sovereignty and agency.

This ambivalence and ambiguity regarding god's sovereignty creates several problems for Major Jones. If god has no coercive power, then Major Jones cannot sustain the claim, which Jones attributes to him, that god liberates the oppressed. If god does have coercive power, then Major Jones cannot explain why god has not used those powers on behalf of oppressed black people. This raises the possibility that god has not liberated Blackamericans because they are being justly punished for prior sin, or that god bears ill will toward them. Major Jones' theology, therefore, falls prey to the charge of divine racism that it has not adequately refuted. His partial retention of the conventional notion of god's omnipotence and rejection of deserved punishment and conventional eschatological theodicies, which places the resolution of human suffering beyond the "earthly life span" of those who suffer, only exacerbates this inadequacy. In turn, these inadequacies expose the shaky foundations of Major Jones' theology of hope, which fails to specify whether hope is ontologically or merely psychologically grounded. To avoid this problem, Jones calls for an anthropology of hope: hope rooted in the natural powers and limitations of humans.

Jones appears to have Major Jones dead to rights. Jones' critique is clearly based on criteria that are internal to Major Jones' theology: black awareness, hope, and a Bonhoeffer-derived conception of divine impotence.[51] It is not clear how Major Jones could respond short of significantly revising his theology of hope with its black eschatological theodicy. Despite my doubts, Major Jones manages a response in *The Color of God* (1987). His misunderstanding of Jones' critique is gross. He confuses humanocentric theism with Jones' preferred position of secular humanism. Jones constructs the former option, a kind of "humanism light," as an escape route for black theologians who wished to remain theists even though convicted by his critique. This basic misunderstanding undermines everything that Major Jones writes in response. Consider the magnitude of the misreading in the following passage:

> Is it God's character or collective man's character which is at stake in Jones' thought? How did God get to be a White racist? Is God's segregationist mind-set part of his inner consciousness or is it an external projection of his ontological being? If God were a White racist, he would have to be an ontological being, possessing a subjective and objective self-consciousness or self-knowledge. If God, the White racist, is merely a projection of the collective American character, which is mostly White and largely racist, William Jones has not told us anything we did not already know. His accusation against God is little more than a sociologically astute but theologically reductionist anthropomorphism.[52]

One can appreciate Major Jones' attempt to respond to Jones' critique, but he clearly is out of his depth. This passage reveals his failure to understand a philosophical argument. The whole point of Jones' critique is that assumptions (explicit or implicit) and claims about the nature of god and god's solicitude for black people—*that are internal to black theology, to the claims that black theologians themselves make*—raise the issue of divine racism. Black theologians cannot evade the logic of their own claims, which makes "Is God a white racist?" the threshold question for black theology. They must address this question *before* their theological project, specifically their claims about a liberating god, can get off the ground. A critique can occur at many levels, with some levels being logically, though not necessarily temporally, prior to others. As a critical discipline, the task of theology is to evaluate the first-order beliefs of the faithful. Major Jones confuses a logical and methodological critique with a sociological claim. He is tone deaf; he cannot hear the frequency at which Jones pitches his argument. We encounter a similar problem in this passage:

> William R. Jones' limited God-concept is not adequate for suffering Black people of faith. Black people need a God who can make the difference, if they are to have faith in God as the subject of their religious quest, liberation, freedom, salvation, and the ultimate salvation of more than just the Black world. God must be worthy of Black worship. Help from God is surely more needed than human assistance, especially from a powerless people. Black theologians dare not conclude upon a God who is less personal and all-powerful: There must be no doubt about the outcome of the Black struggle for justice. An absolute God must equal the difference between Black power and Black hope. With or without the help of human beings, God is our absolute assurance of ultimate success.[53]

This passage merely reasserts the kind of question-begging claims that generated Jones' critique in the first place. Major Jones is his own worst advocate. From his own lips, he confirms Jones' critique. That Major Jones does not recognize this point and the irony of it all is an index of just how deep his misunderstanding is.

J. Deotis Roberts

Like the other black theologians whom he subjects to internal critique, Jones accuses Roberts of begging a crucial question regarding the nature of god: is god benevolently disposed toward black people or "Is God a white racist?" The assumption regarding god's intrinsic goodness stands behind every theological move that Roberts makes. His implicit theodicy, which reduces to a contradictory hodgepodge under Jones' critique, presupposes this very assumption. Jones shows why this assumption cannot hold without begging the very questions it must answer.

Jones provides the following concise statement of Roberts' theodicy: "an affirmation of God's omnibenevolence and omnipotence, aspects of the 'beyond human comprehension' theodicy of Job, a modification of the theodicy of redemptive suffering already analyzed in the discussion of Washington and a doctrine of eschatology that is both 'realized and 'unrealized.'"[54] Dismantling Roberts' theodicy piece by piece, Jones begins by criticizing a feature of Roberts' theology that he shares with Major Jones: his tendency to privilege a "psychology of comfort" over an "ontology of liberation." Psychological security (such as the uncritical assumption that god is intrinsically good and well disposed toward black people) trumps the ruthless critique of everything and the model of counterevidence that liberation demands. Roberts clings to a survival model of Black Religion, which made sense during slavery but is senseless under circumstances that demand a liberation model. The priority of psychological comfort to a liberation ontology reverberates through Jones' critique of Roberts' theodicy. Jones criticizes the psychology underlying Roberts' preference for a conventional view of divine sovereignty that imposes argumentative obligations that Roberts cannot meet. Jones criticizes Roberts' brief, provisional, if not half-hearted, attempt to place black suffering beyond human comprehension, thus saving god from invidious critique. More importantly, Jones attacks Roberts' vacillation regarding the suffering servant motif as a sufficient explanation of black suffering. That suffering appears to exceed the bounds, if not caricature, the very notion of redemptive suffering. Jones concludes that the ambiguities (Is god the sum of god's acts or not?) in Roberts' twofold—realized and unrealized—eschatological explanation is massively confused.

At each step of Roberts' argument, Jones shows how the charge of divine racism rears its grotesque head. Roberts fails to decapitate the monster of divine racism when he fails to adequately refute the theodicy of deserved punishment, which holds that black suffering is a sign of god's disfavor. In turn, the predicate of this failure is his uninterrogated assumption that god is intrinsically good; that is, his failure to answer the question "Is God a white racist?" As with Major Jones, Cleage, Cone, and Washington, Jones has identified the assumptions, implicit or explicit, in Roberts' theology, which he seamlessly melds with his own metacritical categories: the multievidentiality of suffering and god as the sum of god's acts. On the basis of these criteria, Jones concludes that black theology, as represented by these figures, fails to adequately address the threshold question "Is God a white racist?"

Roberts responds to Jones' critique in *Black Theology Today* (1983). One might think that the intervening ten years would have provided Roberts with sufficient time to carefully consider his response. One would be mistaken. Roberts' response is full of misunderstandings and misattributions similar to Major Jones'. In construing William Jones' text as indicative of a methodological crisis in black theology, Roberts asserts that theological method and theodicy should be separate enterprises and that Jones should have approached "method more from an epistemology point of view." He accuses Jones of not having "faith in the integrity of the divine character." He attributes to Jones the claims that god is responsible for black suffering and is a white racist.[55]

Even a cursory reading of Jones' text should have prevented the grievous errors in Roberts' response. Jones goes to great lengths to explain why black theological method and theodicy cannot be separated. It is precisely epistemology—how we know what we think we know, in this case, about the nature of god—that makes theodicy unavoidable for a black theological method. The very premises of black theology—that black suffering is not deserved, that black suffering is disproportionate and unjust, that god is on the side of black people, that god intervenes in history on behalf of the oppressed—demand that black theology be pursued as a theodicy. The contradiction between these assertions and the suffering of black people cries out for an explanation. Roberts has every right to disagree, but he owes the reader an argument. But all we get are passionate expressions of distaste. If this were not bad enough, he attributes to Jones the very claim—god is responsible for black suffering and is a white racist—that Jones identifies as the logical entailment of the images, assumptions, and arguments of black theologians. Roberts consistently confuses subjunctive claims, "if black theologians claim x, then y is true," with declarations: god is a malevolent deity; god is responsible for black suffering; god is a white racist.

Like Major Jones, Roberts struggles to understand Jones' preferred view: "At the moment," he writes regarding Jones, "he wavers between a secular humanism and what he calls humanotheism."[56] Jones is explicit about his own position, which he describes as secular humanism and carefully distinguishes from humanocentric theism, which Roberts transcribes as "humanotheism." Roberts conflates Jones' secular (i.e., nontheistic) humanism with humanocentric theism, which is a theological position intermediate between secular humanism and traditional theism, which Jones offers to black theologians as a lifeline, if not a peace offering. But Roberts will have none of that:

> What William Jones calls humanotheism seems limited to a select few among blacks in the middle class. Many of these blacks cannot handle

> the razor-sharp logic in Jones' position. They have a rather affective grasp of a world view or a religious affirmation. Jones does not make contact with the mass religious or secular movements in the black community.[57]

In a concluding remark, Roberts writes, "My understanding of what William Jones provides is in the nature of black religious thought rather than a black theology."[58] I regret that Roberts found it necessary to play the "elitism card." I suppose it is an effective card to play when you have a bad hand, and Jones' analysis shows us just how bad Roberts' hand is. Roberts' reference to the class limitations of Jones' critique is an evasion. Theology is a learned discipline. It entails critical, technical, and jargon-ridden modes of argument. And so it should be. It is a second-order, academic, critical reflection on first-order religious life that is designed, in part, to correct bad beliefs and practices. The implication of Roberts' criticism is that Jones' analysis is incomprehensible to the proverbial "brother on the block." This unlettered, if not anti-intellectual, "ideal type" becomes the measure for how intellectual work should be done, as if such work should be nontechnical and easily accessible to the untutored "brother on the block." One might be more sympathetic if Roberts' critique revealed a serious engagement with critiques of the international division of labor, power, and status. Then his criticism of Jones might have more bite. But there is little evidence that he has engaged such criticism at all. On the contrary, anti-intellectual and tendentious, his claim of elitism says more about Roberts' inability to mount an argument than it does about the merits and demerits of Jones' critique.

Reconstructing Black Theology

We live in a "deconstructive" age. Derrida's rhetoric, if not his method, has a casual ubiquity in critical circles. One easily recognizes the method's skeletal features: first identify a binary opposition, the subordination of one term to the other and the "violence" that entails; second, invert the opposition or otherwise show how the subordinate term is constitutive of the dominant one, thereby destabilizing the normative relationship between the two. In addition to its widespread critical use, which extends beyond the narrowly technical and professional, a measure of deconstruction's rhetorical ubiquity is its popular function as a synonym for any form of critique or as a verbal sign of sophistication. One can envision would-be sophisticates on television or at dinner parties dropping the term as if it were a talisman. Perhaps it is.

Jones wrote his text before the critical use of deconstruction entered the American academy in a big way. His critical sensibility is different from the deconstructionist insofar as he attempts to supplement his destructive critique of black theology with a *reconstructive* account, the spirit of which recalls John Dewey's effort to reconstruct philosophy by weaning it from dualities and certainties. (As a pragmatic matter, I think that reconstruction, presupposing as it does a critically *destructive* act, is preferable to the purely skeptical outcomes of a norm-destabilizing deconstruction.) If Jones' entire text is a preamble to black theology, then his concept of humanocentric theism is a preamble to a humanistic reconstruction of black theology. This effort is not fully developed, which is not surprising since Jones is not a theologian. If black theology is to be adequately reconstructed, then black theologians themselves must do the heavy lifting. Whether they pick up the baton and carry it to the finish line, if I may switch metaphors, is up to them. Jones provides a track on which the race can be run.

A Debate Deferred

Jones wrote *Is God a White Racist?* in the hope that it would provoke a critical debate among black theologians. That debate never happened. Jones' analysis was clearly Afro-*Eccentric* before the concept of Afrocentricity had even emerged. By highlighting the humanist tradition (theistically skeptical, nonbelieving, and rejectionist) among Blackamericans and pointedly criticizing the image of god in contemporary black theology, Jones stepped outside a theistic, Christian, and Protestant church–based "normative blackness."[59] He became Afro-*Eccentric*. This may explain why the robust debate that Jones hoped for when he wrote his text has not occurred. It certainly explains why Jones attempts to establish a conceptual bridge between him and black theologians. He wants to maintain a critical foothold in a discursive universe dominated by theology. Thus his critique is not merely a deconstructive enterprise but also an outline for reconstructing black theology: a reconstruction that would abandon the twin requirements of apologetics and divine liberation[60] that define the old approach, in favor of an account of black suffering that validates a liberation ontology rooted in anthropology. Jones calls his reconstruction "humanocentric theism." This is truly theism with a human face and a theology that accentuates one of Jones' guiding principles:

the functional ultimacy of humans. As Jones is at pains to make clear, the position he offers, though similar to his own nontheistic humanism, *is for the benefit of black theologians.* He hybridizes traditional theism with secular (non-theistic) humanism. While acknowledging that "humanocentric theism does not honor every pressing demand of a contemporary black theodicy,"[61] he does not specify the nature of those demands.

Humanocentric theism constructs human agency as functionally ultimate. The exalted nature of human power is part of the nature of things, a manifestation of god's purpose. In the strongest versions of this view, humans make their own destiny—god does not predetermine it. Or, to be more accurate, god's exalted regard for humans is evident in the role they play as co-creators of their own activity, choices, and freedom. On this view, the success or failure of the human venture is their responsibility. What humans do redounds to their honor or dishonor. God's self-limitation of his agency is such that he relates to humans only by means of persuasion. Humanocentric theism involves a reconstruction of traditional notions of divine omnipotence and sovereignty. "Its special merits are its capacity to eliminate the charge of divine racism and its unambiguous impulse against quietism."[62] In addition to these virtues, humanocentric theism eliminates "theological and moral escape often used by the white oppressor"[63] to justify black subordination.

Anthony Pinn disputes Jones' claims regarding the quietism-eliminating effectiveness of humanocentric theism. He contends that Jones' initial move of constructing a self-limiting god is illegitimate and violates his own criteria. A self-sovereignty-limiting and noncoercive god might still be malevolently disposed toward black people. This god might work through human or superhuman surrogates. In either case, a god could foresee the consequences of creating beings who could suffer and so such a being (or ground-of-being as the case may be) cannot avoid blame. Whatever the proximate causes may be, a sovereignty-limiting-persuasive god is the distal cause of oppression and other forms of negative suffering. God is still the sum of god's acts. Divine limitation and divine racism are not mutually exclusive. A limited god may very well be a racist god.[64]

In a sense, Pinn provides an internal critique of humanocentric theism. But he is not as explicit as he should have been in noting that humanocentric theism is not Jones' "theological position." As a secular humanist, Jones does not have a theological position. Rather, in a reconstructive act of generosity (and, perhaps, a pragmatic act of survival through bridge-building, which those who move in theological circles, such as Pinn, should understand), he attempts to provide a theological alternative for those who cannot accept his thoroughgoing humanism—what Pinn calls "strong humanism." If this act of extending an olive branch is a failure, it should be understood for what it is: an act of securing discursive space in the face of a marginality-producing normative blackness, which threatens to ignore his critique and to render his perspective discursively invisible.[65] This proviso aside, Pinn's claim that humanocentric theism fails is insightful and pushes the black humanist option forward.

The Limits of Jones' Critique

No critique can do everything. Jones does not claim to address every possible problem with black theology. Rather, he limits the analysis to the threshold question of divine racism to which the internal logic of black theology demands an answer. The problem he addresses is a logical one. But it is not merely logical, if this means abstract, non-causal, and disconnected from concrete social relations. The question of god's disposition toward black people arises within the context of everyday black life; so it cannot be summarily dismissed as many black theologians might wish. As Jones has shown, there is a long tradition of humanism among black people who asked some version of the question "Is God a white racist?" The failure of black theologians to address this question, generated by the logic of their own claims, leads to potential and actual forms of quietism in the face of black subordination.

Before considering a potentially effective critique of Jones' analysis of black theology, let us deal with an ineffective effort. I refer to an allegedly Wittgensteinian critique put forward by the "second generation" black theologian James B. Evans that goes to Jones' so-called misuse of logic. Evans claims that Jones uses a universal logic that abstracts from the particularity (ordinary language) of the black theologians' discursive world. This is not true. Jones knows that logic is discursive and is bound up with social practices.[66] His critique of black theology underscores his agreement with Wittgenstein's canonical remarks: "Think of the tools in a tool-box: there is a hammer, pliers, a saw, a screw driver, a rule, a glue-pot, nails and screws.—The function of words are as diverse as the functions of these objects. (And in both cases there are similarities.)"[67] The whole point of an internal critique is to hold an author to the logic of her own images, assumptions, and claims. Jones identifies various language games played by black theologians, specifically games regarding theodicy. He explicates their similarities (family resemblances) and the forms of life in which they are rooted. Evans is wrong when he claims that Jones employs a universal, external logic in his critique of black theology. Evans' critique, which is surely a caricature of Jones, reads like the caricature of Wittgenstein's view that Kai Nielsen calls "Wittgensteinian fideism."[68] On this view, language games are as hermetically bounded and incommensurate as their forms of life are purported to be. Given this interpretation, black theological apologists can argue that black theological language games and forms of life that embed them are immune to external critique and to changes it might inspire. As with J. Deotis Roberts' tendentious reading, Evans' account tells us more about his view than it does about Jones' critique of black theology.[69]

Speaking of Wittgenstein, Fergus Kerr observes, "In effect, by remarking that theology is grammar, he is reminding us that it is only by listening to what we say about God (what has been said for many generations), and to how what is said about God ties in with what we say and do in innumerable other connections, that we have any chance of understanding what we mean when we speak of God."[70] Jones listened to the claims of black theologians very carefully and took their claims with the utmost seriousness. He saw contradictions between the fact of black suffering and their claim that god liberates the oppressed, of which black people are exemplary; that said liberation occurs on "this side" of the eschaton. These contradictions, he feared, underwrote a quietistic response to white supremacy. So Jones "called out" black theologians, but they failed to respond. Or, where they did respond, it was grossly inadequate. As with Evans, their responses are full of exasperation, suspicion, and mischaracterization. One senses that they take Jones as somehow illegitimate, as having violated a code of solidarity by asking questions that should not be asked. Never mind the fact that these questions are generated by the very claims that black theologians make. Jones' critique is foundational; it challenges the very basis of black theology in ways that many black theologians cannot acknowledge. Perhaps this collective denial is the condition for the possibility of black theology.

In contrast to Evans' Wittgensteinian caricature, an effective way of getting at the limitations of Jones' critique of black theology is to compare it with Cornel West's critique. If Jones is the leading "analytic" philosopher of black theology and religious thought, then West is the exemplary " synthesizer." Where Jones patiently and meticulously explores in depth a single interpretive key (the concept of divine racism), West is the master weaver of disparate discourses. Intellectually curious and impatient, West stitches many patches into a quilt-like critique, while Jones produces something more akin to a seamless garment. Though both of their analyses are in fact inductive, Jones' analysis due to its systematic character has the superficial appearance of a deduction. Both wrote in the midst and wake of the black theological project and can be viewed broadly as "black liberationist" cultural critics. In support of their respective critiques, they marshal different forms of existentialism and interpretations of humanism.

One of the greatest strengths of Jones' critique, its highly contextual nature, is also its greatest weakness. Jones' analysis is limited by the quality of the theologies he analyzes. What they do not explore—such as the internal division of labor, wealth, power, and prestige created by capitalist modernity, and how this reality is an unavoidable horizon for a proper analysis of the black condition in America—he does not explore. In contrast, this sort of analysis, especially as capitalist divisions play domestically, is a major, if not distinctive, aspect of West's critique. But I shall argue that the limitation of Jones' analysis in this regard is more virtuous than "vicious." It is the kind of limitation that is proper to the level of his analysis. Every critique is an act of delimitation that excludes certain matters from consideration because they are not immediately relevant to the analysis or because they exceed the grasp of the critic. There is no knowledge or critique without exclusion. A skeptical critic might argue, nonetheless, that Jones should have attended to the issue of class and the way it cuts among blacks and between blacks and whites in ways that complicate simplistic black liberationist narratives. This is something that Jones fails to do and is obvious when his analysis of black theology is compared to West's account. While important, this limitation does not vitiate Jones' analysis. Given the kind of analysis in which he is engaged, the threshold question of divine racism has logical priority. Other critiques of black theology are relevant *only* if that question is successfully answered in the negative. Were such an answer forthcoming, then a host of profoundly important criticisms of black theology would be relevant, such as West's critique of a deficient class analysis.[71]

If every critique excludes some things for reasons of the critic's fallibility and finitude, then a refined version of the question regarding the limitations of Jones' critique might go something like this:

does Jones' analysis of black theology exclude matters that he ought to have considered given the context and the limitations he properly set for his task? I begin by considering two objections to Jones' critique that might seem decisive but are not. During the last thirty years, gender has emerged as an indispensible category of analysis. Except for his contention that a response to the problem of divine racism that resulted in the validation of divine sexism is unacceptable, Jones does not have a gender analysis. He does not address the male-centered nature of black theology. If Cone ontologizes blackness (anthropological and theological), writing as if race were not gendered, as if the masculine construction of deity was unproblematic, then Jones' analysis is deficient where gender is concerned. But he is no more blameworthy epistemically than is Cone. When Jones wrote the epistemic circumstances were not conducive for a gender critique. Only the rare critic, ahead of her time, engaged such an analysis. To hold Jones blameworthy would be a case of the "historian's fallacy," of attributing our current knowledge and norms to actors in the past. Just as importantly, gender is not germane to his critique of black theology's threshold question. Regardless of gender, the deity—god or goddess—might still be a white racist.

A second possible objection has to do with the time-bound nature of Jones' language: an unreconstructed Black Nationalist rhetoric from which many of us recoil. Critics from a variety of ideological perspectives have made us well aware of the deficiencies of nationalism: the imposition of a normative blackness, hostile to intraracial difference, especially same-sex loving orientations that are often construed as a kind of racial treason; the subordination of women, and the mystification of class. Insofar as Jones channels this kind of language without displacing the unpalatable aspects of nationalism, his language strikes us today as inadequate. One can only imagine how this discourse would handle intersexed bodies and transgendered subjects. Could it even recognize them as black subject/bodies? Could its proponents recognize *queer blackness*?[72] We need to avoid anachronism. Even progressive critics often fail to condemn the gender injustice of normative blackness. In this regard, we should not expect more of Jones than is appropriate given the circumstances. A more appropriate question is how well he did, given his discursive context, in critically capturing his own time in thought. I think he did well.

My conclusion, therefore, is that Jones' critique is limited in both an epistemically nonblameworthy and in a praiseworthy manner. It is limited in the first respect because he does not use gender as a category of analysis. It is praiseworthy because it properly circumscribes its topic. This requires, necessarily, the exclusion from consideration of matters that are meritorious in their own right: for example, the way that racial politics are produced, refracted, and reconstituted by the international and national division of labor, culture, and value. Exclusion is the price we pay for knowledge, which is always fallible and subject to critique and revision. Excluding some matters from consideration is the price Jones had to pay to make any critique at all.

Earlier I remarked that insofar as Jones' purpose was to conduct an internal critique of black theology, it is illegitimate to criticize him for not doing what an internal critique as he understood it constrains him from doing—criticizing black theologians based on criteria external to their normative assumptions. However, there is one criticism of Jones' critique that we might offer on the metacritical level: the level at which he selected the kind of critique he would make. Jones had the option of internal and/or external critique. He chose to limit himself to an internal critique. This choice is open to normative evaluation. Should he have done so? A critic might claim that Jones underestimated the power of external criteria to persuade black theologians. Perhaps they would have responded positively to external criteria where they did not to his attribution of implicit norms they did not acknowledge. After all, their conceptual world is not hermetically sealed; the language games of black theology are commensurate with other games. But then again, maybe not: black theologians seemed determined to resist the substance of the critique. Given this resistance, one can understand Jones' choice. He believed that black theologians were more likely to receive an internal critique sympathetically. He hoped to persuade them by respecting their normative assumptions enough to explain in meticulous detail why they led to the undesirable outcome of theological quietism.

Apparently, Jones assumed that black theologians would respond to his critique in the same measured way that it was offered. That did not occur. Jones underestimated the tenacity of their beliefs. He did not anticipate how vigorous, if not nimble, black theologians might be in denying his attribution of implicit norms, how determined they would be in evading the threshold question "Is God a white racist?" Recall Cone's response to Jones' critique: it's all about methodology, while evading the substance. Cone can then divert attention from the scandal on which his theology is built: a black god of the oppressed who is for Blackamericans but unable or unwilling to liberate them. Thus distracted we do not ponder the conventionality of an account in which Cone's ostensibly radical and revolutionary claims about god liberating the oppressed *are merely rhetorical,* amounting to nothing more than the affirmation that black people are saved through the life, death, and resurrection of Jesus Christ. How conventional. Even fundamentalist and conservative evangelicals would agree. Its linguistic pyrotechnics aside, a "black theology of liberation" is redundant—more showy and honorific than revolutionary. If nothing else, Jones sees this scandal clearly.

Not quite persuaded by this account, an especially persistent (or obnoxious) critic might assert that Jones should have coupled his methodological critique with a sociological analysis along the lines that Cornel West would produce several years later. Much of the power of West's critique, the critic might assert, derives from a sociological analysis that juxtaposes perspectives with radically different norms. This approach conceptually unhinges the reader, familiarizing Marxism while defamiliarizing black theology, meanwhile opening new interpretive vistas. Such a critique would have enabled Jones to push beyond the visionary limitations (and black theology is limited) of those he criticized. But this suggestion presumes that black theologians have successfully addressed the threshold question, which is logically and methodologically prior to the sociological analysis that West provides. There is a division of labor. West's sociological critique, explored in chapter 6, presupposes a successful response (not necessarily an answer) to the question "Is God a white racist?"

As stated in the book's subtitle, Jones conceived his text as a "preamble" to black theology. Its purpose was to clear discursive ground, to open a space within the forest of theological cant and radical posturing where what is really important could appear and black theologians could see their task clearly. If they have not received the message, we should not blame the messenger. As readers, we should not use "merely academic," "logical," and "philosophical" as epithets, thus appealing to the anti-intellectual strain in American culture, as a way of evading the power of Jones' critique. As an analytical critique of black theology and religious thought, Jones' text is unequaled. This is true despite the peevishness of black theologians and students of black religious thought and their failure to adequately engage his critique.

Coda: Is Allah an Anti-black Racist?

I recall comments regarding writing style that I wish to attribute to Reinhold Niebuhr. Since I cannot verify the attribution, the inspiration for this insight will remain anonymous. As I recall, this anonymous author would write a first draft "hot," that is, fully impassioned and rewrite "cold." The penultimate version of this coda was written hot. Excessively polemical, perhaps too self-assured, and littered with gratuitous insults, it did not have the benefit of a "coldblooded" revision where my editorial self said, "This goes too far; that is unfair." The subject of my analysis read that version. Though he had a right to be angry and to respond in kind, he generously described my analysis as "strident." I read his complaint as saying that I did to him what I accuse him of doing to William R. Jones. In response, I have attempted to repair that defect and have blunted the sharper edges of my critique. I suspect, however, that these concessions will not mitigate the complaint that I caricature or otherwise misrepresent his argument. On this point, the question of how Jones is best interpreted, we simply disagree. The reader will have to decide which of us (if either) gets it right. Whatever conclusion the reader draws, our disagreement shows just how contentious theodicy is. Theodicy is about the character of god and its implications for human behavior. What one says on this subject (including whether god is ontological or imaginary, the artifact of our concepts or concept-transcendent) can lead to impassioned exchanges and even nastiness. My revised remarks are contentious and provocative, but I hope they are not nasty.

In this coda, I provide a critique of Sherman A. Jackson's *Islam and the Problem of Black Suffering* (2009). Jackson explores Jones' critique of black theodicy in light of four classical Sunni traditions of Muslim theology. Critical to his comparative enterprise is a proper translation of subject matter from one context to another. Translation is difficult, as anyone who has attempted to learn a "foreign" language can attest. I shall claim that Jackson does not adequately attend to the difficulties entailed in translating Jones' critique of black theology into an Islamic context, specifically in regard to classical Sunni traditions of theology. Though he takes seriously the claim that issues of theodicy arise for any "theistic religion that holds God to be all-powerful and all-good," he does not attend adequately to the contextual specificity of Jones' critique. While spirited and often illuminating, Jackson's critique ultimately misses its mark. He fails to properly raise the question of divine racism in relation to Islam because he misunderstands the grammar embedded in the very question "Is God a white racist?"

I begin with a quote from chapter 3 that provides a useful summary of Jackson's claims:

> For with Ash'arism (and, as I will show, Māturīdism and Traditionalism) we are introduced to a universe of alternative definitions, presuppositions, and ways of viewing things that were neither provided by Mu'tazilism nor considered by the religious and existentialist thinkers Jones relies on. Most notable in this regard is the alternative to the presumed contradiction between divine omnipotence and human agency, the distinction between ontological decree and normative preference, and the religious commitment to a weak rather than a strong moral ontology. Together, these adjustments combine to (1) complicate—if not frustrate—the charge of divine racism; (2) refute the claimed necessity of quietism; (3) question the denial (or indictment) of divine *omnibenevolence* by questioning the categorical evil of black suffering; and (4) reveal, as did Mu'tazilism, the superfluousness of a nontheistic or secular approach.[73]

Jackson provides a similar litany in chapter 5, where he discusses the virtues of Traditionalism, which, going beyond the other schools of Islamic theology, "unequivocally affirms divine omnibenevolence and refutes the connection between it and quietism, as well as the idea that the occurrence of black suffering necessarily disproves God's goodness/justice." Unlike Mu'tazilism, he adds, "Traditionalism joins Ash'arism and Māturīdism in refuting the idea that black suffering cannot be reconciled with God's omnipotence (i.e., God's sovereignty over nature *and* history). Far more unexpectedly, Traditionalism actually joins Mu'tazilism in holding out the possibility for a more *humanocentric* expression of theism."[74]

Let me preface my remarks by saying that I am not an expert on Islam. My only reason for characterizing Jackson's views of Islam is because of the role he assigns classical Sunni theology in his critique of Jones. I may very well get certain details wrong or miss nuances that might irritate an expert. These inadequacies, which come with scholarly but nonexpert knowledge, do not touch my central claim that Jackson mistranslates Jones' critique of black (Christian) theology. With this acknowledgment in mind, I contend that Jackson engages in two critiques: one is a polemic against Jones' critique of black theodicy; the second target is a particular school of theological rationalism called Mu'tazilism. (If one includes his dismissal of distinctively African American (non-Sunni) forms of Islam, then one could say that he has three critical targets.) In Jackson's account,

Mu'tazilite theology is distinguished by its approach to religious knowledge and divine revelation, which are ultimately subordinate to reason; only reason can validate the authority of revelation and particular claims of religious knowledge. Though he may have reservations about Mu'tazilism when compared to other theological schools, Jackson contends that it anticipates Jones' critique of black theodicy. As a response to the problem of theodicy, it is entitled to as much esteem as humanocentric theism.[75]

Jackson's account fingers a primary reason for our interpretive disagreement: where I take secular humanism as Jones's preferred view, with humanocentric theism as a strategic attempt to prevent the outright dismissal of his argument by theologians (a point that Jackson acknowledges[76]), he accents humanocentric theism. Jackson's reading is licensed by an ambiguity if not ambivalence in Jones' account: his decision to offer a theistic companion to his preferred, nontheistic view. To the extent that Jones has not been read the way he might have wished, the fault lies largely with this decision, which dilutes the clarity of his nontheistic account. Here I countersign a point that Anthony Pinn has made elsewhere. Thus Mu'tazilism may compare favorably with humanocentric theism, but this is not a virtue since this ambiguous/ambivalent figure is part of the problem, the point at which Jones' argument fails to be true to its own logic and goes awry. Humanocentric theism introduced an unnecessary ambiguity into an otherwise clear argument; Jones would have been better off had he offered his secular humanism straight, with no "theological chaser."

In his brief for Mu'tazilism, Jackson claims that it can reconcile divine omnibenevolence and omnipotence in a manner that is consistent with black liberation. In contrast, "Jones insists that sustained black suffering cannot be reconciled with belief in the inherent benevolence of God. In his view," Jackson continues, "any honest assessment of the ontological *fact* of black suffering would require that one at least consider the possibility that God is malevolent, at least toward blacks."[77] *Pace* Jackson, Jones makes no such claim. What Jones actually claims is the following: "An examination of the biblical understanding of suffering confirms the crucial premise of the multievidentiality of suffering. One can find biblical statements to support each of the logical possibilities—suffering as an expression of (a) divine disfavor or deserved punishment, (b) divine favor, and (c) neither favor nor disfavor. Accordingly, suffering in the biblical view is inherently ambiguous."[78] In advancing his own position, Jackson minimizes the complexity of Jones' position. Jones does not deny that sustained black suffering and divine omnibenevolence can be reconciled. Rather, it is only in the presence of specific claims that the problem of irreconcilability arises. Required are the claims that god is an omnibenevolent, omnipotent liberator who acts in history and is a partisan of the oppressed (that is, those who suffer unjustly, and where black people are a distinctive class of the oppressed) and that black suffering is inordinate, noncatastrophic, sustained, and nonpedagogical.

The procedure that I just followed of juxtaposing a direct quotation of Jones to Jackson's characterization of his views is one that I shall pursue throughout my assessment of Jackson's text. In this way, I to signal to the reader what she can expect: that this is an argument about interpretation; that some interpretations are better than others; that Jackson commits several attribution errors in his account of Jones' argument. If not attenuating Jones' claims, then he ignores context and the specific ways that Jones qualifies the scope of his claims. Establishing this point requires extensive direct quotation because how he characterizes Jones' claims is integral to my critique of Jackson's account. I shall provide examples where Jackson omits information or mischaracterizes important aspects of Jones' account.

I attribute to Jackson an apologetic desire to vindicate, if not demonstrate the superiority of "classical" Sunni theologies to Jones' critique of black theodicy. If the reader has any doubts about the cogency of this claim, she need only consider a distinction between two modes of vision, central and peripheral, that Jackson borrows from Alan Watts, a scholar of Buddhism. To reprise Jackson's account, central vision is highly focused and narrow in scope; it is especially useful '"for accurate work like reading'" where fastidiousness about detail is more important than the big picture. In contrast, peripheral vision has limited utility for accurate reading. Its virtues are compatible with "regimes of sense that are less rigid, precise, and systematic."[79] Jackson goes on to note that peripheral vision was more characteristic of the interpretive style of the early Muslim community. In contrast, central vision is dominant in Mu'tazilism, while both perceptual styles are operative side-by-side in modern Western societies. The point of all this is that Jackson recognizes that different regimes of sense require different modes of reading. However, he does not apply this fine distinction to his reading of Jones. Jones engages in a careful, philosophical critique of black theology based on theodic reason. This critique often turns on fine distinctions and meticulous qualification. What the reader should have noticed thus far and will discover subsequently is that Jackson employs the wrong "regime of sense," to use his language, when characterizing Jones' claims.

Regarding the art of sense-making, consider Jackson's comparison of Jones' critique of black theodicy and Ash'arite theology. Notice how he characterizes Jones' views in this passage: "Recall that the charge of divine racism rested on the contention that if God is omnipotent, God must have the power to eradicate black suffering. If God does not, this can only mean that God does not want to."[80] Here Jackson quotes Jones' critique of Joseph Washington. Jones uses similar language to characterize the view of the "Blasphemer" in Countee Cullen's poem "The Black Christ," if not to describe Cullen's own view. What he claims regarding the poem is that there is a tradition of black humanist thought in which god's disposition toward black people is questioned. Jones writes, "Jesus' power is unmistakable, according to Cullen, in His victory over death. Thus His failure to exert the same power in behalf of blacks must be regarded not as an indication of His impotence but an admission that he does not want to."[81] In neither case (Washington's nor Cullen's/the Blasphemer's) does Jones claim that god *is* a white racist. What he does claim is that the question inevitably arises for both.[82] The question arises for Washington, and other black theologians, because of his and their (especially Cone's) specifically partisan, pro-black construction of god. I contend that Jackson does not properly distinguish the logic of the views that Jones characterizes from an *endorsement of those views*. It is precisely the logic of those views that leads Jones (when most clear-minded) to advocate abandoning god-talk altogether. This is the import of his concept of the "functional ultimacy of "wo/man."[83]

In the following passage regarding evil, I think that Jackson attributes the wrong views to Jones:

> In his condemnation of black suffering, Jones appears to proceed on the basis of a moral objectivism reminiscent of the strong ontology of the Baghdādī Mu'tazilites or psychological naturalism of Abd al-Jabbār (i.e., that the human psyche is naturally programmed to impose a proper moral order on the world). On this approach, rather than prove his claim—that is, on the basis of an objective, validateable definition of evil—Jones simply *assumes* and *asserts* the evil of black suffering and in doing so effectively places this beyond critique.[84]

Jones does not merely assume and assert; he provides an argument. Contra Jackson, Jones provides criteria for distinguishing among kinds of suffering, which may be morally good, bad, or neutral. This is precisely why he calls forms of suffering that involve subjective agency, if not intentionality—suffering that is maldistributed, negative in quality, enormous, and noncatastrophic—*ethnic suffering*. He also calls it "oppression" to signal its morally negative quality. In contrast, there are forms of suffering, short of ethnic suffering, that can be construed as deserved, pedagogical, or otherwise "redemptive." Under the right circumstances, in light of a noneschatological, non-question-begging, retrospective judgment, these forms of suffering might be judged as "good." Though differential criteria can be specified, they are not dispositive: "suffering in the biblical view is inherently ambiguous." Its positivity or negativity cannot be proven. Suffering is "multievidential." Given this irremediable ambiguity and the peculiar history of black suffering, Jones argues that black theologians *ought to construe* suffering as negative. This construction is most likely to sustain a liberating agency. *Pace* Jackson, this is an argument, not mere assertion.

If, under Jackson's analysis, Jones' critique fails in relation to Ash'arite theology, then Traditionalism exposes its failure as well. Jackson claims that traditional Muslim theology, unlike black theology under Jones' critique, affirms that all humankind (not committed to god) is subject to the wiles of Satan and of other humans. On his view, Jones seems disinterested in what Blackamericans do with their agency, an issue that cannot be effectively addressed outside a conscious commitment to god. Jackson bases this claim on the authority of the Traditionalist theologian Ibn Taymīya.[85] Constructing an invidious comparison between Jones and Ibn Taymīya, Jackson claims that the latter assigns a greater role to humans in eliminating suffering; indeed, they bear primary responsibility.[86] Jackson concludes his comparative analysis of Islamic Traditionalism and Jones' critique of black theodicy by criticizing the secular mind-set that, ironically, or so he claims, attempts to minimize human responsibility while maximizing God's responsibility for human well-being:

> Thus, for example, while Jones insists on the functional ultimacy of man and an all-is-in-man's-hands approach, he also insists that the very fact of black suffering calls into question not humans' effectiveness, wisdom, or level of discipline, sacrifice, or commitment but the sovereignty and goodness of God! God, in other words, regardless of the action or nonactions of blacks, remains ultimately responsible for guaranteeing Blackamerican welfare. From Ibn Taymīya's perspective, however, for God to be good, just, wise, and all-powerful does

> not mean that God must effectively function as a divine Santa Claus, regardless of whether God's wards are naughty or nice. This, however, is hardly enough to render God a divine racist.[87]

In detailing the nature of divine racism, Jones remarks: "It should be recalled that my objective is not to demonstrate that God is a white racist or an anti-Semite. Rather, it is to question the theological frameworks within which these charges legitimately surface."[88] This is a serious method of inquiry. Notice that it has none of the silliness of Jackson's reference in the passage above to "a divine Santa Claus." Jackson confuses a methodological question, "Is God a white racist?" designed to improve the critical reasoning of black theologians with an affirmative answer. He conflates Jones' critique of black theodicy with an endorsement of a divine Santa Claus view of god. Let's consider in detail what Jones actually says:

1. The first purpose [of his critique of black theology]...is to identify the combination of theological categories that makes it necessary to ask, Is God a white racist? The issue of divine racism surfaces whenever a specific type of suffering, which I identify as *ethnic suffering,* is joined with particular interpretations of God's sovereignty over human history and His activity within human history or both.
2. If one dichotomizes between negative and positive suffering, oppression is a variety of negative suffering....The theologian of liberation, by definition, is committed to annihilate oppression, which is to say, to eliminate the suffering that is the heart of oppression. Thus he must provide an explanation that perceives the suffering as negative. He must show that the suffering that is oppression is not God's will or sanctioned by nature. He must, in sum, desanctify the suffering in question, or else the oppressed will not regard their suffering as oppressive and will not be motivated to attack it.
3. The black theologian is obliged to reconcile the inordinate amount of black suffering, which is implied in his claim that the black situation is oppressive, with his affirmations about the nature of God and God's sovereignty over human history.
4. [T]heodicy is the controlling category for black theology...because black theology defines itself as a theology of liberation.
5. [T]he issue of divine racism is in fact forced by the black theologians' own conclusions and presuppositions.
6. The critical test I utilize is whether the black theologian consistently disproves the charge of divine racism and whether his account of black suffering provides a coherent and sturdy foundation for the theology of liberation advanced as its explicit purpose.

7. I suggest that what I term *humanocentric theism* and *"secular" humanism* are the best candidates [for an authentic black theodicy]. The essential feature of both is the advocacy of the *functional ultimacy of man.*[89]

Jones is a secular humanist: god, for him, has no reality apart from the human imagination; god is neither ontic nor ontological. To claim that Jones contradicts himself, both holding humans responsible for their own destiny and holding god responsible when they fail, is, to put it mildly, a bad reading. Jackson conflates Jones' actual position—"the functional ultimacy of wo/man"—with the logical implications of the claims that black theologians make. Though Jones' prose is clear, economical, and nonornamental, with few ambiguities of style, he may be partly responsible for Jackson's (mis)reading. His generosity in offering the olive branch of humanocentric theism (a peace offering to black theologians) seduced some readers such as Major Jones and Jackson into attributing that perspective to Jones himself.

This may be a good place to comment briefly on Māturīdism (the fourth tradition of classical Sunni theology explored by Jackson) and to offer a summary analysis. Though Jackson knows that humanocentric theism is a compromise, he writes as if it is Jones' preferred view. He writes, furthermore, as if classical Sunni theologies and black theologians are speaking the same language, as if the latter make claims about black suffering and the nature of Allah that are comparable to the claims Jones discerns in black theology. Thus he can dismiss Jones' charge of quietism by remarking that "Māturīdism, no less than Mu'tazilism or Ash'arism, provides a powerful theistic incentive to revolt against domination and equally powerful assurances that sustain the oppressed in case of defeat."[90] But Jackson is comparing carrots and sticks. His passionate assertion doesn't touch Jones' point. Jackson fails to establish a comparison relevant to the specificity of Jones' critique. This is my principal objection (one I do not think can be overcome) to Jackson's analysis.

But Jackson does identify a potential problem in Jones' account of the relationship between agency and hope. Unfortunately, he commits additional attribution errors along the way. He attributes to Jones, for example, the contention "that God is or must be a white racist."[91] And he attributes the view that there is a "necessary connection between belief in divine omnipotence and quietism."[92] He claims that Jones assumes as a "universal given" the "legitimacy of black interests and the propriety of revolution."[93] As my argument has attempted to establish, I think that these claims are false. But in case these points have not been adequately made and at the risk of being repetitive, Jones does not assert that god is a white racist, he poses the question "Is God a white racist?" This question is a methodological device designed to force black theologians to clarify their arguments, to make them less vulnerable to the question. The reader should remember what Jackson forgets: Jones is a secular humanist for whom god is merely an imaginary reality. (But even imaginary realities have real-world effects; hence Jones' critique of the quietistic implication of black theodicy.) Jones' claims are not universal but particular and highly contextual, rooted in the specificity of black Christian theology and life. They remain particular despite Jackson's apologetic-driven desire to universalize them, to make Jones' critique of black theodicy a critique of theodicy as such, to create a pretext for trumpeting classical Sunni theology.

These attribution errors notwithstanding, I think that Jackson is right when he remarks that "Jones' humanocentric theism, with its 'functional ultimacy of man' and its 'all in man's hands approach,' is ultimately about agency." Jackson simultaneously poses two questions: Are humanocentric theism and secular humanism any better than conventional black theism in avoiding the problem of quietism? To sharpen the question, doesn't conventional theism do a better of job of sustaining hope, which is a fundamental ingredient of agency? Hope is what we have when reason and evidence are against us. It sustains us against the odds. A form of conscious and unconscious illusion-making, hope is the midwife of a counterfactual reality that exists only in our imaginations and that we try to bring into a new order of being. This is especially true when hope is embodied in mythopoetic forms with heroes and gods who act on our behalf. Jackson makes the same point as follows: "As the celebrated Christian theologian Reinhold Niebuhr (d. 1971) once noted, 'contending factions in a social struggle require morale; and morale is created by the right dogmas, symbols and emotionally potent oversimplifications.' "[94] Jackson raises these issues of quietism, defeatism, and hope most effectively in his book's third chapter, titled "Mu'tazilism and Black Theodicy." He remarks:

> Having laid this theoretical groundwork, Jones appears to leave the question of practical effectiveness to mere chance. Having succeeded, in other words, in bringing Blackamericans to see themselves as functionally ultimate and endowed with the independent ability to direct

> their efforts toward crushing oppression, Jones leaves a singularly glaring question unanswered: What if Blackamericans' oppressors are more numerous, more powerful, more resolved, better organized, and possessed of bigger, better, and more guns?[95]

This is a fair question. As Jackson notes, Jones poses a version of this question himself. He is well aware of the argument that Jackson makes regarding defeatism as the flip side of the quietism he criticizes. Hope exceeds what we know, even what we ordinarily believe. It is a kind of pragmatic, prudential, and existential modality *in extremis*. To reiterate, hope sustains us when experience, reason, logic, and, for that matter, "bigger, better, and more guns" are on the other side. Hope is a pragmatically productive form of wishful thinking. It might be fair to say that Jones does not attend enough to the hope dimension of agency. To that extent, his critique of theological quietism may be vulnerable to Jackson's critique of humanistic defeatism. Not to worry. Those of us who are naturalistic and humanistic in orientation have myths and heroes too, even if we are not as accomplished on the mythopoetic level as the adherents of theistic traditions. We do not simply deny the reality of g/God so much as bring g/God down to earth, recognizing g/God as personification and idealization of human and other natural powers or of powers we imagine as nature-transcendent. *Thus the gods are real, their mode of existence is the human imagination, and they have effects in the lives of those who believe in them.* Having said that, I think it fair to say that whether quietism or defeatism is the bigger problem for emancipatory agency is an open question. Open because many proponents of theistic superiority take the correlation between theistic beliefs and a robust agency as causal. It may be. But we do not know whether there is *in fact* a correlation. What we do know is that "correlation is not causation." In any event, Jackson does a fine job in bringing attention to the matter of hope and agency in Jones' account.

In conclusion, I turn to the distinctively Blackamerican forms of Islam that Jackson dismisses. I know that he chose to focus on classical Sunni theologies. And that is certainly his scholarly prerogative. Insofar as his subject is Islam and black suffering, however, it is hard to understand why he excludes these forms of Islam. I offer the following conjecture: Jackson wishes to promote a particular, normative vision of Islam among Blackamericans, which seduces him into dismissing as heretical those forms of African American Islam such as the Moorish Science Temple and the Nation of Islam to which Jones' critique of black theodicy might be applicable. Consider the words of the "Honorable" Elijah Muhammad from his collection of sermons and teachings entitled *Message to the Blackman in America*:

> The Black people of America have been swallowed by the slave-masters, who are a race of devils, says all-wise God, Allah, and now refuse to let us go free without hinderance and hold us a prey against the will of Allah in the person of Master Fard Muhammad, who now seeks our deliverance, since our people love the enemy more than God.
>
> For God to fulfill his promise to deliver us from our enemies, He must go to war against the enemy and break the enemy's power of resistance to free us. War is inevitable. The so-called Negroes must come to the knowledge of Truth, that they have no future in their enemies who are the enemies of almighty God, Allah. God must come to put an end to war and, that is to say, destroy those who love to make war and delight in making mischief.[96]

As Mattias Gardell remarks, "The Nation of Islam had to struggle with the problem of doctrinal theodicy."[97] If Allah is good, is black, and has a covenantal relationship with his people—"Original Man," the Tribe of Shabazz, founders of the Holy City of Mecca—then why did he permit a renegade, big-head, mad scientist named Dr. Yacub to graft the Devil (the white race) from the stock of Original Man? Why didn't he spare Blackman the horrors of slavery? Why did a black god allow his chosen people to suffer "the burden of white supremacy?" Why, as the Nation's popular song puts it, is the white man's heaven the black man's hell?

Jones' critique of black theodicy is clearly applicable to the theology of the Nation of Islam and may be applicable to others such as the Moorish Science Temple. If Jackson had a less jaundiced view of distinctively Blackamerican forms of Islam, then he might have taken the Nation of Islam as a worthy object of analysis. Doing so might have served his apologetic interests better. He could have demonstrated how the issue of divine racism emerges from the very conclusions and presuppositions of Nation of Islam theology. Then he could have provided an invidious comparison of classical Sunni theologies and Nation of Islam theology. Jackson certainly has every right to be a Muslim "classicist," if not a "traditionalist." However, to engage Jones' critique of black theodicy in relation to "classical" Sunni theologies makes little sense. Or it would only make sense with a lot of preparatory work, which Jackson does not do, and many qualifications of the claims he wishes to make. For his project to even get off the ground, Jackson would have to show, first of all, that there is a classical Sunni tradition of Muslim theology comparable to Christian black theology. Like the latter, this Blackamerican classical Sunni Muslim theology would have to make claims regarding god's partisan disposition toward Blackamericans. As a "black Muslim James Cone" might put it, Allah must be for black people and against white racists, or Blackamerican Muslims should kill him. Or, like a "black Muslim Joseph Washington," they must construe Blackamericans as Allah's contemporary suffering servant. Or, like a "black Muslim Albert Cleage," they must claim that Allah is black and that the Prophet Muhammad and the original Muslim community were black. *Absent these kinds of claims, Jackson has no project.* Classical Muslim theologies are not analogous to the black Christian theologies whose claims compelled Jones to ask, "Is God a white racist?"

Lest I be misunderstood, none of what I've said should be construed as suggesting that distinctively Blackamerican forms of Islam are "true" Islam, or that they are superior to Sunni Islam, or that Blackamerican Muslims have a special obligation to them. I know that there are sites of bigoted ignorance where the complexity and diversity of the Blackamerican Muslim community is reduced to the Nation of Islam. That bigoted agenda is not mine. My only point is that the Nation of Islam is a better subject of Jackson's critique than is classical Sunni Islam. There is a *relevant* basis of comparison between the Nation and black theology.

Finally, to emphasize the problem that Jackson's approach encodes, imagine Cone responding to Jones' critique of his theology by reference to the theodicy of Karl Barth or, worse, to Patristic theologians such as Irenaeus of Lyons and Athanasius of Alexandria or, even worse, to the classical Sunni theological traditions of Mu'tazilism, Ash'arism, Māturīdism, and Traditionalism. Jones would rightly retort, What do these theologians have to do with my critique of black theology? Jones does not claim that divine racism is a threshold issue for *all* forms of theology. Barth, the Patristics, and classical Sunni theologians do not make claims that force them to consider the question "Is God a white racist?" They do not claim that god is black; that black suffering, given its inordinate, disproportionate, and chronic character, is oppressive and, therefore, against god's will; that black suffering is undeserved and nonpedagogical, and that god acts in history to liberate the oppressed. These are essential aspects of Jones' critique that Jackson does not consider in his work of translation from black (Christian) theology to classical Sunni theologies. Jackson's nonrecognition of these aspects makes Jones' arguments appear unmotivated or otherwise weak. To reiterate, Jackson constructs Jones' argument as universal claims about theology rather than particular claims about a historically specific form of Christian theology that might be applicable to non-Christian "theologies" insofar as they make similar claims. In light of this analysis, I conclude that Jackson gets Jones' critique of black theology wrong. I wonder whether this is related to his desire to promote a normative view of Islam among Blackamericans. *Islam and the Problem of Black Suffering* is an interesting effort to engage Jones' critique of black theodicy that is well worth reading. But it misses the mark as a comparative Christian–Islamic, black theological–classical Sunni analysis of black theodicy.

Chapter 6

The Prophet

Attunement: A Personal Note

I have never met William R. Jones, and I have interacted with Theophus Smith (the subject of chapter 7) on a single occasion, where I queried him on the role of Rene Girard in his text. My relationship with Charles H. Long is more substantial. David Carrasco, Long's former student at the University of Chicago, introduced him to me when I was a graduate student at Princeton University. Carrasco had invited Long to lecture at Princeton in the hope that a center could be established that would archive and preserve his work. I still recall the rhetorical effect of Long's cryptic phrase, "the imagination of matter," that had a kind of incantatory power until I acquired a fuller sense of its meaning within the phenomenological tradition in which he worked. Aware that Long once held a dual appointment in religious studies at the University of North Carolina and at Duke University, I sought his advice regarding a job offer from Duke and its suitability for a person such as me. I will not share his advice but am thankful for his wisdom, candor, and clairvoyance. No doubt, he has made a far greater impression on me than I have on him. We are casual acquaintances. In stark contrast, my relationship with Cornel West, the subject of this chapter, is both personal and professional. He is both mentor and friend. My ongoing encounter with him over twenty-plus years as student and colleague has shaped me in ways that I cannot calculate. There was a time when I could not determine where his thinking ended and mine began, when he had already thought my best thoughts.[1] My debt to him is such that the only proper payment is gratitude. Of course, there are different ways of showing gratitude. In the spirit of the Emerson he taught me, I take West not as my instructor but as provocation for my own thinking. On this Emersonian view, a student who does not "bite" his teacher's hand is a poor student. As Nietzsche, Emerson's best European student, put it: "One repays a teacher badly if one remains only a pupil."[2] In this chapter I strive to be a good (former) student and to repay my teacher well by "biting" the hand that I love. I write under the twin signs of Emerson and Freud. Given West's status as one of my intellectual fathers, the oedipal thematic, at least as I see it, is unavoidable. The reader must determine whether I avoid debilitating forms of oedipal desire, whether a Bloomian "anxiety of influence" detracts from my argument as opposed to adding complexity, texture, and spice.

Between Marx and Kierkegaard

In *American Evasion of Philosophy: A Genealogy of American Pragmatism* (1989), West describes the difference between American philosophy and its European antecedents as the former's "evasion" of the latter's epistemology-centeredness. For American philosophers, ethics and politics are first philosophy. Their evasion of epistemology is tantamount to refusing to answer a question poorly asked, whose premise is incorrect, answers to which would only lead to confusion. In this chapter, I explore West's prophetic construction of Black Religion. I do so by addressing two broad questions: How does West's prophetic construction of black church and theology fare in light of Long's threefold challenge—does it take it up or pursue a different path, illuminate or obscure Black Religion? What is the relationship between West's and William R. Jones' respective critiques of black theology; specifically, how do they construct relations among existentialist orientation, humanism, and emancipatory agency in Black Religion? The place to pursue these questions is *Prophesy Deliverance! An Afro-American Revolutionary Christianity* (1982), which West wrote at the youthful age of twenty-eight. It is the most important source for his concept of prophetic Christianity, and the only text that deals with the topic at length. As West is now fifty-something, one might expect some change in his views since that time. One of the remarkable things about West, however, is how little his views have changed. Like Athena, West seems to have sprung fully formed from Zeus' head. The stability of his views from youth to mature fifties is either a measure of his precociousness and untimely wisdom and/or the mark of a certain intellectual stubbornness, an unwilling to revise his claims in light of criticism. Whatever the case may be, I expect to encounter some changes and will take note and qualify my claims where appropriate. Unless I find explicit modifications or repudiations, I will take the views he expressed in *Prophesy Deliverance!* and in contemporaneous essays as his current views.

West is excellent at providing concise encapsulations of his views. The following is his description of an Afro-American revolutionary Christianity. "A black Christian position contains four central elements: the philosophical methodology of dialectical historicism, the theological world view of prophetic Christianity, the cultural outlook of Afro-American humanism, and the social theory and political praxis of progressive Marxism."[3] A correlation and synthesis of prophetic Christianity and progressive Marxism is the heart of this perspective. Prophetic Christianity and progressive Marxism each supply the defect of the other; that is, they shore up the weaknesses in the other perspective by filling in the gaps. According to West, prophetic Christianity lacks a social theory and political praxis; it does not understand the productive relations between wealth and power, which progressive Marxism supplies.[4] In contrast, progressive Marxism is "unmusical" and has a tin ear when it comes to religion: specifically, its cultural theory is deficient, flat, one-dimensional, and otherwise unimaginative. Christianity overcomes the deficiencies of Marxist cultural theory with a powerful hermeneutic that works in the receptive, transformative, and dialectical interspace of Christian lives and through the imaginative power of the Bible.[5] Where there is no defect, as in their common dialectical methodology, they mutually reinforce the other's strength.

A dialectical methodology is the critical interplay of negative and positive judgments that simultaneously preserve, cancel, transform, and elevate. This concept of dialectics is Hegelian rather than Socratic. In its Marxist iteration, dialectics corresponds to what Marx took to be objective historical processes, historical-materialist transformations in the mode of production that had ramifications for all aspects of society. The most important point regarding West's dialectical methodology is antidogmatism: dialectics keep the Peircean road of inquiry open and enable the unmasking of falsehoods, hidden agendas, systematic misunderstandings, and mystifications that are endemic but not limited to capitalist societies. Organic to West's Afro-American humanism, this methodology enables the unmasking of deficient cultural perspectives. West identifies the Afro-American humanist tradition dialectically. Indeed, it becomes a visible and distinctive tradition only through his construction and critique of alternative responses to white supremacy. As he constructs it, the humanist tradition preserves the strengths of the exceptionalist, assimilationist, and marginalist traditions of response while negating their antiprophetic and antiprogressive elements. West's critique of their defects are these: that the exceptionalist tradition is often little more than a subterfuge for class mobility by "*an emerging opportunistic Afro-American petite bourgeoisie*"; that the assimilationist tradition is defined by "self-hatred, shame, and fear," which leads to a rejection of Afro-American culture; and that the marginalist tradition is excessively individualistic and often apolitical, substituting *moral sermonizing* for political organizing. Through a dialectical "yes" and "no" to these traditions, West constructs the humanist tradition as his preferred tradition of response to white supremacy. He remarks:

> The humanist self-image of Afro-Americans is one neither of heroic superhumans untouched by the experience of oppression nor of pathetic subhumans devoid of a supportive culture. Rather, Afro-Americans are viewed as both meek and belligerent, kind and cruel, creative and dull—in short, as human beings. This tradition does not romanticize or reject Afro-American culture; instead, it accepts it for what it is, the expression of an oppressed human community imposing its distinctive form of order on an existential chaos, explaining its political predicament, preserving its self-respect, and projecting its own special hopes for the future.[6]

Largely but not exclusively defined as a response to white supremacy, West's cultural perspective dovetails nicely with his views regarding theology. I describe West as a *Kierkegaardian liberationist*.[7] He combines the liberation theologian's emphasis on a revolutionary eschatology that prefigures the kingdom of god in history with Soren Kierkegaard's accent on truth as subjectivity: a Christian inwardness that is so deep and *radically private* as to make systematic theology and perhaps any theology absurd, inducing a kind of aphasia. West's theology is situated, dare I say stuck, between Kierkegaard and Ernst Troeltsch: between the latter's thoroughgoing historicism, which relativizes the truth of Christianity, and the former's reason-defying "qualitative leap," which leaves objective historical considerations behind and burrows deeply into a subjectivity that Kierkegaard construes as truth.[8] Even when West calls himself a "Chekhovian Christian,"[9] which so far as I can tell he began to do sometime during the early 1990s, I hear Kierkegaard's *Concept of Dread* and *Sickness unto Death* beneath Chekhov's voice. Chekhov is a puppet for a Kierkegaardian ventriloquist. Or to put it differently, Kierkegaard is the theological spirit behind the mask of the agnostic playwright. I would go even further and say that Chekhov, Coltrane, Tolstoy, and Toni Morrison (as exemplars of a kind of "existential seriousness") are *dramatis personae,* pseudonyms of the master name of Soren Kierkegaard. With his idiosyncratic Christian voice, Kierkegaard is a recurring figure in West's cultural critique. Though usually present *only* in the form of a citation or allusion, Kierkegaard is the preeminent representative of existential seriousness and depth on which West places a lot of weight. Reading West on Kierkegaard can be as frustrating as reading Kierkegaard. West uses "Kierkegaard" like shorthand but never provides a longhand explanation. Kierkegaard has a furtive presence. There is little translation and no interrogation. This shorthand mimics and underwrites a Kierkegaardian evasion of explication—"a qualitative leap" beyond investigation and explanation.

The Kierkegaardian-induced, aphasic theology that I am attributing to West is not absolute, as he has something to say about black theology. He approaches black theology dialectically, which in this case also means obliquely and comparatively. West describes the alliance of prophetic Christianity and progressive Marxism as "a last humane hope for humankind."[10] In the spirit of a materialist version of Hegel's logic, West constructs the alliance by staging a dialogical encounter in the hope that each will sublate *(aufheben)* the other: negating the bad, preserving the good, while mutually transforming, binding, and lifting the other higher. To the Marxist critique that Christian praxis is impotent and based on an ill-formed assessment of the human predicament and an incorrect analysis of social change, the Christian partner in this staged dialogue responds by acknowledging the historical impotence of Christianity while asserting the impotence of every historical project of radical transformation.[11] West neither specifies the standard of measurement (the standard cannot be perfection) nor acknowledges the relativity of historical powerlessness. Projects of radical transformation are not equally powerless. (As West surely knows, genuine politics inhabits the interstices of the more or less, the better or worse.) The only compelling question is the prospect of relative success or failure. Imperfection and uncertainty cannot be the standards. As Voltaire taught us, perfection is the enemy of the good. West does not provide criteria for distinguishing the "more" from the "less," the "better" from the "worse." Such differential judgments, often painfully incremental, are the whole point of politics.

To the Marxist charge that Christian truth claims are rationally and scientifically unfounded, the Christian responds with a Kierkegaardian leap to faith. But West must surely know that "truth as subjectivity" (the "existential appropriation of Jesus Christ") is only one Christian conception of truth among many.[12] West's account obscures the differences among prophetic Christians. (Indeed, there may very well be more disagreement among Christians regarding the nature of truth than between Christians and non-Christians.) Not all accept Kierkegaard's retreat into the "absurd." West implies that such a retreat is prerequisite for a prophetic outlook. The limitations of West's claims are apparent when we consider them in relation to Walter Rauschenbusch and Martin Luther King, Jr. (both liberal, and perhaps the two preeminent prophetic American Christians of the twentieth century).[13]

To the Christian critique that Marxist praxis is "narrow, naive, and nearsighted," West remarks that the Marxist responds by acknowledging the critique while simultaneously arguing that its utopian and Promethean exaggerations of human possibilities are inspirationally and pedagogically necessary. Furthermore, its narrow focus on politics, economy, and society is analytically productive, providing unparalleled knowledge of the systematic operations of capital.[14] But here the unbalanced nature of this dialogical encounter becomes apparent.[15] West construes the scientific desires and pretensions of Marxism as totalitarian, monopolistic, and manipulative. He claims that the modern world-picture of science, technology, and Enlightenment hold Marxism captive. But Kierkegaard is no less captive. There is no qualitative leap, truth as subjectivity, or existential appropriation of Jesus Christ without scientific and enlightened modernity. Kierkegaard and Auguste Comte, absurd leaps to faith and positivistic conceptions of knowledge, share the same modern assumptions, have the same "picture" in view, and are two faces of the same captivity.

I would be remiss if I did not accent a central claim advanced by West, namely, that both prophetic Christianity and progressive Marxism are fundamentally the same in their desire to transform current realities according to the norms of individuality and democracy. One wonders about the democratic character of the prophetic tradition based on the sectarian revelation of "Thus sayeth the Lord." Isn't the "Lord God" to the prophetic tradition what wealth is to capitalism, an undemocratic power whose authority and privilege is exempted from democratic debate and regulation?

West's Account of Black Theology

I preface my assessment of West's account of black theology by briefly considering the views of Mark David Wood (2000)[16] who rejects West's prophetic Christianity–progressive Marxism synthesis. Skeptical of the Christian partner in the dialogue, Wood advances three basic claims. First, and perhaps most importantly, he criticizes West's lack of generosity in describing notions of human nature within the Marxist tradition. As West construes it, Marxism is excessively optimistic regarding the human capacity to transform its circumstances, which is anchored by a Hegelian-inspired notion of historical inevitability, the notion that success is metaphysically guaranteed. (This is the flip side of the theological notion of divine providence.) While acknowledging that there are highly Hegelian forms of Marxism that accent historical inevitability, Wood argues that there are important strains that deny it. West subscribes to this radically historicist interpretation in his doctoral dissertation that was published under the title *The Ethical Dimensions of Marxist Thought* (1992).[17] If humans are the makers of their own history and nature, then there are no inevitable constraints on their creative capacities except finitude.[18] (While West does not subscribe to the concept of original sin, he does subscribe to *a* notion of sin as an offense against god.) Thus there is a contradiction between his Marxist (Emersonian and Deweyan) anthropology of self-creation and his Christian anthropology of dignity and depravity.

I think that Wood's analysis is correct, which leads to his second claim: that West's notion of the tragic is metaphysical rather than historical. Wood remarks: "Given humanity's ontoformative powers, we have no stake in establishing a priori limitations on the possibilities for individual and collective development."[19] Providing such limits is precisely what he takes West's notion of the tragic and tragicomedy to do. As Wood reads him, West holds that engaging the evil, tragic, and absurd dimensions of life is prerequisite to any effort to humanize social and natural relations. Wood is skeptical. Too much attention to such matters, staring too long into the abyss, only paralyzes; it enervates rather than invigorates. I think this claim is true. Knowing when to avert one's eyes and to forget is just as important to a robust agency as acknowledging tragedy. Wood contends that the existential engagement that West commends essentializes/fetishizes the abyss; mystifying the extent to which, evil, tragedy, and absurdity are the product of social relations that humans create.[20] It underwrites the kind of pessimism that compelled Heidegger to claim that "only a god could save us."

Wood's third claim is this:

> To the extent that liberation theology maintains a conception of human nature, the universe, and history as governed by forces that remain beyond theoretical cognition and practical control, such that liberation is, in the last instance, the result of God's will being done here on Earth as it is in Heaven, liberation theology sacralizes the linchpin of ruling-class ideology. Whereas bourgeois political economists invert the relationship between commodity producers and the commodities they produce, liberation theologians invert the relationship between religion producers and the religion they produce.[21]

Even though he fudges this claim with the introductory phrase "to the extent that," Wood applies this criticism to West, whose prophetic pragmatism he construes as a form of liberation theology. Keep these points in mind as we consider West's Marxist-informed critique of black liberation theology.[22] Is West gored by his own ox?

With this preface in mind, I note that West further circumscribes his topic by taking "the prophetic Christian tradition in the Afro-American experience" as exemplary of prophetic Christianity in America. Given his focus on ideas, the choice of black theology as subject of critique is appropriate. Black Theology of Liberation as Critique of Slavery is the first of five historical stages of development that West surveys. According to West, this first stage was consolidated between the 1650s and the First Great Awakening (1740s), and it lasted until 1863. The end date, presumably, has something to do with the Civil War, the Emancipation Proclamation, and the effective end of slavery. The longest of the five stages, it closely tracks the 246-year duration of legal slavery (1619–1865) and the struggle for emancipation.

That black theology should be preoccupied with slavery and liberation is not surprising. Slavery was the most important hermeneutical context for theological reflection. The sad fact of slavery was the starting point for black theologians. They had to grapple with tough questions. Why had god permitted black people to become slaves? How long would he allow this injustice to go on? Perhaps they asked a more disconcerting question: was their slavery unjust at all? Perhaps black people were being justly punished (like the idolatrous Israelites) for sinning, and slavery was their Babylonian Captivity. Perhaps white supremacists were right when they claimed that black people were the descendants of Cain and bore his mark, the odious color of their skin, as a sign of god's disapproval. How else could one account for such unforgivable blackness? Or maybe they bore the curse of Ham, son of the biblical patriarch Noah, who exploited his father's nakedness by gleefully failing to cover it. Recall the story: Ham is amused by the sight of his father who, normally sober and clothed, is drunk and naked. After recovering his sobriety, a spiteful Noah (perhaps he was still drunk) does something rather odd: he curses his grandson Canaan for his father's disrespectful behavior. Misdirected and disproportionate to the offense, Noah declares that Canaan's descendants will be slaves in perpetuity. Not merely the reaction of an angry father, this is a striking example of divine madness. For white supremacists the story was certainly divine, because it provided a convenient rationale for racial slavery.[23] Their twisted interpretation went something like this—black people had been slaves for a long time; wherever one looked in the world of European modernity, slaves were predominately black; ergo, black people must be cursed, they must be the descendents of Ham. The Bible sanctioned slavery. Jesus did not condemn it. Could there be a better justification for the enslavement of black people? Competing with white supremacist justifications of racial slavery was the "suffering servant" interpretation in which the enslavement and unjust suffering of black people was redemptive. Black suffering was a divine strategy for saving white people (a version of which is reproduced in the theopolitics of Martin Luther King), thus glorifying god and bathing Blackamericans in reflected glory. Such interpretations were bound to make black people blue. In the cacophony of competing biblical interpretations, I can imagine slaves asking, "Why do black people 'catch' so much hell?" Why are we enslaved, lynched, and stigmatized? Why, as the Negro spiritual puts it, have we been " 'buked, scorned, and talked about?"

I find it peculiar that such questions are virtually absent from West's account of black theology, given the huge role that he otherwise assigns to the struggle with "evil" and existential anxieties. Is there any anxiety greater than the fear that the "cosmic deck" is stacked against you: that the cosmos is fundamentally against black people; that god is a white "trickster" who plays games of chance with the fortunes of Blackamericans the way Yahweh played with Job; that god is a white racist who, like Indra in the *Rig Veda*,[24] hates your very blackness; that the unjust, disproportionate, chronic, and nonpedagogical nature of black suffering is not merely a contingent human reality but a necessary consequence of divine animus? There is a peculiar *lack* of anxiety regarding such questions in West's account of black theology.

In the first stage of West's evolutionary account of black theology there were few formally trained black theologians. Whether enslaved or free, black people had little or no access to education. We know that a few such as Harriet Jacobs were taught to read by "benevolent" masters; some, such as Frederick Douglass, were both autodidacts and taught by sympathetic whites; others, such as David Walker, were free persons who acquired some formal training. Walker might rightly be called a black theologian, even without West's expansive concept of theology that cuts against the predominant notion that theology is an elite discourse, a second-order reflection on popular piety. If we accept this expanded view, then Gabriel Prosser was a theologian who saw himself, according to West, as a black Samson pulling down the temple of white supremacy onto the heads of white American Philistines. Joining Prosser in the theological ranks were Denmark Vesey and Nat Turner. West claims that Walker's *Appeal to the Colored Citizens of the World* (1829) is the most significant theological document of Stage One black theology. Among the most prophetic words ever written, Walker condemned the sins of slavery, white supremacy, and the heresy of white Christianity. As critics of racial slavery underwritten by Christianity, Prosser, Vesey, Turner, and Walker were abolitionists in the most significant and first-order sense of the word. Curiously, West does not connect their individual theological voices with abolitionism as a social movement of slaves, free black people, and a significant cadre of dedicated white people. The most significant social movement in the late eighteenth and the nineteenth centuries, abolitionism was a social formation, a cloud of well-known and anonymous witnesses and antislavery freedom fighters that enabled black theologians.

On their shoulders stood the theologians of Stage Two: Black Theology of Liberation as Critique of Institutional Racism. Extending from 1864 to 1969, Reconstruction and the black power movement frame this stage. During this period black theologians reflected on the nature of god and world in relation to the plight of Blackamericans. They had a lot to consider: the neoslavery of debt, tenant farming and vagrancy laws in the service of peonage, and other forms of forced labor that were precursors of the contemporary prison-industrial complex. From the infamous draft riot in New York City during the Civil War to the murderous *coup d'état* in Wilmington, North Carolina, in 1898, the Red Summer of 1919, and the destruction of the black section of Tulsa, Oklahoma (1921)—which was firebombed from an airplane, as were the members of MOVE sixty years later—thousands of black people were terrorized and murdered, often with the complicity of government. Such was the anatomy of white terror in a racialized state that defined nationality in terms of whiteness. Given these ugly circumstances, black theologians had to find words of comfort and analysis, compelling arguments about the nature of god and the causes of Blackamerican suffering that would preserve life and sanity in the face of the deepest despair.

Suicide and homicide are two faces of despair. When we suffer from our suffering (one definition of despair), we want to know why and, more importantly, what we can do about it. Of course, we may despair of our despair, in which case we simply become numb, blinking at things that should make us shudder. Where despair has not overwhelmed a person, theodicy may answer the "why" with implications for the "what" of their suffering. It is the implications of theodicy for the "what" of human agency that some people find troubling. As we saw in chapter 5, theodicy constructs evil as a logical and metaphysical problem. That logic sounds something like this: If only we could get our arguments right, then the innocence of god (the fundamental goodness of the cosmos) would be established. Doubts about god's moral attributes inspired by the existence of evil would be overcome. Whatever the causes of evil, god would be exempted from scrutiny or blame. Granted, there is a certain metaphysical comfort in this solution. But as a logical "solution" to a practical problem it is pernicious. Such solutions do nothing to overcome evil as an ensemble of practical problems of everyday living. Despite the singular form of the word, evil is a plural reality. If evil is primarily a practical question of what "we" should do in the face of a *plurality of specific evils*, then metaphysical preoccupations with the justice of god and the *singular* logic of evil are displaced by pragmatic efforts of destruction and mitigation. Even folk wisdom understands this point: how you got into a hole is irrelevant; what matters is getting out. On this folksy view, erudite but metaphysically arid discussions of the "problem of holes"—that is, *the* problem of evil and the moral attributes of god—are so much sound and fury signifying nothing when they displace ethical and political struggle against concrete evils. Preoccupation with "the" problem of evil is a case of *misplaced abstraction*, a class-based luxury, a form of *hiding*.

It would seem that black theologians could not afford to hide. West's account of Stage Two black theology suggests that they turned practical and political. The prominent voices during this period included Bishop Henry McNeal Turner and Martin Luther King, Jr. Turner's theological reflections led him to conclude that there was no justice for black people in America. Several years before Marcus Garvey became the leading advocate of the "back to Africa" movement, Turner was urging Blackamericans to emigrate to Africa. (Turner and Garvey's desire for African repatriation was part of a larger white-inspired desire, once shared by Lincoln, to send black people back to Africa. Emancipation and repatriation, antislavery and anti-blackness, were two dimensions of the same desire. This is not to deny that there were always Africans, from the beginning of the transatlantic trade, who hoped to return to "Guinea" (Africa) when they died. (The story of "Ibo Landing" in Marshall's *Praisesong for the Widow* expresses this desire beautifully.) Turner concluded that African emigration, replicating the biblical Exodus, albeit in reverse, was god's will. Turner's African dream never materialized. But we learn something from his efforts. His response to the evil of racial oppression was pragmatic. This is not to say that Turner did not hold views about the nature of god and the evil of black people's suffering that could generate the classical questions of theodicy. But the metaphysical impulse to ruminate on "the" problem of evil was subordinated to the practical and political effort to solve the specific evil of white supremacy, indeed, problems even more specific such as the endemic occurrence of lynching. The problem of evil white folks did not become the problem of evil. Black suffering was a specific problem calling for a specific response.

This same orientation is evident in the life of King. West considers King the outstanding nonacademic theological voice during the latter period of Stage Two. King was trained as a theologian.[25] His most significant work of academic theology (some of which he plagiarized) was his doctoral dissertation: *A Comparison of the Conceptions of God in the Thinking of Paul Tillich and Henry Nelson Wieman* (1955). On a nonacademic level, his most significant "theological work" is contained in the many sermons, lectures, speeches, essays, and books that he wrote and that were ghostwritten. By the late 1960s Benjamin Mays, Howard Thurman, and George Kelsey were the deans of black theology. According to West, their success in codifying their theology was unrivaled among black theologians. But they worked in relative obscurity behind the "veil" of white supremacy and within the segregated world of black scholarship and intellectual life. Outside the veil, their pioneering work received little critical attention. Though their academic and professional contributions as theologians are more significant than those of King, they have not received their due. Mays wrote important books such as *The Negro's Church* (with Joseph W. Nicholson, 1933) and *The Negro's God, as Reflected in His Literature* (1938). Thurman did interesting work on black mysticism, spirituality, and the contemplative life—prefiguring, as I construe it, a mini-tradition that includes Julius Lester and Albert Raboteau. Thurman's *Jesus and the Disinherited* (1949) is a classic. Kelsey wrote *Racism and the Christian Understanding of Man* (1965), a fascinating and powerful critique of white supremacy. Using the theological categories of Reinhold Niebuhr, he construed white supremacy as idolatry, that is, the racist conflates god with race and worships it; in America, whiteness is god. Mays, Thurman, and Kelsey influenced King.

If West has done black religious studies a great service by focusing attention on important figures in Stage Two, he says little about Stage Three: Black Theology as Critique of White North American Theology. This stage lasted only nine years, from 1969 to 1977. Between its emergence and the pioneering efforts of the Stage Two theologians—Mays, Thurman, Kelsey, and King—there was little in black theology that West regards as worthy of note. Stage Three black theology emerged from the tumultuous events of the 1960s. It seems obvious in retrospect that the Black Nationalist radicalism of Malcolm X and the black power movement would influence the development of black theology. Cleage published *The Black Messiah* in 1968. The following year Cone published *Black Theology and Black Power.* With the publication of Cone's text, followed quickly by *A Black Theology of Liberation* (1970), this new intellectual project commanded wide attention. In Detroit, Cleage founded the Church of the Shrine of the Black Madonna, where he preached what he wrote: the original Jews were black people, Jesus was black, and blacks were god's chosen people. This was not the first time that such claims were made. But Cleage's work gave birth to a small nationalist movement and several churches affiliated with his. In a practice that is now part of black "mainstream" Christianity, images of a black Christ replaced the white Christ, often behind the pulpit, above the baptismal pool. Though an inspiration, if not co-founder of the new black theology, Cleage is not an academic scholar. His book is devoid of scholarly conventions of argument and apparatus. In contrast, Cone has worked tirelessly within the theological academy. An emeritus professor at Union Theological Seminary, Cone has mentored a generation of black theologians. During the late 1970s, he was West's senior colleague at Union and an important interlocutor.[26] Stage Three tracks Cone's theological development from his nationalist manifesto in 1969 to his more nuanced work of the middle 1970s. I read it as West coming to grips with the challenge to his neo-Marxist, anti-nationalist, and pragmatic perspective that Cone's resolutely Black Nationalist view represented.

West describes three virtues of Stage Three black theology: that god acts on behalf of the oppressed, that religion can kill or give life to the spirit of rebellion, and that racism is the core malignancy of America's exploitive, capitalist social order. This sounds like high praise until West details the vices:

1. Its absence of a systematic social analysis, which has prevented black theologians from coming to terms with the relationships between racism, sexism, class exploitation, and imperialist oppression.
2. Its lack of a social vision, a social program, and concrete praxis that defines and facilitates social-economic and political liberation.
3. Its tendency to downplay existential issues such as death, disease, dread, despair, and disappointment, which are related to, yet not identical with, suffering caused by oppressive structures.[27]

Is this a fair critique? Or is West is guilty of a "category mistake" when he criticizes black theology as bad cultural and political-economic theory? While theologies necessarily imply theories of culture and political economy, these discourses are not the primary languages of theology. Theology is about story-telling: the way a particular people describe their encounter with the cosmological powers that be. To be sure, theologians tell stories about god, humans, and the world that are relevant to how social relations might be imagined. But to argue that they ought to do the work of social, cultural, political, and economic theory is misplaced. West criticizes theologians for doing poorly what they do not intend to do and what, to make a stronger claim, they should not be expected to do. It seems to me that they have done their job well when their stories help their communities determine how they should live, which by definition has some relevance for how they might normatively contextualize economy, society, and culture within a larger, Christo-cosmological frame.

West may be on to something, however, when he speaks of the existential deficiencies of Stage Three black theology—but then again, maybe not. Maybe the dearth of commentary on existential anxieties is consistent with tradition. Without a doubt, expressions of such anxiety can be found throughout the sources on black religious life. Let us assume for the moment that West is correct when he says that these anxieties are inadequately represented in Stage Three black theology. It is still not clear why they must appear in the manner that West desires. The phenomenology of black people's existential anxieties might not have a Kierkegaardian shape. I can only speculate. But what West sees as a lack may be a sharp difference between black theology, in all the stages he describes, and the Kierkegaardian-inflected theology that he prefers. Blackamericans may have been sick of death, but it is not clear that they experienced a Kierkegaardian *sickness unto death*.[28] Lest readers draw the wrong conclusion, let me be clear about what I am not saying in criticizing West's reliance on Kierkegaard's theological anthropology and existential psychology. This is not a version of the specious claim that some of James Cone's critics made: that his theology was travestied by his reliance on European thinkers such as Karl Barth.

I do not claim that I have provided a sufficient argument regarding the relative insignificance of Kierkegaard-like thinking in the Blackamerican tradition. It is a claim, however, that West ought to address given the weight he asks Kierkegaard's theological anthropology to bear in this argument and throughout his work. Since the charge of "shallowness" is a standing critique of any perspective that does not address death and its intimations (disease, dread, despair, and disappointment) in a Kierkegaardian manner, West owes his readers a fuller account of why other perspectives, such as Spinoza's *affirmative equanimity* or Nietzsche's *affirmation laughter,* to limit the candidates to the Western philosophical tradition, are deficient. Could it be that the dearth of existential reflection in black theology as West construes it provides indirect evidence that Blackamericans are more Spinozist than Kierkegaardian? Or just maybe they are "blues people." Kierkegaard was certainly blue, but I can't imagine him playing the blues. If this affirmative stance (humor and playfulness in blue) is true, then we might take Blackamericans' "denial of death"[29] as a life-sustaining strategy rather than the avoidance and trivializing of the depth dimensions (sickness unto death) of human experience that West criticizes.

Here I transition sharply from Kierkegaard to Marx, the inspiration behind Stage Four: Black Theology as Critique of U.S. Capitalism. West roots this stage in a tradition of black socialist Christians such as the Reverend George Washington Woodbey, a pastor of the Mt. Zion Baptist Church in San Diego, California. That Woodbey thought seriously about the relations between Christianity and socialism is underscored by the texts he wrote and that West cites: *What to Do and How to Do It, or Socialism vs. Capitalism* (1903), *The Bible and Socialism: A Conversation between Two Preachers* (1904), "Why the Negro Should Vote the Socialist Ticket" (1908), *The Distribution of Wealth* (1910), and "Why the Socialist Must Reach the Churches with Their Message" (1915). West does not describe the content of these texts, but one can infer much from the titles. West notes the contributions that he and Cone made to the development of Stage Four black theology. But Woodbey seems like the ideal representative: a black pastor and pulpit preacher who combines Jesus and Marx. Far more explicit and less ambivalent than West, Woodbey would appear to be as good as it gets when it comes to Black Theology as Critique of U.S. Capitalism.

With his Kierkegaardian theological reticence (though Kierkegaard's takes the form of a studied, if not ironic, logorrhea), West says little about Stage Four black theology that is "doctrinally" theological. Is this good or bad? Bad—if you regard progressive Marxism's nearly complete absorption of black theology on the level of ideas as undesirable. This judgment may be too hasty. After all, West criticizes the fourth stage for failing to preserve the distinctively theological heritage of black theology. One would like to know what West means, for him to unpack statements such as "the prevailing conception of black theology of liberation remains inadequate. I believe that a new conception of black theology of liberation is needed which preserves the positive content of its earlier historical stages, overcomes its earlier (and inevitable) blindnesses, and makes explicit its present challenges."[30] To what does he refer when speaking of "positive content" that was lost during Stage Four, and that an emergent Stage Five black theology would restore? One thing is clear: even at this fourth stage, black theology is not dialectical enough. In their analyses, theologians of the fourth stage have not appropriated the power of "the Hegelian-Marxist negative." I interpret this to mean that black theology's critical capacities are insufficiently creative. But this does not explain how fourth stage black theology fails to preserve its distinctively theological heritage or what the "positive content" of that theology is. Again, one would like to hear more. Working with what he does provide, one would expect significant changes between Stage One and Stage Three black theology given the radical sociological changes that occurred among Blackamericans: transitions from slavery to freedom, rural to urban, nonliterate to literate, agricultural to industrial to postindustrial, and from Jim and Jane Crow to a status that has achieved, however imperfectly, "first-class" citizenship. But West does not specify what worth preserving has been abandoned and where it is evident in the transition from Stage Three to Stage Four.

Stage Five: Black Theology as Critique of Capitalist Civilization radicalizes the previous stage, extending the critique of capitalism beyond its American instantiation and a narrow focus on economy and society to the entire civilization. Just as importantly, this stage accents proto-Kierkegaardian concerns with existential depth. Would it be churlish for me to suggest that if the forth stage closely tracks Cone's theology, then Stage Five is a thinly disguised cipher for West's own views; that the proto-Kierkegaardian concerns he finds are his own, and that his account is not descriptive but constructive, what black theology would become under his critique?

From West's account of Stage Four and Stage Five black theologies, I distill the four claims. One: the prevailing relations of wealth and power are a matter of Christian concern. In light of the biblical concern for the poor and the wretched of the earth, this concern requires a sophisticated analysis of who has wealth and power, how they got it, and how the production and distribution of power and wealth can be made more equitable and just. Two: black theology combines radical faith commitments with radical politics. Three: the goal of black theology is a humane social order that prefigures the kingdom of god. Four: in its black theology of liberation incarnation, prophetic Christianity must embody a Kierkegaardian perspective on the depth dimensions (disappointment, despair, disease, death, and evil) of human existence.[31]

Let me belabor a point. West does not tell us what we need to know regarding the positive content of a radicalized black theology. His claim about the failure of the fourth stage to preserve the black theological heritage is ironic, to say the least, given his own unwillingness to theologize, even the minimal theologizing[32] that a sympathetic critic must do. This is doubly ironic given the terms of the proposed marriage between black theology and progressive Marxism. This refusal to theologize introduces an unavoidable asymmetry into the "marriage contract" that makes it more likely that the theological partner will be merely a helpmate.[33] Black theology becomes whatever its progressive Marxist spouse desires. All the powerful ideas and the critical energy appear to be on the Marxist side. Black theology has a veneer-like appearance.

Analogies are always imperfect. But when I consider West's great refusal to speak theologically in relation to Franz Hinkelammert's *Ideological Weapons of Death* (1982), a brilliant Marxist-Christian theology of capitalism, I cannot help but think that West's reticence serves him poorly. His Marx and Kierkegaard do not talk to each other. They do not even appear to be in the same room. In an odd division of labor, West consigns Kierkegaard and Marx to incommensurate spheres of critique. In this space of incommensurability, Marx cannot interrogate Kierkegaard who has a critique-free pass in West's account. At the very moment when West ought to be most dialectical, exploring the creative insights of the "negative," he opts for Kierkegaard over Marx. He subordinates dialectics, which he otherwise argues is essential to prophetic Christianity and progressive Marxism, to a kind of Kierkegaardian "either/or." (Here I use the distinction loosely.) It is hard not to regard this move as dogmatic.

To speak of spheres is to conjure Weber and to think again, though in a different context, about Troeltsch. Earlier I claimed that West is stuck between Kierkegaard and Troeltsch. I am even more convinced of this claim now than when I initially made it. West is perpetually on the verge of making the Kierkegaardian qualitative leap to faith, which presupposes "the objective truth of the Christian revelation and the validity of its doctrinal expression."[34] But he is constrained by Troeltsch's sober conclusions about the historical relativity of all religions. With Troeltsch, Christianity and the "leap" are historicized and relativized. For all his love of Kierkegaard—the *Kierkegaardian absurd sublime*—West cannot forget Troeltsch's liberal, anti-Kierkegaardian theological insights. This makes it difficult for West to theologize, even in the minimalist manner of Kierkegaard, who claims, properly speaking, to be a "religious thinker" rather than a theologian.

Of course, I may be wrong. Consider West's characterization of black theology and Marxism in table 6.1. If not brilliant, this comparative typology and analysis is certainly provocative.

According to this schema there is a convergence between prophetic Christianity (black liberation theology) and progressive Marxism. This convergence is an artifact of West's dialectical method in a double sense: one, he compares and contrasts various alternatives within black theology and Marxism respectively; two, he uses theological categories to expose the inadequacies of Marxism, Marxist categories to expose the inadequacies of black theology, and black theology

Table 6.1 West's characterization of black theology and Marxism.

CHRISTIANITY	MARXISM
Virulently Racist and Fundamentalist Theologies	*Stalinism is to Marxism what the Ku Klux Klan is to Christianity: a manipulation of the chief symbols yet diametrically opposed to the central values.*[35]
Conservative Evangelical Theologies	*Leninism and Trotskyism are to Marxism what conservative evangelicalism is to Christianity: orthodox and fundamentalist outlooks which give self-serving lip service to truncated versions of the major norms.*[36]
Neo-Orthodox Theologies	*Gramscianism is to Marxism what neo-orthodoxy is to Christianity: an innovative revision of dogmas for dogmatic purposes.*[37]
Social Gospel Theology	*Bernsteinianism is to Marxism what the social gospel is to Christianity: powerful critiques tied to abortive practices.*[38]
PROPHETIC CHRISTIANITY	PROGESSIVE MARXISM
Black Theology of Liberation as Critique of: Stage One—Slavery; Stage Two—Institutional Racism; Stage Three—White North American Theology; Stage Four—U.S. Capitalism; Stage Five—Capitalist Civilization	*Councilism is to Marxism what liberation theology is to Christianity: a promotion and practice of the moral core of the perspective against overwhelming odds for success.*[39]

as an honorific to describe the most progressive forms of Marxism. West concludes that "*Councilism is to Marxism what liberation theology is to Christianity: a promotion and practice of the moral core of the perspective against overwhelming odds for success*" (emphasis added). Meanwhile, fifth stage black theology is the critique of capitalist civilization. And yet, in these very formulations, does not the asymmetry between Marxist and theological partners reappear? Let me be clear. I am not complaining about this asymmetry. In some ways, it suits my metatheoretical views (naturalistic and humanistic) just fine. However, West should be concerned given his claims for progressive Christianity, especially in its black theology version. It appears that progressive Marxism, despite the black theological "baptism" it receives in West's account, is doing most of the heavy (critical) lifting. Critically speaking, black theology is little more than a veneer.

There is an important ambiguity in West's correlations. He is persnickety in describing what counts as progressive Marxism but quite generous where prophetic Christianity is concerned. Black theology in all stages qualifies as prophetic. But should it? It seems odd to count all black theology while limiting progressive Marxism to the Councilist stream. If the social gospel does not qualify as prophetic because its praxis failed, then Stage Four black theology should not qualify either. If anything, its failure as praxis is greater than the social gospel, whose extra-academic effects were more significant. It is not clear that Stage Four black theology has had extra-academic effects at all. This failure to influence the world outside the theological academy may have negative implications for the practical success of Stage Five black theology, which West construes as a kind of organic development. In any event, if Bernsteinianism does not qualify as progressive Marxism because of "abortive praxis," then neither should Councilism. Both are abortions. Neither has left a significant trace in actually existing or formerly existing Marxist regimes.[40] Beyond this, I question whether practical success should be used as a measure of how progressive a particular option is. There is no guarantee that the more progressive option will succeed. Even though the analogies are very imperfect, and without denying progressive elements, West's description of Stalinist, Leninist- Trotskyite, Gramscian, and Bernsteinian forms of Marxism—as fundamentalist, conservative evangelical, neo-orthodox, and Social Gospel, respectively—provides more compelling analogies for black theology than the uniform prophetic description he prefers.

Long's Challenge

West's correlation between prophetic Christianity and progressive Marxism is one of the most interesting and distinctive approaches to Black Religion, even if its scope is limited to Protestant Christian thought. As such, his analysis does not explicitly address Long's threefold methodological challenge to those engaged in the academic study of Black Religion. Nor does he take up the comparative dimension of Long's challenge. There is little evidence that Long's challenge is a consideration in West's analysis at all. So it is wrong to suggest that he *evades* Long's challenge through inattention, inadvertence, or intentional default. He has his own construction of Black Religion. With these interpretive differences in mind, I use Long's criteria to assess West's account of Black Religion. This analysis is executed in both indicative and subjunctive moods: I assess the account that West actually provides and the one he might have provided had he taken up Long's criteria as his own.

A phenomenological account of Black Religion, in Long's sense of the term, can be distilled from West's account of black theology as a distinctive version of prophetic Christianity. It can be identified, at the very least, by observing black worship style. West provides such an account in a handful of suggestive concepts that are more condensed than underdeveloped. I quote at length:

> The principal African resources in black Christianity were threefold. First, a *kinetic orality* permeated black sermons and songs, black prayers and hymns. A sense of community was constituted and reinforced by an invigorated rhetoric, rhythmic freedom, and antiphonal forms of interaction. Fluid, protean, and flexible oral stylizations of language gave black church life a distinctively African-American stamp—a stamp that flowed from black cultural agency in a society that tried to deny and downplay any form of black cultural agency and black creativity. Second, a *passionate physicality* accented black control and power over the only social space permitted to them in American society—that is, their bodies. Self-assertion of *sombodiness* enacted by bodily participation in stylized forms of spiritual response in black church liturgy signified a sense of *homefulness* for an exilic people. Last, *combative spirituality* was promoted and promulgated by the central roles of preacher, deacon, and choir. Each had to meet a weekly challenge of feeding the flock, encouraging the discouraged, and giving hope to the downhearted. This stress on the performative and pragmatic, on pageantry and the histrionic put a premium on prospective moral practice or forward-looking ethical struggle for black Christian parishioners. This sense of struggle paradoxically cultivated a historical patience and subversive joy, a sober survival ethic and openness to seize credible liberation opportunities.[41]

I take these categories—kinetic orality, passionate physicality, and combative spirituality, augmented by subversive joy and revolutionary patience—as West's phenomenological description of Black Religion. This is how it appears to the critical observer. Even though *Prophesy Deliverance!* is limited to Protestantism, the phenomenology described in this passage from *Prophetic Fragments* (1988) is presupposed by black theology, is relevant to how West views Black Religion, and, perhaps, is relevant to how "we" should view religion across Black Atlantic cultures.

West does not avail himself of the resources that a comparative approach to the study of Black Religion might provide. Though remarking that he is in some sense "a Bible-thumping" Christian,[42] West has little to say about god; in fact, he avoids god-talk assiduously in his work. His critique of black theology reads more like a sociology of black theologians than an assessment of theological ideas, especially the central idea of god. West's reticence regarding god-talk is curious: firstly, this self-described Bible-thumping Christian does not consistently and vigorously demur when others describe him as a theologian or a lay-preacher; secondly, he chooses to approach Black Religion under the umbrella of theology rather than philosophy or critical theory; thirdly, there is nothing peculiar to a sociological account of black theologians that would prevent an analyst from describing the kind of god that a particular social form is likely to produce. One thinks of Weber's brilliant analysis of the social basis of different forms of religiosity; or, in the American context, H. Richard Niebuhr's rich assessment of Protestant Christianity. Given West's fierce interest in forms of critique that keep track of the depredations of capital, he might have assessed the relationship between degrees of support for capitalist values and various conceptions of god in black theology. Mapping the god concept within black theology in relation to various stages of capital, with their ever changing regimes of racial ideology would have been breath-taking. But perhaps I am asking too much of a twenty-something intellectual writing his first book. But maybe not: after all, West sets very high standards for black intellectuals. His judgment about their relative success is quite severe. As most are mediocre, they fail to meet the high standards that intellectual work demands. It is only fair that West be held to the same demanding standards. In light of these standards, he may be vulnerable to his own critique. In sociological terms, West does not produce anything on the level of Benjamin Mays' *The Negro's God, as Reflected in His Literature*. Nor does he provide, as Jones does, a philosophical critique of the god symbol in relation to black political agency, whether "revolutionary" or "quietistic." Though his self-description suggests otherwise, West seems remarkably disinterested in god.

Perhaps there is a different way of understanding that disinterest. In his essay "Is Cornel West Also among the Theologians?" Victor Anderson distinguishes between "maximal" and "minimal" views of transcendence; the latter "does not lead naturally into the idea of God." According to Anderson, there is a deep ambiguity, if not ambivalence, in West's work regarding transcendence. Maximally conceived, transcendence refers to "God as the absolute, transcendent subject who meets all humanity, regardless of their particular narratives or stories, as the creator."[43] Anderson associates this conception with Barth, in relation to whom, at least most of the time, West is a minimalist. For West, god is not "a radically transcendent/ontotheological subject who commands absolute loyalty."[44] But occasionally, when pinned down, as he was in an interview with George Yancy, he acknowledges his theological maximalism. Anderson sees this Barthian maximalism as the subordinate position, so he purses the implications of West's minimalism: the identification of Christian faith with "individuality" and radical democracy, which West baptizes as fundamentally Christian, and the reduction of Jesus Christ to "a set of ethical mandates." Anderson offers this construction despite West's vigorous denial (responding, perhaps, to the critique of Stanley Hauerwas) that democracy is his religion. In West's dominant, minimalist mood, Anderson suggests, god is little more than a cipher for democratic powers and desires. This is befitting since West once referred to himself as a Deweyan pragmatist.[45]

The image of Africa is not a prominent feature of West's interpretation of Black Religion. But the involuntary presence of black people in America is a basic consideration. If Long speaks of America as the hermeneutical context for Black Religion, then West explores it from three converging perspectives: cultural insecurity and alienation, a genealogy of racism, and traditions of responding to both. In broad strokes, West describes the transformations in European social organization and knowledge that preceded and were contemporaneous with the emergence of the United States. The consequences of the way America was founded produced a deeply ingrained sense of provincialism, the feeling that in comparison to Europeans Americans were not quite good enough. "It resulted primarily," he remarks, "from the geographical displacement of European peoples from that European civilization whose superiority they openly acknowledged. Adding to this, an antagonism to the indigenous American peoples and an unwillingness to mingle with unchristian African slaves created an alienated, intensely self-conscious, and deeply anxiety-ridden society."[46] The upshot of West's account is that the black freedom struggle (slavery to postindustrialism) occurred against the backdrop of identity struggles among European Americans. On this view, the double consciousness among Blackamericans (Negro and American) that DuBois describes mimics a duality (American and European) that white Americans experienced. Beyond DuBois' account, West argues that Blackamericans experienced a "triple crisis of self-recognition." First, they were African in phenotype and unconscious mores within a society dominated by the European phenotype and norms, where citizen equaled white. Second, they were subjects of "involuntary displacement to America without American status." Third, they lived amid culturally insecure European Americans who were alienated from Europe *and* beholden to its norms.[47] The crowning paradox that West traces throughout American history is this: just when black Americans began to attain first-class status within America's industrial order, it was displaced by a postindustrial order that rewarded a different set of skills.[48]

White supremacy was a decisive feature of the provincial culture West describes and a major hermeneutical context for Black Religion. Drawing loosely on Nietzsche and Foucault, West produces a genealogy of modern racism, arguing that racism is a discursive artifact of modern discourse. Rhetorically, this suggests a more Foucauldian than Nietzschean account. West adopts a genealogical approach to avoid the base-superstructure reductions of vulgar Marxist historiography and to emphasize the subjectless (anonymous) nature of white supremacy as a discursive power.[49] This approach dovetails with his description of the structural features of modern discourse: "the controlling metaphors, notions, categories, and norms that shape the predominant conceptions of truth and knowledge." Ocular metaphors helped produce a "normative gaze" during the first stage of modern racism's emergence. Normed by this gaze, black people were consistently degraded aesthetically, which stereotyped white perceptions.[50] During the second stage—West likes "stage" language—this anti-black aesthetic marries the "scientific" disciplines of skull reading (phrenology) and facial reading (physiognomy). Not surprisingly, black people were routinely seen as deficient in intelligence and character; modern discourse denied "black equality in beauty, culture, and intellectual capacity." Whether the emergence of racism was inevitable or a contingent feature of modernity (West is ambivalent), it cannot be reduced to capitalist exploitation. It encompasses the whole range of cultural affects, ideas, and objects, including ideas of beauty that were bound to alienate black people.[51]

Finally, by way of establishing the hermeneutical context for Black Religion, West describes four traditions of responding to white supremacy and racial ideology: exceptionalist, assimilationist, marginalist, and humanist. Though I alluded to these traditions in an earlier section, a fuller presentation of West's emphatic remarks regarding their features will help set up my next point. I present them without the italics that appear in the original account:

> The Afro-American exceptionalist tradition lauds the uniqueness of Afro-American culture and personality.... The exceptionalist response to the challenge of self-image and self-determination is this: a romanticization of Afro-American culture that conceals the social mobility of an emerging opportunistic Afro-American petite bourgeoisie.[52]
>
> The Afro-American assimilationist tradition considers Afro-American culture and personality to be pathological.... The assimilationist response to the challenge of self-image and self-determination is this: a rejection of Afro-American culture and total assimilation into American society.[53]
>
> The Afro-American marginalist tradition posits Afro-American culture to be restrictive, constraining, and confining.... The marginalist response to the challenge of self-image and self-determination is this: a candid acceptance of personal marginality to both Afro-American culture and American society plus moral sermonizing to all Americans.[54]
>
> The Afro-American humanist tradition extols the distinctiveness of Afro-American culture and personality.... The humanist response to the challenge of self-image and self-determination is this: a promotion of an individuality, strengthened by an honest encounter with the Afro-American past and the expansion of democratic control over the major institutions that regulate lives in America and abroad.[55]

These responses condition expressions of Black Religion and consequently are an important hermeneutical context. Though impressive, they are also problematic. Consider Lewis Gordon's trenchant remarks in "The Unacknowledged Fourth Tradition." This title refers to West's neglect, if not belittlement and certainly exclusion, of black revolutionary thought from the list of fundamental sources—pragmatism, Marxism, and Christianity—that inform his intellectual project.[56] I focus on Gordon's remarks regarding the consequences of exclusion. Gordon contends that West reproduces, though without essentializing, the black intellect-deprecating logic that critics attribute to Lêopold Senghor: whites produce theory and blacks produce art.[57] Hence, West's excessive celebration of black musicians and preachers, specifically, their verbal artistry—and to a lesser extent, his celebration of literary artists such as Ellison and Morrison—is the flip side of his denigration of black intellectuals.[58] Though his account of West is harsh, but no harsher than West's critique of the alleged mediocrity of black intellectuals, Gordon's view has merit.[59]

Without discounting Gordon's critique, I offer a final remark on West in light of Long's challenge. Along with his discursive account of racism and the insecurity-inducing cultural duality within white Americans that produced a "triple crisis of recognition" among blacks, West not only meets the second criterion of Long's challenge, "the involuntary presence of blacks in America," but pushes it in a creative and radical direction.

Existential Seriousness and Depth

Let me begin with a skeptical note on the very concept of existential seriousness and depth, concepts that are very important to West. This skepticism is inspired by Theodor Adorno's critique of contemporary German existentialism in *The Jargon of Authenticity* (1973). While the immediate subjects of Adorno's critique are Heidegger, Jaspers, and Buber, among others, I think that the following remarks about existential seriousness and depth, which he calls the jargon of authenticity, are also applicable to Kierkegaard's highly influential work:

> The jargon secularizes the German readiness to view men's positive relation to religion as something immediately positive, even when the religion has disintegrated and been exposed as something untrue. The undiminished irrationality of rational society encourages people to elevate religion into an end in itself, without regard to its content: to view religion as a mere attitude, as a quality of subjectivity. All this at the cost of religion itself. One needs only to be a believer—no matter what he believes in. Such irrationality has the same function as putty.
>
> That religion has shifted into the subject, has become religiosity, follows the trend of history. Dead cells of religiosity in the midst of the secular, however, become poisonous. The ancient force, which according to Nietzsche's insight nourishes everything, should enter completely into the profane; instead it preserves itself in an unreflected manner and elevates limitation, which abhors reflection, to the level of virtue.[60]

This reads like a sharp critique of the Kierkegaardian absurd sublime with its "truth as subjectivity" and qualitative leap or what many call "the leap of faith." Other than noting that West construes the leap as an act of hope where Adorno spies despair (where Kierkegaard,[61] trapped by his love of the "despair sublime," speaks of the leap[62]), I draw no conclusions as to whether West's Kierkegaardian Christianity functions as putty, filling holes in his prophetic project. But I raise that possibility by way of establishing the background of this inquiry.

However one construes it, depth has much to do with the questions one is willing to consider. Existentially speaking, Jones cut deeply when he asked a rhetorical and methodological question, "Is God a white racist?" This question cuts more deeply than Nietzsche's claim that god is dead. In relation to Jones' question, Nietzsche's claim is a relief. In posing his provocative question, Jones asked black theologians to consider a frightening possibility in order to clarify what the liberation (well-being) of black people required. The question I wish to ask is this: does West's perspective obligate him to refute the charge of divine racism? Hence I conclude this section by triangulating West, Jones, and Long. Specifically, I wish to tie together West's and Jones' respective critiques of black theology in light of Long's third programmatic suggestion for the study of Afro-American religion. To refresh your memory, the three methodological principles that should guide such study are:

1. Africa as historical reality and religious image
2. The involuntary presence of the black community in America
3. The experience and symbol of God in the religious experience of blacks

Jones' text, which is largely silent on Long's first principle, is rooted in the second and inseparable from the third. To reprise that view: black people are in America principally because their ancestors were transported here in the transatlantic slave trade. Racial slavery and its legacy of pathological animosity toward black people—their virtual reenslavement through debt, peonage, vagrancy and Jim and Jane Crow laws, anti-black riots, lynching, and other forms of racial cleansing, economic exploitation, and political exclusion—exemplify what Jones calls "ethnic suffering." By "ethnic," Jones signifies that such suffering is maldistributed, negative, enormous, and noncatastrophic, a description to which black suffering, historically speaking, appears to conform. In the absence of an argument to the contrary, which forswears the assumption that god is good, refutes the theodicy of deserved punishment, acknowledges the multievidentiality of suffering, and employs a method of counterevidence, the charge of divine racism cannot be refuted. Is West vulnerable to this charge? Does he consent to black theology's liberationist construction of god by failing to criticize it? In short, does he fail to address the threshold question—"Is God a white racist?" These questions go directly to West's own criterion of existential depth: to how deeply an analysis cuts, how fearlessly it explores our deepest anxieties.

One thing is clear: West is not vulnerable to an explicit charge of opening the door of divine racism since he is virtually silent on the question of god, who has a spectral presence in his discourse. Unlike the black theologians whom Jones criticizes, West does not make explicit claims regarding god's character and agency; or more accurately, he rarely makes such claims, so rarely, in fact, that one is hard pressed to find any reference to god at all. But one can still raise the question of whether his failure to explicitly refute black theological constructions of god, particularly by his chief interlocutor Cone, is a form of tacit consent. Now an argument from tacit consent is necessarily different from the explicit assertion that West reproduces a version of the defective theodicies that Jones attributes to black theologians. Searching West's corpus for comments resembling the assertions that "god liberates black people in history" or "blacks are god's suffering servants" would be a vain endeavor. West is too sophisticated a thinker to be caught making such claims. If an argument is to be made, it must regard West's tacit commitments. Recourse to a tacit argument concedes the fact that an explicit argument cannot be made. In a subjunctive mood, I explore how West might respond to the charge that he gives tacit consent to black theologians who evade the threshold question of black theology: "Is God a white racist?"

Hypothetical I.

West might frankly concede the gist of Jones' argument as I have constructed it: that divine racism is the unacknowledged threshold question in black theology; that black theologians presuppose the intrinsic goodness (pro-blackness) of god; that various assertions about the nature of god and the relationship between god and black people create severe problems for black theodic reasoning; and that the consequence of the defective theodicies implicit in black theology is ethical-political quietism in the face of white supremacy—in short, these theodicies provide a prop for oppression where black people are complicit in their own subordination.

If this was his response, he would acknowledge the quietistic implications of his reason-defying Kierkegaardian perspective while asserting, nonetheless, its sanity-preserving role in *his* life and the lives of those who share his sensibility. He would acknowledge, furthermore, the sanity-preserving role of the assumption regarding god's intrinsic goodness. To question this assumption by arguing, as Jones demands from the possibility of a demonic god, and thereby teasing out the potentially liberation-undermining qualities that the assumption of god's intrinsic goodness may conceal, would be to hesitate before the "leap" that West's Kierkegaardian-inflected faith entails. This concession would underscore Jones' claim that the unexamined, sacrosanct, oppression-sustaining assumption regarding god's intrinsic goodness, and the desire to hold on to this assumption at all costs, is more basic for black theologians (and fellow travelers such as West) than black liberation. To adequately respond to this claim West would have to explicate more clearly the relationship between the prophetic and the revolutionary in his version of Christianity.

Hypothetical II.

West might frankly concede Jones' point but relativize its critical bite by relegating the relevance of that critique to an earlier incarnation of himself. After all, he was twenty-eight when he expressed these views. The subject of those views was a more radical version of him (before the apparent collapse of the international socialist project) who spoke of revolutionizing Christianity and used Marxism as his critical *lingua franca*. In controversies between nationalist parochialism and Marxist universalism, he was always an enthusiastic partisan of the latter. Intellectually, this earlier self was often located professionally in a divinity school context and was invested in theological discourse in a way that is unmatched in his subsequent work. Presumably he would acknowledge that much of his intellectual work during this period was devoted to reconciling Marxist-inflected cultural criticism and his black Baptist Christian commitments: his politics, racial identity, and religious orientation. Though he continues to interact with many church elites, I should think that he would have to acknowledge that the Black Church and black theology no longer possess him *intellectually* the way they did during his early phase; that to some extent their grip on him was situational, a matter of institutional location—seminary and divinity school. West might insist that he has already done the work that this critique calls him to do; that he said what he had to say on these matters in his writings during the 1980s. Of course, he might push back against my analysis and reassert his anti-nationalist desire to see beyond narrow geographical, ethnic, and masculine-constructed racial identities. He could insist that his guiding intuition is unchanged: reminding readers that nationalism is related to the rise of the modern state and the globalization of capital, labor, and cultural markets; accenting the way that capitalism structures an international division of wealth, power, and status; emphasizing the cultural conservatism and petit bourgeois character of nationalist formations. But wouldn't he be obligated to acknowledge that a quasi-nationalist rhetoric now frames most of what he says, and seems to have eclipsed the revolutionary socialist in him? West might acknowledge that he is no longer a revolutionary (few contemporary socialists are) but insist that socialism is still the critical grammar underlying and qualifying his quasi-nationalist syntax and vocabulary. In substantive terms, West could argue that his views have not changed much: that his arguments in *Democracy Matters* (2004) are remarkably similar to those in *Prophesy Deliverance!* If this response fails to satisfy those who insist that West has become too cozy with unreconstructed nationalists and that he has "gone soft" on capitalism, is too "pink" (not "red" enough), or even worse is a "pale," anodyne, reformist liberal,[63] then it may also not save him from the reach of Jones' critique as I have constructed it: namely, that West's Kierkegaardian perspective toward black theology has quietistic implications.

Hypothetical III.

West might go on the attack and charge Jones with failing to take existential matters with sufficient seriousness. If this was his response, he would acknowledge the unparallel quality of Jones' critique but accent its deficiency: "Its tendency to downplay existential issues such as death, disease, dread, despair, and disappointment which are related to, yet not identical with, suffering caused by oppressive structures." This is the point that West made earlier in regard to black liberation theologians and that I see him extending to Jones. This point merits emphasis. West would acknowledge the power of Jones' critique by limiting it to the sociological specificity of black people's suffering while accenting its failure to address forms of suffering rooted in human existence as such: suffering that is quasi-independent of the ways in which they are sociologically constructed. This response might have merit. Jones appears to limit ethnic suffering to oppressive social relations; specifically, to the encounter between Africans and Europeans, the reign of white supremacy and the various regimes of race that has characterized it over time. But I see nothing in Jones' analysis that requires this sociological reduction. His focus is purely strategic. His analysis can accommodate the quasi-independent, existential, human-all-too-human forms of suffering that West enumerates and still claim that their negative quality is intensified by the shadow of divine racism.

Unlike West, Jones takes the suffering of Blackamericans—their suffering unto death, to riff on Kierkegaard's term—so seriously that he constructs an analytic framework designed to expose the liberation-defeating aspects of black theology. What West takes as an axiom—that black theology, as a "structure of motivation" and agency, is liberation theology—Jones construes as "begging the question." Meaning, West assumes as true what needs to be argumentatively established. If Kierkegaard is to have more than a citational presence in West's account of existential depth (seriousness), and if his claims are to have the force he wishes them to have, then he must provide an argument comparable to Jones' argument. Such an argument would no doubt be fascinating. West would have to work his way through *The Sickness unto Death* and show why the forms of despair that Kierkegaard describes are more than reflections of his personal peculiarities and pathologies. (It is not clear to me that they should or can be generalized; he provides a philosophical anthropology we do not need.) West must move beyond broad rhetorical gestures. He needs to construct an analysis that actually supports "black liberation," an Afro-American revolutionary Christianity, "existential democracy," or any other term he might use to describe his notion of human flourishing.

Augmented by the existentialism of Sartre and Camus, Jones makes the case for the "impious" stream of the black humanist tradition, which West completely ignores. Along the way, he identifies defective theodicies that are inimical to black liberation. These theodicies characterize the suffering of black people as redemptive, deserved punishment (a sign of divine disfavor), vicarious (a sign of divine favor), or beyond human understanding. Jones exposes the black unconscious, the repressed anxiety of black theologians and nontheologians alike: the fear that god might be a white racist, or that the cosmos is stacked against black people, or simply that black people are "losers," beyond good and evil, in a cosmic game of chance. This accounts for Jones' claim that divine racism is the threshold issue for black theology. If we translate Jones' claim into the Kierkegaardian language that West prefers Ernest Becker's *Denial of Death* (1975), then divine racism can be interpreted as specifying the "death anxiety" and its various intimations among Blackamericans, concretizing the question regarding the "evils" of black suffering that DuBois addresses to god—"What meaneth this?"[64] In contrast to West's Kierkegaardian-Wittgensteinian aphasia regarding this issue, Jones poses the diagnostic question "Is God a white racist?" and recommends the method of arguing from counterevidence.

Conclusion

In this chapter, I explored Cornel West's prophetic construction of Black Religion. Construing Black Religion primarily in theological terms, West analyzes various developmental stages in black theology and streams of Marxist thought. Construing black theology as prophetic in all its developmental stages, he correlates it with the most progressive stream of Marxism. Through their dialectical interaction, each repairs the defects of the other. The product of West's Whiggish account is his own prophetic, Afro-American revolutionary Christianity. I assessed West's account in relation to the competing accounts of Black Religion provided by Charles H. Long and William R. Jones. I argued that Jones' critique of black theology could be construed as reasserting and intensifying Long's second principle for the study of Afro-American religion—the role of the god symbol in the Blackamerican experience. Thus I compared West and Jones on the relation between the god symbol and the existential dimension of human experience that is so important to West's account. If existential matters (death, disease, despair, dread, and disappointment) and moral evils (cruelty and indifference) are as important to a proper understanding of black theology, the black religious experience, and the prospects of black people as West claims, then my analysis suggests that Jones does a better job of explicating them. This is due to Jones' meticulous critique of the god symbol in terms of theodic reasoning. Though highly creative and a significant contribution to black religious studies, I conclude that West's analysis is deficient regarding the god question. Though questioning the cogency of the prophetic-Christian, progressive-Marxist alliance, I conclude that West's prophetic construction of Black Religion and his phenomenology of Black Church religiosity are deeply insightful. The prophetic critique of this scholar-as-prophet pushes against the limitations of the Standard Narrative of Black Religion.

Chapter 7

The Conjuror

Conjurational Spirituality: An Overview

Theophus Smith is among a growing number of scholars interested in Black Atlantic forms of religion and spirituality, a literary representation of which we considered in chapter 3. He situates his book *Conjuring Culture* (1994) "between the historical and social scientific study of religion on the one hand, and the black theology of liberation movement on the other."[1] In this chapter, I read Smith's distinctive project on its own terms but also in relation to Long's programmatic challenge for the study of African American religion, West's prophetic construction of black religiosity, and Jones' critique of black theodicy.

I begin with an overview of Smith's argument: his claim that African spirituality is a potent source of Black Religion. Smith uses "conjurational spirituality" as the root metaphor for this influence. He remarks that "Conjure is fundamentally magic,"[2] a way of transforming reality. Conjuring culture refers to "(1) ritually patterned behaviors and performative uses of language and symbols (2) conveying a pharmacopeic or healing/harming intent and (3) employing biblical figures and issuing in biblical configurations of cultural experience."[3] Evident in traditions such as Vodou, Santeria, Candomble, and the Black Church, conjuring culture involves a double initiation, conversion, or "passing over" as biblical narratives are Africanized and African spirituality is Christianized. Blackamericans conjured their identity under the conditions of slavery, amid the encounter of African spirituality and biblical narratives, especially those drawn from the Hebrew Bible. Accenting the prominence of Hebrew figures, places, and events in their imagination, Smith describes black people as Afro-Hebraic cultural hybrids. Within this Afro-Hebraic cosmology, black North Americans imagine themselves as the children of Israel. As their ideal leader, Moses is construed as a diviner, herbalist, and "semi-divine wonder-worker" whose *minkisi* (sacred medicine or *pharmacosmic* power) transforms reality. Moses models god's wonder-working agency (thaumaturgy); god is Moses' divine double: the god of Abraham, Isaac, and Jacob and a god (orisha) of Africa. Smith's account centers on this conjurational transformation (magical and medicinal) of biblical narratives, on the extraordinary act of imagination and bricolage that is Black Religion.

Drawing on the Romantic poet William Blake, for whom the Bible is "the great code of art" in Western Civilization, and Northrop Frye, who extends Blake's idea in *The Great Code* (1981), Smith suggests that the Bible is both the code and the key to the conjurational identity of Blackamericans. Seven major typologies comprise Frye's code. Each is dyadic, with a prototype-antitype relationship; the antitype recapitulates and extends its prototype. Genesis (prototype) and Exodus (antitype) are the preeminent example. Postbiblical events such as the Puritan "errand into the Wilderness" are interpreted as antitypical recapitulations of a biblical prototype. If Exodus recapitulates and extends the story of Genesis, then Smith recapitulates and extends Frye's typological schema. He does so by adding two additional typologies, "Spirituals" and "Praxis," that reflect a distinctively Blackamerican appropriation of biblical narrative. The respective biblical typologies of Frye and Smith is shown is Table 7.1.

Smith completes his theory of biblical typologies by triangulating Blake and Frye with Werner Sollors' concept of "typological ethnogenesis," the formation of peoplehood through biblical typology. On this view, Blackamericans (like white Protestant Americans or any people for whom the biblical text has a paradigmatic importance) engendered themselves as a people by imagining themselves as antitype to the ancient Israelite prototype. Smith calls this interpretive tradition, which "links biblical types or figures to postbiblical persons, places, and events,"[6] a biblical configuration. The appropriation of the Bible through African patterns of spiritual discernment makes black identity distinctive. Doubly bicultural, black identity is African and European, African and Hebraic. Under this inheritance, Black Religion seeks to transform the world, to conjure god for freedom. The Bible is a conjure book, a magical formulary, *materia medica* that facilitates the performative and mimetic transformation of reality. In brief, Blackamericans seek to transform the world "through

Table 7.1 Biblical typologies of Frye and Smith

Northrop Frye	*Theophus Smith*
Old Testament	*Hebrew Scriptures*
1. Genesis	1. Genesis (cosmology)
2. Exodus	2. Exodus (God-conjured-for-freedom)
3. Law	3. Law (curing violence "prototype")
4. Wisdom	4. Spirituals (psalms and aesthetics)
5. Prophecy	5. Wisdom (proverbs and worldview)
	6. Prophecy (oracles and vocation)
New Testament	*Christian Scriptures*
1. Gospel	1. Gospel (curing violence "antitype")
2. Apocalypse[4]	2. Praxis (Acts and activism)
	3. Apocalypse (revelation and judgment)[5]

ritually improvised applications of biblical models" to their current historical circumstances.[7]

The Genesis-Exodus Dyad and the "Law"

Moses has a special place in the self-understanding of black North Americans. Mosaic imagery is connected to images of god. In black folk culture, Smith remarks, god is sometimes portrayed as the great conjuror and creation as the greatest act of conjuration. In the art of conjuration, Moses plays antitype to god's prototype. Smith claims that an interesting inversion occurs when god is occasionally represented as the divine double (*supernatural* doppelganger) of Moses. Mosaic agency, so to speak, is the prototype of god's antitypical agency. Smith supports his expansive claims by citing Zora Neale Hurston's *Moses: Man of the Mountain* (1939), which is informed by her ethnological work in Haiti, where Moses is described as "the finest hoodoo man in the world."[8] He adds Raboteau's remark that "Damballa-wedo…is sometimes identified with Moses because of the miracle of the brazen serpent."[9] And drawing on Lawrence Levine (1989), Smith remarks:

> Judging from the songs of his black soldiers, [United States] Colonel Higginson concluded that their Bible was constructed primarily from the books of Moses in the Old Testament and of Revelations in the New: "all that lay in between, even the life of Jesus, they hardly cared

> to read or to hear." "Their memories," he noted at another point, "are a vast bewildered chaos of Jewish history and biography; and most of the great events of the past, down to the period of the American Revolution, they instinctively attribute to Moses."[10]

If Genesis is about creation (beginnings), then Exodus is the story of the "creation of a people, Israel, out of Egyptian bondage."[11] Genesis prototypes Exodus, and Exodus antitypes Genesis: from the creation of the first man of god to the creation of the first people of god. The narrative structure of the Exodus Configuration includes biblical *figures* such as bondage and oppression, liberation, wilderness, and the Promised Land. Exodus is the most important of the nine biblical configurations in the formation of black identity. Smith underscores this claim with a detailed analysis. Again, Moses is the central figure, and his importance can be seen most clearly in the Mosaic construction of black leadership. Smith identifies Harriet Tubman, Sojourner Truth, Abraham Lincoln, and Martin Luther King, Jr., as prominent examples of Moses-like emancipators. Perhaps it was inevitable that ordinary Blackamericans, reflecting on the meaning and significance of the Emancipation Proclamation, would see strong parallels between their own situation and the biblical story of "the miraculous exodus of the Hebrew slaves out of Egyptian bondage."[12] According to Smith, Lincoln's presidential order demonstrated that biblical events of the past could be repeated in the present. That slaves would find this idea compelling should not surprise us. Smith claims that a plurality of black converts were convinced that they might inherit the promises of freedom and prosperity that god had made to the ancient Hebrews—where he promised to be their god if they would be his people—if they were dutiful in obedience, prayer, and righteousness. Their slave status was the obvious association, the crucial typological link to the biblical model. "That singular instance, the link between Lincoln's role in the emancipation and Moses' role in the Exodus, would distinguish itself as a kind of paradigm. In this manner a new development in the ancient tradition of biblical typology emerged in the collective psyche of a displaced people."[13] The Exodus became a prototype of black emancipation: from the Underground Railroad, to the Emancipation Proclamation, to the "Exodusters"[14] on their way to the "free" territory of Kansas, to the great migration north between world wars.

Smith accents the light side of the Exodus narrative. Take Mosaic leadership, an important figure in the Exodus Configuration, that revealed itself decisively within the wilderness episode. One need not look too closely to recognize a lot of darkness in Moses' leadership style. Aaron Wildavsky (1984) claims that Moses' leadership style is a function of the political regimes that he had to cope with: from the autocracy of slavery to the anarchy of newly won freedom, from the equity of voluntary association to the hierarchy of a fully routinized charisma with its justifying notion of divine right.[15] One might wonder about similar effects on black leadership, given its charismatic and authoritarian cast. The authoritarian aspect of Moses' leadership style is most evident in the golden calf episode. Recall the story: Moses descends Mount Sinai, where he had gone to pray, with the Ten Commandments in hand. He discovers his people worshipping a calf casted in gold from their collected jewelry and ornaments. Angry, Moses orders the most draconian punishment for the ringleaders of this idolatry, which included melting the calf and pouring the molten gold down their throats. Through this brutal act, Moses reasserted his leadership. In *Moses in Red,* Lincoln Steffens calls it a purge: prototype of Soviet purges in the early twentieth century. Noting the fear and cruelty involved in forging a new nation, Steffens remarks, "whenever a nation is setting up a new system of laws and customs, it has a red terror; whenever it is defending an old system it has a white terror." Steffens attributes to Moses the view that such terror though bad is natural and even divine.[16] Smith does not address this aspect of Moses' leadership and whether it stereotyped African American leadership styles. I think that Wildavsky is probably right: "Moses is not meant to be a paradigm of leadership." After all, he is variously depicted in biblical narrative as "wriggling out of responsibility" and encouraging his followers to assume covenant responsibilities when they are clearly ill-prepared. Underscoring his skepticism, Wildavsky adds: "Are future leaders supposed to kill off a significant part of the people or to delay their maturity until a generation has died off?"[17] Smith does not consider such questions in his "delightful" account of the Exodus Configuration. While insightful, it is "too bright" by half.

This creative appropriation of biblical narratives is further evident in the interpretative tradition of Ethiopianism that draws its prophetic and rhetorical power from Psalms 68:31—"Princes shall come out of Egypt; Ethiopia shall soon stretch out her hand to God."[18] It is a trope that conjures god for the freedom of black people through a ritualistic use of scripture: as *minkisi, materia medica,* a veritable pharmacopoeia of sacred medicine. Smith cites the following passage, from

David Walker's "Appeal to the Colored Citizens of the World," as exemplary of the Ethiopian figure within the Exodus Configuration:

> Though our cruel oppressors and murders, may (if possible) treat us more cruel, as Pharaoh did the Children of Israel, yet the "God" of the Ethiopians, has been pleased to hear our moans in consequence of oppression, and the day of our redemption from abject wretchedness draweth near, when we shall be enabled, in the most extended sense of the word, to stretch forth our hand to the Lord our God.[19]

Walker conjures Blackamericans in the image of Hebrew slaves, and simultaneously "Ethiopia stretching out her hand to God—becomes prophetic with respect to the situation and destiny of black people in early nineteenth century America."[20] Those cast down will be exalted. Blackamericans will have their day. In this act of interpretative imagination, Ethiopia is black people writ large and Egypt is transformed from a symbol of black people's bondage into a symbol of their once and future greatness. An incredible metamorphosis occurs as imagery of Ethiopian princes displaces slaves coming out of Egypt. In an Afrocentric gesture before Afrocentrism, the "stolen legacy" of black people is reclaimed as black civilizations once destroyed are restored. To reiterate, this act of "stretching out their hands" to god mimes the prophecy in Psalms 68:31. By conjuring god-for-freedom, black slaves induced him through the mimetic and performative power of "conversion, prayerful outcry, and longsuffering" to do for them what he had done for the Hebrew slaves of old.[21] This kind of ritualized oral performance (conjuring) is constitutive of the black sermonic style.

A schematic reproduction of Smith's account of the Exodus Configuration might look something like this:

1. *Egypt* as America: a trope for slave-trading Africans; the genesis of black civilization, the Promised Land
2. *Moses* as an orisha: god's semi-divine double; conjuror (magician and medicine man); the prototypical leader—Harriet Tubman, Sojourner Truth, Abraham Lincoln, Martin Luther King, Jr.
3. *Exodus* as the Underground Railroad, the Emancipation Proclamation, and the great migrations after the Civil War and between the two world wars
4. *Wilderness* as the post-Reconstruction period: neoslavery, Jim and Jane Crow, the post–civil rights period, any period of confusion and doubt
5. *Promised Land* as freedom: Kansas, Chicago, Canada, or anywhere north; civil rights, and a "color blind" society

6. *Ethiopianism* as the regeneration of Africa: decolonialism, the rise of Afro-America, and contemporary Afrocentrism

Conquest: The Unspoken Figure

In his presentation of the Exodus Configuration, Smith left something very important unsaid. He is silent regarding the biblical story of the conquest of Canaan by the emancipated Israelites. This story has long troubled sensitive readers. It became a controversy within intellectual politics in 1986 with Edward W. Said's trenchant critique of Michael Walzer's *Exodus and Revolution* (1985). This section is an extended excursus on that controversy, the way Said's theme, if not his hermeneutic of suspicion, was later taken up by liberation theologians, and its relevance to Smith's account of the Exodus Configuration.

In her provocative book *Sisters in the Wilderness* (1993), Delores Williams criticizes the androcentric character of black theology. In particular, she questions the uncritical reliance on the Exodus narrative as a paradigm for black liberation:

> Womanist theologians, in concert with Womanist biblical scholars, need to show the African-American denominational churches and black liberation theology the liability of its habit of using the Bible in an uncritical and sometimes too self-serving way. This kind of usage has prohibited the community from seeing that the end result of the biblical exodus event, begun in the book of Exodus, was the violent destruction of a whole nation of people, the Canaanites, described in the book of Joshua. Black liberation theologians today should reconceptualize what it means to lift up uncritically the biblical exodus event as a major paradigm for black theological reflection. To respond to the current issues in the black community, theologians should reflect upon exodus from Egypt as *holistic* story rather than *event*. This would allow the community to see the exodus as an extensive reality involving several kinds of events before its completion in the genocide of the Canaanites and the taking of their land. The community would see the violence involved in a liberation struggle supposedly superintended by God.[22]

Viewed holistically, the Exodus story is full of violent acts of god and god's Hebrew surrogates: acts of genocide in Jericho, Makkedah, Libnah, and Canaan. Williams remarks that critical reflection on the whole story as opposed to a discrete "historical" event, cherry-picked from the larger narrative, would enable "black theologians to show the black community the awful models of God projected when the community's understanding of God becomes normative for the black community's understanding of how God relates to its life." This is not the most artful formulation, but her point is clear enough. Williams adds that a holistic account would "explore the moral status of violence" in the biblical story, forcing black theologians and the community to raise critical questions about any account of divinely sanctioned violence.[23]

As her brief in favor of the "wilderness experience" illustrates, Williams is not opposed to the paradigmatic use of the Exodus story. Rather, she calls for a critical appropriation. While I think that her distinction between black experience and African American experience is merely verbal, I do find her remarks about the wilderness trope instructive. Gender and family-inclusive, it accents human initiative, circumvents the sacred/secular distinction, emphasizes "female-male intelligence and ingenuity in the midst of struggle," and symbolically exemplifies female leadership, something that many accounts ignore. The wilderness trope captures the difficulties and discontent with newly attained freedom—the murmuring of ex-slaves—as they struggle to make their freedom real.[24]

Williams was not the first liberation theologian or fellow traveler to express negative judgments regarding the Exodus story. Robert Allen Warrior, a member of the Osage Nation, published "A Native American Perspective: Canaanites, Cowboys, and Indians," an essay that originally appeared in the *Christian Century* (1989).[25] Noting a preoccupation with the Exodus narrative as a paradigm in liberation theologies, he remarks, "I believe that the story of the Exodus is an inappropriate way for the Native Americans to think about liberation."[26] As the essay's title suggests, Warrior sees troubling parallels, ancient and modern, between perpetrators and victims of genocide. He remarks:

> The obvious characters in the story for Native Americans to identify with are the Canaanites, the people who already lived in the promised land. As a member of the Osage Nation of American Indians who stands in solidarity with other tribal people around the world, I read the Exodus stories with Canaanite eyes. And it is the Canaanite side of the story that has been overlooked by those seeking to articulate theologies of liberation. Especially overlooked are those parts of the story that describe Yahweh's command to mercilessly annihilate the indigenous population.[27]

Smith's laudatory account of the Exodus Configuration ignores the genocidal dimension as do the accounts of prominent black theologians such as Cone. This is significant since Smith triangulates historical, social-scientific, and black liberation theology. Warrior accents what liberation theologians ignore. He will not permit escape from the ethical predicament that arises when praise of the Exodus narrative obscures the destruction of the Canaanite nations. Genocide is evil. Attempts to escape the moral implications of the narrative usually take the form of the claim that the "conquest" was not an actual historical event. The destruction of the Canaanite nations, the argument holds, is inaccurate, an exaggeration within the biblical text designed to accent god's power and opposition to Canaanite "idolatry." But this does not account for the historical power of the narrative. The issue is narrative, not history; the status of the indigenous population and the kind of theology the story underwrites. Within this theology, Yahweh has no concern for the well-being of indigenes when they stand in the way of his chosen people. To put it crudely, indigenous people, at home in their own promised land, have no rights that the Israelites or cowboys are bound to respect.

Warrior hammers this point, and we hear it ring when he remarks, "Many Puritan preachers were fond of referring to Native Americans as Amelkites and Canaanites—in other words, people who, if they would not be converted, were worthy of annihilation." When these sermonic, theological, and political writings are critically examined, he adds, we "understand how America's self-image as a 'chosen people' " underwrites a domination-mystifying rhetoric.[28] Warrior contends that this rhetoric of Indian extermination and dispossession (the only good Indian is a dead Indian) is exacerbated by contemporary developments in biblical interpretation that emphasize "catechetical (Lindbeck), narrative (Hauerwas), canonical (Childs), and Bible-centered Christian base communities (Gutierrez)." He wonders how readers within these communities of interpretation can "differentiate between the liberating god and the god of conquest," the god who frees slaves and the god who exterminates. In the absence of a "mechanism of differentiation" (this reminds one of Jones' demand that black theologians identify the liberation-exaltation event in black history), the genocide and dispossession of indigenous peoples "becomes just one more redemptive moment."[29]

In conclusion, Warrior remarks:

> The indigenous people of this hemisphere have endured a subjugation now 100 years longer than the sojourn of Israel in Egypt. Is there a god, a spirit, who will hear us and stand with us in the Amazon, Osage County, and Wounded Knee? Is there a god, a spirit, able to move among the pain and anger of Nablus, Gaza, and Soweto? Perhaps. But

> we, the wretched of the earth, may be well advised this time not to listen to outsiders with their promises of liberation and deliverance.[30]

The Canaanite Question

> *There is no Israel without the conquest of Canaan and the expulsion or inferior status of Canaanites—then as now.*
>
> —*Edward W. Said*[31]

Two self-described secular intellectuals provide the most penetrating accounts of the contemporary implications of the Exodus story: Michael Walzer, the political philosopher and Edward Said, the cultural critic. Walzer is a prominent Jewish American; Said, a prominent Palestinian American. Both are men of the "left." Walzer is the longtime editor of the socialist journal *Dissent*. Before his death, Said was long associated with the Palestinian liberation movement and with anti-imperial struggles. Against this backdrop, Said published "Michael Walzer's Exodus and Revolution: A Canaanite Reading" (1986). Sharp and hard-edged, the review essay led to a bitter exchange of letters. This contretemps focused on the question of representation; specifically, the untoward political and ethical implications, as Said construes it, of contemporary appropriations of the Exodus narrative. "With clarity, subtlety, and simplicity, which are the signature of his neo-Orwellian style,"[32] Walzer argues that the Exodus narrative provides a paradigm for revolutionary politics. Said's stinging review ensured that the book would receive the careful analysis it merited. The vitriolic exchange of letters between Walzer and Said, an ascending spiral of fury—hard-edged review, angry rebuttal, and surrebuttal—tell us that something important was at stake. At stake were competing concepts of secularism, of how a religious narrative should be represented and, most important, what a just resolution of the Israeli–Palestinian conflict requires. Said construes Walzer as a sophisticated Zionist (for Said this is a bad thing) whose text, though ostensibly liberal and generous as prose, legitimizes the Israeli occupation of Palestine. As such, the book is a historical repetition, "both tragedy and farce," of the conquest of Canaan.

Before connecting the Said–Walzer contretemps with Smith's Exodus Configuration, I will briefly outline Walzer's argument. Walzer offers an ethical and political argument regarding the historical consequences of the Exodus narrative. He notes that the Exodus story has inspired historically and geographically distinct people such as English Puritans, South African Boer nationalists, members of the African National Congress, and the black leadership of the American civil rights movement. They read the narrative as revolutionary, a this-worldly account of liberation from oppression. In the book's final paragraph, the message they received from the story was this:

> —first, that wherever you live, it is probably Egypt;
> —second, that there is a better place, a world more attractive, a promised land;
> —and third, the way to the land is through the wilderness. There is no way to get from here to there except by joining together and marching.[33]

Walzer provides an arresting picture of Hebrew bondage. "Egypt," he writes, "is like a hot summer day," except that it is "infinitely worse, of course."[34] Pharaoh was a cruel tyrant who made the lives of the ancient Israelites miserable. On Walzer's bill of particulars were infanticide, alienating and forced labor, humiliation, and repression of every kind. This description of bondage resonates with the Blackamerican experience and informs Smith's account of the Exodus Configuration. But one need not accept the anachronistic component of Walzer's narrative that construes Egypt as a historical anticipation of the Nazi death camps. That would be a teleological construction that denied contingency and rob "history of the innocence to which it is entitled."[35] Though history is a "slaughter bench," we must distinguish between different acts of slaughter. At night, all cows are black. But in the daylight of critical scrutiny, we see the differences: all cows are not black, every case of slaughter is not the same, and ancient Egypt was not the Third Reich.

Said is impressed by Walzer's skill as a writer but not so impressed by Walzer the historian, especially when he conflates Pharaoh and Palestinians. To reiterate and elaborate, Said construes Walzer's text as "a thinly veiled apology for the policies of the state of Israel."[36] By recasting the Exodus story as "the birth of a new polity, one that admits its members to a communal politics of participation in political and religious spheres," he simultaneously recasts the nature of the contemporary Israeli state.[37] On this interpretation, Exodus and the modern state of Israel are not stories of conquest, dispossession, and occupation. Symptomatic of Walzer's apology, according to Said, is his reading of (failure to read) the Promised Land episode. This absence of a critical reading must be interrogated. In constructing the Exodus Configuration, why is Smith (like Walzer) silent on the destruction of the Canaanite nations and its possible prototype-antitype relation?

Perhaps Said's critique of Walzer provides reasons that, properly qualified, also apply to Smith. According to Said, Walzer is far too sanguine about a narrative in which a sanguinary god is a major actor. Yahweh's bloodlust is writ large within the Bible, especially in those books—Leviticus, Numbers, Deuteronomy, and Joshua—that encompass the Exodus narrative. Indeed, the three gods of Abraham—Yahweh, the Trinity, and Allah—share this lust for blood. This explains Said's opposition to "monotheistic politics," which he believes undermine Walzer's desire for a "secular and decent politics."[38] As a theologian, Smith is more attuned to such matters. His metaethical views regarding biblical interpretation might provide cover from the sharper edge of Said's critique. Smith remains vulnerable, however, where Walzer is, with respect to what he strategically cuts in stage-setting the narrative he constructs and regarding those aspects of the Exodus narrative that he avoids. How does the appropriator of this narrative separate the destruction of the Canaanite nations, which is essential to the integrity of the Exodus story, from postbiblical antitypes such as Indian-killing Puritans and the founding fathers of apartheid? This is a difficult question.

Canaanite Genocide: A Biblical Interlude

> However, in the cities of the nations the LORD your God is giving you as an inheritance, do not leave alive anything that breathes. Completely destroy them—the Hittites, Amorites, Canaanites, Perizzites, Hivites and Jebusites—as the LORD your God has commanded you. Otherwise, they will teach you to follow all the detestable things they do in worshiping their gods, and you will sin against the LORD your God. (Deuteronomy 20:16–18 NIV)

> The LORD listened to Israel's plea and gave the Canaanites over to them. They completely destroyed them and their towns; so the place was named Hormah. (Numbers 21:3 NIV)

> Joshua took all these royal cities and their kings and put them to the sword. He totally destroyed them, as Moses the servant of the LORD had commanded. Yet Israel did not burn any of the cities built on their mounds—except Hazor, which Joshua burned. The Israelites carried off for themselves all the plunder and livestock of these cities, but all the people they put to the sword until they completely destroyed them, not sparing anyone that breathed. (Joshua 11:12–13 NIV)

To pick up the thread of my account, Said's critique of Walzer is elbow-sharp. Said's question is tough. Walzer needs to answer it. And in my extension of this analysis, so does Smith. As postbiblical, antitypical imitations of the biblical prototype demonstrate, the Exodus narrative has an effective history that may very well be different from its historical actuality. According to some historians, the "conquest of Canaan" was no conquest at all. The Israelites entered Canaan through a slow and relatively bloodless process of infiltration, more like immigration than military invasion.[39] But this ignores Said's point, which is about the *effective history*, the inspirational and paradigmatic power of narrative. According to Said, right-wing Zionists, in their antitypical reenactment of the conquest episode, are more honest interpreters of the Exodus narrative than Walzer.

In determining what the Exodus story means, Walzer gives more weight to the later rabbinic tradition than to (near) contemporaneous traditions. (I think that this is appropriate since the conquest narrative has no effective history among Jews until after the creation of the modern State of Israel in 1948. So in this respect, I think that Said is wrong about the comparative honesty of Walzer and right-wing Zionists.) In contrast, Said gives greater weight to the Puritans' "errand into the wilderness," where they constructed themselves as new Israelites and Indians as New World Canaanites. Walzer wants to protect contemporary Judaism by disassociating it from the worst part of the Exodus narrative—the divinely sanctioned genocide of the Canaanite nations—and from any analogical (prototype-antitype) associations that might be made between the biblical story and contemporary Palestine. Said wants Walzer to take more seriously the ugly but effective history of this narrative for Indian-killing, Promised Land–conquering Puritans; apartheid-practicing South African Boer nationalists, and contemporary right-wing Zionists—and, I might add, their American right-wing Christian supporters. Indeed, Said's critique is more apropos of the latter.

Said worries about this postbiblical, antitypical, effective history of the Exodus narrative because it places Canaanites (read: Palestinians, black South Africans under apartheid, American Indians, etc.) outside the ark of safety, excluding them from the world of moral concern. As an over-heated Kanye West might say, "god and Israelites do not care about Canaanites." I extend this expression of concern to Smith's account of the Exodus Configuration in the Blackamerican experience. Or, to put this concern in the form of a question, does Smith's Exodus Configuration reproduce the exclusions that Said condemns?

Smith *might* respond by noting that Said is right: that liberal, progressive, and leftist commentators who take the Exodus narrative as a politically attractive paradigm of social change, people such as Walzer and himself, obscure if not ignore the destruction of the Canaanite nations. Ignoring the dark side of the Exodus narrative, they do not attend to the antitypical use of this story for conquest, dispossession, colonialism, and other pernicious purposes. Of course, Smith might wish to disassociate himself from Walzer's not-so-benign neglect of this issue and from Said's critique. True, he does accent positive uses of the Exodus narrative by Blackamericans, but he does not completely neglect the dark side. There is an oblique, near reference to the two-sided, light and dark, reality of the Exodus narrative as effective history. Drawing on the observations of Vincent Harding, Smith notes the very different ways in which blacks and whites in America appropriated the story. They had inverse views: America as Egypt versus America as the Promised Land. Though it often had a geographical referent (the North, Kansas, and Canada), Blackamericans did not associate the Promised Land with the conquest of the land and dispossession of its inhabitants. There is no analogue to Indian-killing Puritans within the Blackamerican figural imagination. On the contrary, the image of the Promised Land expressed black people's desire for *self-possession*. This insight has to be teased from Smith's account through a generous reading. He does not address the destruction of the Canaanite nations (as textual reality, as historical actuality, or as effective history) and consequently provides no hermeneutic to deal with this unacknowledged threat to his analysis. His silence makes him vulnerable to Said's critique. Though Smith does not reproduce the uncritical reading of the Exodus narrative that Williams attributes to black liberation theologians, his neglect of the conquest episode is a huge oversight that might leave "Canaanite readers" such as Said and Warrior suspicious.

Despite this major oversight, Smith's argument for the Exodus narrative in the biblical formation of black identity is more persuasive than his account of the Law Configuration. While illuminating, the connections that he makes are looser, if not strained. Unlike the Exodus Configuration, what distinguishes this account is his conscious attention to the ethical-political duality of law. Smith remarks that the Law Configuration deals with "the historical moment when a culture first establishes its identifying tradition of law."[40] Legality has to be distinguished from illegality, freedom from anarchy, as cosmos displaces chaos. The primary foci are the law as a *pharmakon* (poison/cure), black people as *pharmakoi* (scapegoats), and the wilderness as a trope for the legal regimes during the early colonial era, post-Reconstruction period, and the late nineteenth century.[41] Under each regime, law presented a dual reality: a source of despair, codifying the mistreatment of black people, and a source of hope that mistreatment could be overcome. Potentially, the law could poison their hopes *or* cure their despair. It was a *pharmakon*. The legal regime was supported by white terror: the festive, *communitas*-establishing[42] blood rite of the white (anti-black) riot, lynch mob, and racial cleansing. Under this quasi-legal regime, Blackamericans were a collective scapegoat *(pharmakoi)*, a race of sacrificial victims. Lynched on a thousand crosses, they were hung, castrated, fed their own severed genitals, burned, and shot; their dismembered body parts were carried away by relic-hunters, worshipping at the altar of white supremacy. Such was the quasi-legal regime of Blackamerican-scapegoating. Against these dual regimes, according to Smith, Blackamericans conjured the law as a way of curing white violence.

This act of conjuration would have to be a mighty trick indeed. Considering the magnitude of the challenge, Smith poses the following questions: "How does one reconfigure the embodied person herself or himself, who is configured by the culture as a victim or scapegoat, using biblical forms and democratic traditions revered by the society and its institutions? How has black America solved the problem of rendering American law and religion as cures for violence?"[43] Rhetorical and leading, these questions are designed to produce an affect while leading, simultaneously, to an obvious conclusion. Blackamericans learned to walk the razor's edge, conjuring the law for curative purposes while recognizing its ability to sanction violence. This struggle against and for the law, conjuring biblical republicanism and democratic ideas for emancipatory purposes under circumstances where black freedom was subject to severe attack during the wilderness years of the post-Reconstruction period, defines the Law Configuration. According to Smith, Martin Luther King, Jr., was the great conjuror, the most successful practitioner of this curative art in the Blackamerican experience. He led a spiritually audacious, if not *arrogant*, movement (I say this as a compliment) to save America's soul. (Only a clear perception of injustice—"Ain't gonna let nobody turn me around"—and unshakable conviction regarding the righteousness of one's cause can produce this kind of liberating "spiritual arrogance.") If the Emancipation Proclamation initiated a curative regime of struggling with and for the law and the Civil War

Amendments and the Civil Rights Act of 1875 provided a "booster shot," so to speak, against white violence and its despair, then the King-led movement was its sweetest twentieth-century fruit.

The Spirituals-Wisdom-Prophecy Triplet

If the Genesis, Exodus, and Law Configurations constitute what Smith calls "ethnological perspectives" on the topic of conjurational spirituality, then the Spirituals, Wisdom, and Prophecy triplet provide "theoretical perspectives." An improvisational addition to Northrop Frye's sevenfold typology, the Spirituals Configuration is defined by an aesthetic polarity of ecstatic and iconic expression. Smith's argument is quite interesting, emphasizing the dominance of the ecstatic pole while arguing for the importance of the neglected iconic pole. By emphasizing the iconic, Smith makes an important opening to the much-neglected visual dimension in black culture.[44] But that opening quickly narrows as Smith moves away from the image, narrowing his focus almost exclusively to the iconics of the written word. In his account, as in most, kinetic orality trumps literature, which trumps the visual. But I am getting ahead of myself and certainly ahead of a fuller description of Smith's account. Informed by the *Africana* philosophy of Lucius Outlaw, the literary theory of Henry Louis Gates, and the linguistic analysis of Morton Marks, Smith seeks to reveal forms of black expressive culture that are often concealed by various kinds of meaning-reversal, signifying, and code-switching; processes, he argues, that are integral to the biblical configuration of black American culture.[45] Following Long's programmatic suggestions, Smith mines the spirituals, the black folkloric tradition, and the tradition of black prophetic speech.

The upshot of Smith's analysis of the ecstatic-iconic polarity in spirituals is their incantatory, inducing, and transformative intent. The "sorrow songs," whether the spirituals or the blues, are ironic in form and homeopathic in effect—that is, they do not always say what they mean, and they use the *dis-ease* of black people's lives to cure their sorrow or immunize them against despair. Transcending their circumstances, affirming and transvaluing their identity, the ecstasy generated by each of these expressive forms allows Blackamericans to transcend themselves. An iconics of transformation augments this transformative ecstasy by imagistically employing "biblical types to configure black experience": Moses as liberator, Exodus as emancipation, and the Promised Land as destiny.[46] This sounds like a persuasive account of black aesthetics. But I am not persuaded that Smith has made the connection between this account and the biblical text in the black imagination. Thematically speaking, it would be absurd to deny the biblical formation of the spirituals. My only claim is that evidence for the spirituals-psalms connection in the black imagination appears to be weak. Smith does not present anything comparable to the Mosaic construction of black leadership or the figure of the Promised Land in the Exodus Configuration. The fact that Smith fails to make the connection does not, in my view, undermine the value of his account. But it may require that he amend his claim that the Spirituals Configuration is a rhetorical-performative-historical phenomenon in a straightforward and biblically derivative way as opposed to a construction that serves his interpretive aims. To reiterate, he does not provide the kind of textual evidence that he does with respect to the Genesis and Exodus Configurations. The evidence of black people making this connection (he cites Alain Locke) is rather sparse. Again, this does not prevent a constructive rather than a descriptive account of spirituals in the biblical formation of black identity. If this is Smith's intent, then he has made a valuable contribution to that end.

Smith's claims for the Wisdom and the Prophecy Configurations present a different set of issues insofar as they put him in direct dialogue with Long and West, even when he does not explicitly mention them. Long challenged scholars to take black folklore seriously as a data source for the black religious imagination. Smith takes this challenge very seriously, finding in black folklore an indigenous wisdom tradition. From hoodoo to the Signifying Monkey to High John the Conqueror, Smith discerns a conjurational spirituality: mimetic and pharmacopeic in method, transformative in intent, and conjunctive in form.[47] Smith remarks: "I have referred to this conjunctive feature as a wisdom tradition in black culture which, commonly with other wisdom traditions, readily conjoins categories such as visible and invisible, everyday and immemorial, ethos and cosmos."[48] Black folk wisdom, he observes, goes beyond conventional forms of conjunctive thinking by conjoining opposites in every domain of human experience. In short, the tradition is thoroughly conjunctive. While Smith successfully makes the case for the "conjurational intentions" of the black wisdom tradition and does a fine job exploring its rhetorical technique of signification, the antitypical connection to biblical persons, places, and events, the components of what Smith calls a biblical configuration, are barely evident. How does the black wisdom tradition signify on the biblical wisdom tradition? This is a question that Smith does not properly answer because it is never properly asked. Things are pretty much the same regarding the Prophecy Configuration. His account of Sojourner Truth as the personification of the black prophetic tradition is compelling. One might even say inspired: inspired because of the quality of the analysis where Truth, as a conjure-woman, employed homeopathy designed to cure the disease of white supremacy that (like Moloch) ate black people body and soul. It is inspired because it defies our gendered expectations regarding prophetic authority. But there is that nagging question about textual connections. There is no Amos, Hosea, or Joel in this account; no "wheel in the middle of a wheel," "valley of dry bones," "lion's den," or "fiery furnace." Smith does not identify figurative relations between Sojourner Truth and biblical persons, places, and events. He does not *show* us a prototype-antitype relation (but he does an admirable job of *constructing* one). David Walker seems to be a better match for this purpose than Truth. His rhetoric is closer to the eighth-century Hebrew prophets.[49] It is hard to imagine a stronger prototype-antitype relation.

The Gospel-Praxis Dyad and the Apocalypse

Does theology (construed as dogmatic assertion) trump ethnology in Smith's account of Black Religion? Consider the structure of Smith's account. It moves from ethnology to theory to theology. Is this structure normative? Does each successor category provide a perspective superior to its predecessor? In Smith's triadic imagination, the Genesis-Exodus-Law triplet provides "ethnological perspectives" on the conjurational spirituality of black North Americans, while the Spirituals-Wisdom-Prophecy triplet provides "theoretical perspectives." The last group of biblical configurations, the Gospel-Praxis-Apocalypse triplet, provides "theological perspectives." If not already apparent, the *constructive* character of Smith's enterprise should now be clear. He is *inventing* "Biblical Formations of Black America" as much as discovering them. Except for the Exodus Configuration (and perhaps Genesis and Apocalyptic Configurations) where the prototype-antitype connections between biblical text and the black figural imagination are obvious and substantial, Smith is essentially telling us how the tradition *can* and perhaps *should* be read rather than describing an actual tradition of interpretation. However, to reiterate a previous comment: this should not be taken as a negative assessment. I admire what he has done. But I have a number of questions about the Gospel-Praxis dyad and the *orphaned* Apocalypse Configuration that center, more or less, around Smith's reliance on Rene Girard's theory of sacred violence.

The Gospel Configuration, according to Smith, is a tradition of identifying with Christ through acts of mimesis (the imitation of Christ). Blackamericans identify their suffering at the hands of white people with Jesus' suffering on a Roman cross. They conjured their suffering into a redemptive act. Never a dominant tradition *as a matter of praxis*, this method of dealing with white violence extends from slavery to King, where the idea of redemptive suffering provides the bedrock of his nonviolent philosophy. Nonviolence is an attempt to cure the victimizer through the victim's willingness to become a scapegoat. Bearing the cross of the white man's sins of racism, as Christ bore the sins of the world, makes redemption possible. This is the most audacious (and absurd) example of conjuring in the Blackamerican tradition. Through this act of conjuring, the suffering victim is transformed into a redeemer, a Christ-like figure. Through black people's suffering, violence is cured: a cure, presumably, that goes beyond the curative power of the law. (The supersessionism in Smith's account is apparent in this contrast between Jewish law and Christian gospel, which I suppose is apropos given his reliance on Girard.) As the suffering servant and willing victim of scapegoating sacrifice, King disrupted the spiral of mimetic rivalry—the loss of social differentiation (mimetic doubling) and the threat of difference-restoring catastrophic violence. His case exemplified a homeopathic application of *sacred nonviolence*. According to Smith, King accomplished this feat by displacing the *mimetic rivalry*, which Girard had shown to be endemic to human culture, with a historically unique exception, the *mimetic intimacy* made possible through a mutual imitation of Christ.[50] In light of this claim, I pose the following question: Is Girardian theory a useful analytic for explicating the Gospel Configuration or primarily an apology for Christian supersessionism; specifically, a dogmatic assertion of Christian superiority that muddies the water and obscures our view of this biblical configuration in the formation of black America?

I shall defer answering this question and turn to the Praxis Configuration, which Smith correlates with the Acts of the Apostles. Concerned with traditions of nonviolent social activism and closely related to the Gospel Configuration, the Praxis configuration attempts to enact the idea of redemptive suffering: to cure the racist violence to which black Americans have been subjected historically; to cure the racist soul of America, however difficult the task, through conversion and redemption rather than violence and destruction. To paraphrase Smith, all participants in the King-led wing of the civil rights movement had to ask themselves certain questions: "How do I overturn my status as a victim without creating new victims?" and "How do I accept the abuse of those who treat me like an animal without becoming one?" According to King, the solution lay in the victim's body itself. Black freedom fighters would present their bodies as *living sacrifices* to the perpetrators of white violence. Through their nonviolence performances, their civic passion plays, these *pharmakoi* (scapegoats) were simultaneously *pharmakeus* (magicians/sorcerers) and *pharmakon* (medicine/poison), giving their bodies homeopathically to cure the disease of racism structured by white supremacy.[51] Questions: Is this analysis compatible with Girard's analytic of sacred violence? Does homeopathy solve the problem of sacred violence or reproduce a sacrificial logic? Again, I defer answers pending a brief exploration of the Apocalypse Configuration.

If the Gospel Configuration is about the imitation of Christ through redemptive suffering and the Praxis Configuration is about translating redemptive suffering into a strategy of nonviolent struggle, then the Apocalypse Configuration is a counter-memory of a different Christ. This configuration provides a competing image of Jesus: not the meek and humble lamb but a lamb of wrath, a sword-toting and blood-letting avenger. Apocalypse refers to the violent climax of a cosmic and historical struggle between good and evil. As Smith notes, apocalyptic thinking is common among people under great duress such as Jews under Roman domination in first-century Palestine and the peoples of Africa, Australia, and the Americas under the imperial/colonial machine of modernity. Oppression generates anger. Bloody dreams of revenge and retribution displace forgiveness and reconciliation. As Smith notes, this configuration channeled black rage, empowering various nationalist, religious, and revolutionary social movements. The tradition of Ethiopianism that we encountered earlier has apocalyptic tendencies. This interpretive tradition harbors the view that some kind of general catastrophe, a violent end to the way things are, is a precondition for the redemption of black people. Smith claims that the most articulate twentieth-century examples of the Apocalypse Configuration are found in the writings of the Nation of Islam and Eldridge Cleaver. Both associate America with Babylon, "the consummate wicked city in the book of the Apocalypse"[52] that god promised to utterly destroy. Smith sees a problem: the Apocalypse Configuration lacks measure; its logic is one of disproportionality. Apocalyptic thinking is absolutist. The "cosmic defeat of evil" entails the utter exclusion and/or genocide of enemies.[53] On Smith's account, the Apocalypse Configuration (curing violence with violence) is the opposite of the Gospel Configuration (curing violence through nonviolent, mimetic performances). The most important exemplar of the Apocalypse Configuration is the visionary preacher Nat Turner. Also a visionary preacher, King is the most important opponent. Even though there is stronger prototype-antitype evidence for the Apocalypse than for the Gospel and Praxis Configurations, Smith distances his analysis, normatively, from the desire for retribution. Vengeance remains a divine prerogative or simply drops out of his ethical thinking completely.

To the list of questions awaiting answers, I add a fourth: how does Smith's devotion to Girardian theory affect his assessment of the Apocalypse Configuration? I have doubts about the utility of Smith's Girardian-informed account. While the Girard of *Violence and the Sacred* (1972) provides a highly illuminating quasi-ethnological account of violence in human culture, the Girard of *The Scapegoat* (1986) and later texts provides analytically dim and thinly veiled apologies for Christian exceptionalism. By substituting apologetic theology for ethnology, he undermines his own credibility. Curiously, as I noted previously, there is an analogical shift in *Conjuring Culture* from the "Ethnological Perspectives" of the earlier part of the book to the "Theological Perspectives" of the later part. As I have argued, the prototype-antitype connection that Smith posits as the *sine qua non* of biblical typologies is tenuous in the Gospel and Praxis Configurations when compared to the descriptive wealth of the Genesis and Exodus Configurations analyzed under the rubric of "Ethnological Perspectives." Perhaps this shift is just coincidental. That the "Theological Perspectives" section, excluding the Apocalypse Configuration, tells us less about "conjurational spirituality" than the rest of the book is not coincidental. Girard is a distraction. And Smith appears distracted when he remarks, "'Conjuring culture' through the incantatory use of biblical figures like Exodus and Promised Land, requires a specifically theological, rather than a merely rhetorical or literary, figural reading. By 'theological' here I mean that biblical figures are employed in synergy with a Deity who cooperates in the concrete historical realization of such figures."[54] I find this claim gratuitous. Why should we read DuBois' invocation of the wilderness figure in *The Souls of Black Folk* (1903) as requiring a "theology?" This "requirement" says more about Smith's apologetic needs than it does about the conjuring efficacy of DuBois' rhetoric. I think that a strictly ethnological analysis supports the efficacy of that rhetoric quite nicely. Smith implicitly excludes naturalistic conceptions of deity (where god is a creature of the human imagination that emerges from our multifarious interactions with the natural world) without arguing for that exclusion. He attenuates the conjunctive capaciousness of the black wisdom tradition for which he argued so persuasively, excluding figures such as William R. Jones and naturalistic forms of religion. I can make sense of this attenuation only as an apologetic strategy. Smith's concluding remarks on conjuring culture are an unpersuasive attempt to valorize a particular way of thinking about divinity and about the efficacy of human agency.

Conjuring Theodicy

As I noted earlier, Smith situates his project in relation to black theology and the rhetoric of *Prophecy Deliverance!* Though innovative, *Conjuring Culture* is among other things a work of theology. If not liberation theology, it certainly expresses a liberationist desire. If the charge of divine racism hangs shroud-like over black liberation theology, as Jones contends, then Smith fails to address the threshold question: "Is God a white racist?" Answering this question is all the more pressing given Smith's apparent reliance on a theory of redemptive suffering. Underlying this theory is the notion of the suffering servant, which Jones describes as the least desirable theodicy. As the reader should recall, Jones presents his critique of the suffering servant theodicy in assessing Joseph Washington's *The Politics of God*. This theodicy leaves Washington vulnerable to the charge of divine racism because he fails to adequately refute the theodicy of deserved punishment. Before one can claim the status of suffering servant, Jones argues, one must refute the possibility that the suffering in question is deserved. This is a logical prerequisite. Even if one could meet this logical burden, classifying black people as god's (collective) contemporary suffering servant is a bad idea. It potentially underwrites suffering in perpetuity. Jones contends that his critique of Washington, when slightly modified, is applicable "to any black theologian who adopts the theodicy of vicarious suffering, including Martin Luther King."[55] Smith's claim that King is the exemplary practitioner of the suffering-servant model of social transformation and Jones' claim that King's praxis of vicarious suffering embodies the worst possible theodicy call for a comparative analysis.

King as Nonviolent Homeopath

Before exploring Jones' critique of the suffering-servant theodicy, I will briefly recap Smith's account that I detailed earlier under the Gospel and Praxis Configurations. Smith claims to derive an Afro-American praxis of curing violence through nonviolent conjurational performances from sources extending from slavery to the King-led civil rights movement. Confronted by "the existential agony of impotence" in the face of rage-producing circumstances that left them seething with violent, vengeful impulses, slaves adopted an ethic of forgiveness. This ethic was as much a product of pragmatic necessity as theological idealism. Given their circumstances, there was not much that slaves could do. Idealizing the ethic of forgiveness served their short-term interest in sheer survival. This pragmatic move on the level of theological doctrine, Smith claims, had a correlate in praxis: an African American folk tradition of conjurational spirituality: ritualistic, incantatory, and pharmacopeic strategies designed to heal the bodies, minds, and souls of black victims *and* white perpetrators.

King channeled this folk tradition rhetorically and through embodied acts of protest whose dramaturgy was designed to heal the soul-sickness of white racist America. To put it starkly, King was the preeminent conjuror in the Blackamerican tradition—the hoodoo and conjure-doctor supreme. Smith explicates King's healing arts using the Greek terms we have encountered before: *pharmakeus, pharmakos, pharmakon*. As conjuror-in-chief, King was simultaneously a victim of the scapegoating practices of white supremacy, a *curative toxin* that killed the malignancy while healing the damage it caused, and a sorcerer-magician who incanted and ritually produced freedom. As the inspiration of nonviolent mimetic intimacy, King was no ordinary scapegoat. The traditional scapegoat, Smith comments, is "the most accursed and toxic figure in the community" who purges communal fears and animosities by dying. The violent mimesis of conflicting rivals is resolved on the bloody body of the scapegoat—the sacrificial victim. Once accursed and now deified, the deceased scapegoat becomes the repository of salvific power, a Pandora's Box in reverse, so to speak, enclosing and sequestering the violent contamination that disordered the community.

Like the conventional scapegoat, King was the screen onto which his antagonists projected their racialized fears and animosity, what I have elsewhere described as a pathological animosity toward black people that cuts across American history like an ugly scar. Under this paranoia-inducing hatred, "respectable," prominent, and ostensibly sensible white people described King as the most dangerous man in America. Smith notes the construction of King as a lecherous criminal and communist-sympathizing traitor. He draws a fundamental distinction, however, between the conventional scapegoat and King. Where the former is the victim of a violent, bad, othering-mimesis, King was a victim who inspired a nonviolent, good, intimacy-producing mimesis. Smith claims that King "reenacted the gospel story in a salvific rather than a sacrificial mode." King inspired "violent others" to imitate his nonviolent model, as ostensibly he imitated Christ, saving victims and perpetrators of violence without creating new victims. This is a big claim that Smith does not support. He cites no evidence, provides no argument, and does not consider possible objections such as the multievidentiality of suffering. Nor does he address his claim regarding a "good mimesis" in light of the widespread violent reaction to King's assassination. This reaction was certainly the most spectacular, if not the largest and the most intense, that King ever inspired. This suggests that King's performance was not nearly as effective as Smith claims.

Smith asserts that King (and Blackamericans), like Christ, had a dual status as *pharmakos/pharmakon*—victims who cure and poison.

> The cure prescribed is homeopathic on the basis of a nonviolent model, in which the victim's own body and person serve as materia medica—toxic to the victimizer if violation ensues, but tonic if victims are saved. To this end public displays of victimization in which any violation of the victims' bodies could clearly reveal their scapegoat status were devised. In such displays precisely what is toxic for victimizers if abuse occurs—that is, public recognition of their identity as persecutors and scapegoats—can become tonic if scapegoating is terminated and prospective victims are saved.[56]

Smith adds:

> By pragmatically discovering that homeopathic formula in the context of American scapegoating traditions, King and his associates provided a solution to racist violence that had eluded generations of his predecessors.[57]

Where the traditional scapegoat creates culture through violent communitas (generative violence), King conjured a culture of freedom through nonviolent homeopathy. To summarize Smith's position, King conjured a culture of emancipation by inspiring violent others to imitate his nonviolent example by submitting his body (and his followers') as a "living sacrifice." The dramaturgy of this morality play captured the imagination, "turning the souls" of civil rights antagonists from opposition to support of the movement. It seduced them into imitating King as King imitated Christ—the nonviolent god. The King-led wing of the movement severed the connection between mimesis and the violent, scapegoating production of culture that Girard describes in his theory of sacred violence. I see four problems with this argument: first, there is nothing nonsacrificial about self-sacrifice; second, self-sacrifice may victimize victims a second time by requiring them to be better than their victimizers not merely as a prudential and strategic matter but morally, with a kind of "purity of heart" and goodness of will rooted deeply in the self; third, self-sacrifice may be ethically inferior to violent struggle against the perpetrators of oppressive violence—up to and including the act of killing them, especially where "third parties" are involved; fourth, the historical success of King's model is much more ambiguous than Smith suggests.

A suffering servant by any other name, such as nonviolent homeopath, is still a scapegoat. I think that Jones' critique of the suffering-servant theodicy is applicable to Smith's account of King. Let us reexamine Smith's account point-by-point in light of Jones' critique of Joseph Washington, which he summarizes in four points:

1. "Before the theodicy of vicarious suffering can be legitimately utilized, the theodicy of deserved punishment must first be convincingly refuted."
2. "Given the multievidentiality of suffering, the employment of the theodicy of vicarious suffering requires another difficult demonstration: One is pushed either to regard all suffering as vicarious or to provide the criterion for distinguishing redemptive from non-redemptive suffering."
3. "The theodicy of redemptive suffering collapses into a form of quietism."
4. "Once the black Christian concludes that God Himself has died and suffered for the other, how can he refuse to follow in His footsteps?"[58]

I contend that points one and three are directly relevant to Smith's nonviolent homeopathy while two and four are indirectly relevant.

Jones argues that it is extremely difficult to demonstrate that the suffering of black people is undeserved, which is precisely why adopting this theodicy is ill advised. (One might recall from chapter 5 that this is a point that the Muslim scholar Sherman Jackson, in his attempt to provide a comparative Muslim-Christian analysis of Jones' critique of black theodicy, does not understand.) However, this is precisely the theodicy adopted by Washington, which Jones captures in the following syllogism:

> If blacks are the suffering servant/chosen people,
> The charge of divine racism is disproved.
> Blacks are the suffering servant/chosen people.
> Therefore the charge of divine racism is disproved.[59]

In the absence of an "exaltation-liberation event" that demonstrates in accordance with the biblical model that their suffering was undeserved, how do we know that blacks are god's contemporary suffering servant? Granted, black people have suffered a lot. There is considerable evidence that their suffering exceeds "normal" patterns of distribution: it is maldistributed, enormous, and noncatastrophic. But is this enough to make the case? As Jones remarks, one would expect suffering servants to suffer excessively. Otherwise what is the point of the suffering-servant model? What this model cannot tolerate is noncatastrophic suffering, suffering without end, unrequited suffering. If the suffering servant must suffer to achieve god's purposes, then she must also be vindicated. In the absence of vindication, there are alternative explanations of black suffering such as the theodicy of deserved punishment, the perversity of god, or the notion that god is a white racist.

Smith appears to evade the reach of Jones' critique by accenting the nonviolent dimension of suffering servant–hood rather than sacrifice: "The Jesus of the gospels saves by virtue of constituting the will-to-save as the preeminent divine attribute, in contradistinction to other representations of deity in biblical religion itself wherever it claims that God requires sacrifice for the sake of atonement or forgiveness of sins. In this nontraditional reading, Jesus' divinity consists in his virtual identity with nonviolent deity."[60] On this reading, Smith can plausibly claim that he is not playing the same suffering-servant language game as Washington. As such, he is not subject to the same critique. But not so fast: though there is some incommensurability between their games, there is commensurability too. Both require suffering by the agent of transformation/salvation.

But there is an even more serious and I think decisive objection: Girard's theory does not comprehend racial conflict. Smith's adoption of that theory, which he tweaks with his nonsacrificial reading of Jesus, cannot obscure a sobering fact: black victims remain the objects of sacrifice. In Smith's reading, King and his followers present themselves as living sacrifices in the hope that their "nonviolent" performance will produce nonviolent responses on both sides of black–white racial conflict. *Note well: it is black victims who are called to offer themselves in sacrifice; there is no reciprocal obligation on the part of victimizers.* Blackamericans are called to suffer for the black-victimizing white other. King accented the alchemy of unmerited suffering, its redemptive and transformative power. In contrast, Smith accents nonviolence: suffering is redemptive insofar as it is endured without violent retaliation, seduces other blacks to similar acts of self-sacrifice, and inspires mimetic intimacy between black victims and white victimizers. In light of this, I pose a question: doesn't the power of nonviolence, including the nonviolent homeopathy Smith commends, lie precisely in the unmerited suffering of victims? Smith's attempt to pry apart nonviolent mimesis and suffering does not work. Nonviolence depends on the sacrificial logic of unmerited suffering for its inspirational power and efficacy. The refusal of the violated to respond violently is the power of nonviolence. Despite Smith's claim, the price of mimetic intimacy is the sacrifice of black people. There is precious little evidence of mimetic intimacy in Blackamericans' struggle against white supremacy. If this phenomenon exists at all, its occurrence must be rare indeed, as there is no discernable tradition of commentary. It certainly does not reflect the views of King, the hero of Smith's account. On the contrary, King regarded unearned suffering as redemptive. It educates, transforms, and makes one's opponents more amenable to reason. Here King channels the remarks of Mahatma Gandhi. Quoting Gandhi, King writes: "Rivers of blood may flow before we gain our freedom, but it must be our blood."[61] Though these are Gandhi's words, they truly reflect King's view. *Brutal white violence against black people caused King considerable sadness and anguish. However, his inability to maintain strict adherence to nonviolence among his black followers seems to have troubled him more.*

Smith does not acknowledge the difference of interpretation between King and himself. If he is attributing this nonsacrificial notion of mimetic intimacy to King, it was clearly an *unconscious* possession, the logic of which King does not express in writing or speech. His actual comments are rooted in the sacrificial logic of the cross: "The cross is the eternal expression of the length to which "God" will go in order to restore community."[62] If the resurrection symbolizes god's triumph over forces that block community, then blacks who love white people "while they are yet white supremacists" demonstrate sacrificial love. As King remarks, "Since the white man's personality is greatly distorted by segregation, and his soul is greatly scarred, he needs the love of the Negro. The Negro must love the white man, because the white man needs his love to remove his tensions, insecurities, and fears."[63] Need I add that the author of these remarks is not the King that Smith describes?

If King-like nonviolent homeopathy is a species of the vicarious, redemptive, suffering-servant theodicy, then doesn't it collapse into a form of quietism? In his critique of Washington, Jones decries the quietistic implication of making suffering redemptive/positive. It removes most incentives to destroy the causes of such suffering. The difficulty of distinguishing redemptive from nonredemptive suffering only heightens the prospects for quietism. Smith seems to evade any direct hit that this critique might have. Unlike Washington, Smith does not accent redemptive suffering so much as he does nonviolent servant–hood and the mimetic intimacy it creates. This frees him, or so it seems, from the obligation to defend the concept of suffering or provide criteria for distinguishing redemptive from nonredemptive kinds. In light of its actual efficacy, King-style nonviolence and redemptive suffering does not exhibit the quietism that Jones claims we should expect. King and his followers actively confronted powers they regarded as oppressive, which produced nonredemptive forms of black suffering. Maybe nonviolent agency is underdetermined by redemptive intent. The most Jones could claim is that there is a gap between the logical (quietistic) implications of King's theory of nonviolence and the consequences of its practice.

The causal relation between beliefs (the concept of redemptive suffering) and actions (political quietism) may not be as linear and tight as Jones believes. Beliefs do not necessarily fund actions. Jones might object that this observation misses the point: his point being the logical relation between beliefs-as-motives and actions-as-outcomes, and the preponderant rather than absolute effect of the former on the latter. Granted, there is not always a tight, linear relation between beliefs and actions (circumstances and inconsistency matter) but there is a relationship. Moreover, Jones can stop a certain species of criticism underwritten by "Wittgensteinian fideism" in its tracks: the claim that Western academic modes of logic are language games embedded in forms of life that are inapplicable to black theology. As I remarked in chapter 5, black theology *is* a Western academic discourse and not an expression of first-order, black popular piety. As critical reflection it employs standard tools of logic such as the principle of noncontradiction. Black theology is subject to the same standards of logic employed in its critique of white civilization and theology. This is precisely the task that Jones undertakes. But even if we accept this response and renew a Jonesian critique, we encounter another problem. As Jones acknowledges, King did not view black suffering as redemptive per se. Rather, suffering is redemptive when it occurs in the context of black people's proactive efforts to create tensions between them and the latent violence of the white supremacist order. King and his followers were "nonviolent provocateurs" who sought to elicit acts of white violence. They did so in the hope that exposing this now latent, now manifest violence would prick the conscience of sympathetic white people (people of good will) and motivate them to act—to abolish segregationist laws and mores and, over time, to change racist hearts. Jones claims that King does not provide criteria for distinguishing redemptive from nonredemptive suffering. It may be true that he does not provide explicit criteria, but we can distill implicit criteria from the actual campaigns of direct action that he led. Moreover, to reiterate my previous point, Smith's concept of nonviolence is different from King's.

If Jones' critique of the theodicy of redemptive suffering is to be generalized beyond his critique of Washington and applied to Smith, then it needs to be significantly modified. If Smith's concept of nonviolence is different from King's, then King's concept of redemptive suffering is considerably different from Washington's, not the least because it is limited in scope and more specific. Ironically, I think that Smith's account of nonviolent homeopathy is more vulnerable to Jones' critique of quietism than King's position. I take this claim to be true despite the fact that Smith explicitly rejects the idea that suffering is redemptive. Smith is more vulnerable because he reduces violence by white perpetrators and black victims to the same ethical-political status. He does not allow for distinctions between force and violence or just and unjust forms of violence. Also absent in Smith's account is Gandhi's invidious distinction between courageous acts of violence and nonviolence motivated by cowardice, where the former is preferable to the latter. (A critic might reasonably claim that King does not adequately distinguish them either and that the difference I see between King and Smith is illusory.) On Smith's view, violent resistance to the violence of white supremacy creates new victims: white supremacists. I can think of no better or more troubling example of the effects of Girard's theory on Smith's conjurational purposes.

I have reservations, however, about the efficacy of this conjurational performance that are historical as well as theoretical. Does nonviolent homeopathy work? Is it truly nonsacrificial? Does it actually try to avoid violence or doesn't it, in fact, seek to provoke violence so as to expose its social latency? As these questions suggest, I do not see the evidence for the mimetic intimacy and nonviolent alchemy Smith describes. If an explicit apology for the uniqueness and superiority of Christianity underlies Girard's later theory of sacred violence, especially *Things Hidden since the Foundation of the World* (1987), then Smith's concept of nonviolent homeopathy and mimetic intimacy, as exemplified by Martin Luther King, Jr., is an African American elaboration. My answers to questions I posed earlier should now be apparent. Girardian theory *is not* a useful analytic for explicating the Gospel Configuration but primarily a dogmatic assertion of Christian superiority that muddies the water and obscures our view of this biblical configuration in the formation of black America. Though Smith's notion of homeopathy may be compatible with Girard's analysis, neither provides a nondogmatic solution to the problem of sacred violence and sacrificial logic.

Conclusion

Smith's concept of conjurational spirituality is a highly creative contribution to the discourse of Black Religion. In this chapter, I construed Smith as accepting Long's programmatic suggestions for the study of Afro-American religion: that students should account for representations of Africa, the consequences of black people's "involuntary migration" to America, and the role of the god symbol in the black experience. In addition, Long argued that folklore should have a larger role in interpretations of Black Religion. Smith makes good on Long's suggestions by integrating theological, theoretical, comparative, and folkloric sources like no one else. By accenting African-derived spirituality and Afro-Hebraic hybridity, Smith breaks free of the Standard Narrative of Black Religion as the Black Church to a degree that West does not. If we take Jones as intensifying Long's methodological question regarding the "god symbol" in the black experience, then both West and Smith are vulnerable, in different ways and degrees, to Jones' critique of black theology and religious thought.

Chapter 8

Concluding Remarks

Here are my final thoughts about the Standard Narrative of Black Religion that I developed in chapter 2 and elaborated and contested in subsequent chapters. Signifying on Afrocentrism, I coined the term Afro-*Eccentricity* to grab attention and signal a different approach to what some construe as an isomorphism between black identity and Black Religion as the Black Church. Afro-*Eccentricity* is a critical pun and trope that accents the internal plurality of blackness, the *different* in what is often construed as the same and self-identical. Afro-*Eccentricity* emphasizes minor traditions, contrarian orientations, and "heresies" that have always been part of that motley called Blackamerican identity.

Now: to the four theorists of Black Religion that I approached under the dramatis personae of Archaeologist, Renegade, Prophet, and Conjuror. Charles H. Long provides a model for contesting the Standard Narrative. I do not suggest, however, that his is the only possible model. Indeed, I have my reservations. On my view, Long continues to subscribe to some notion of a "religious given"—or some Jamesian "more," the sacred, the holy, or g/God that is archaic, transcends, and is generative with respect to human construction. With this reservation in mind, I draw the following conclusions. Theophus Smith conjures a black religious imaginary that *relativizes* the Standard Narrative by situating the church within a larger set of Afro-Atlantic conjurational practices. These practices, however, are framed and normalized by a Protestant Christian theological imagination that attenuates the radicality of Long's three-pronged programmatic challenge. Cornel West *embroiders* the Standard Narrative by staging a dialogue between prophetic Christianity and progressive Marxism. As such, he broadens the "terministic screen" of the Black Church; he provides an innovative angle, or an additional dimension like a 3-D movie, while sharpening the resolution of what we see. In contrast to Smith and West, William R. Jones works outside the Standard Narrative altogether. At the very least, his "secular humanism" shows what doing so might entail. In this regard, he is closest to Long. Through a black humanist critique, Jones *discloses* the ironies of the Standard Narrative's theological-liberationist voice and *exposes* its "logical complicity" with the subordination of black people. However, there is a gap between logical (formal) and historical (actually existing) complicity that Jones does not adequately acknowledge or address. Though I find no evidence that his analysis was influenced by Long's challenge, Jones' counter-evidential critique of the "god symbol" (from the assumption of divine racism, where god is the sum of god's acts) provides the best example of how a serious response might look. Jones "queers" the Standard Narrative by placing it within the metaphilosophical context of humanism and naturalism. As a comparative phenomenologist, Long *circumvents* the Standard Narrative with a multifocal counternarrative that combines archaic remains with contemporary forms. Whether embroidering, conjuring through and beyond, or circumventing, queering, and working outside the Standard Narrative, these four writers are among the most innovative students of Black Religion we have.

Notes

Preface

1. Nancy Frankenberry, ed., *Radical Interpretation in Religion* (Cambridge: Cambridge University Press, 2002), 170.
2. Though I clearly have Michel Foucault's notion of discourse in mind, I do not commit myself to all of the implications of his theory.
3. Jonathan Z. Smith remarks, "Religion is solely the creation of the scholar's study. It is created for the scholar's analytic purposes by his imaginative acts of comparison and generalization. Religion has no *independent* existence apart from the academy." See Jonathan Z. Smith, *Imagining Religion: From Babylon to Jamestown* (Chicago: University of Chicago Press, 1982), xi. I agree with everything he says except for the hyperbole of "solely."
4. See Donald Davidson, "On the Very Idea of a Conceptual Scheme," *Proceedings and Addresses of the American Philosophical Association* 47 (1973–1974): 5–20.

1 Afro-*Eccentricity*: An Introduction

1. See William David Hart, *Black Religion: Malcolm X, Julius Lester, and Jan Willis* (New York: Palgrave Macmillan, 2008), x.
2. Victor Anderson, *Beyond Ontological Blackness: An Essay on African American Religious and Cultural Criticism* (New York: Continuum, 1995), 11.
3. Anderson, 13.
4. Anderson, 13–14.
5. Anderson, 16–17.
6. Anderson, 131–32, 142–43.
7. See S. Hall, "New Ethnicities," in "Black Film, British Cinema," ed. Kobena Mercer, *ICA Documents* 7 (1988): 27–31.
8. David Morley and Kuan-Hsing Chen, eds., *Stuart Hall: Critical Dialogues in Cultural Studies* (New York: Routledge, 1996), 443.
9. Morley and Chen, 444.
10. Kimberlé Crenshaw, "Mapping the Margins: Intersectionality, Identity Politics, and Violence Against Women of Color," *Stanford Law Review* 43, no. 6 (July 1991): 1241–99.

11. Nell Irvin Painter, *Sojourner Truth: A Life, A Symbol* (New York: W. W. Norton, 1997), 224.
12. Patricia Hill Collins, "Learning from the Outsider Within: The Sociological Significance of Black Feminist Thought," *Social Problems* 3, no. 6 (December 1986): 519.
13. Collins, 520.
14. Collins, 521.
15. Patricia Hill Collins, *Black Feminist Thought: Knowledge, Consciousness, and the Politics of Empowerment* (London: HarperCollins*Academic*, 1990), 225, 227.
16. Collins, *Black Feminist*, 230.
17. Nick Merriman and Tim Schadla-Hall, eds., *Public Archaeology* (London: Taylor and Francis, 2004), 153.
18. William D. Hart, *Edward Said and the Religious Effects of Culture* (Cambridge: Cambridge University Press, 2000), 66.
19. Giorgio Agamben, *What Is An Apparatus? And Other Essays* (Stanford: Stanford University Press, 2009), 51.
20. Ato Sekyi-Otu, *Fanon's Dialectic of Experience* (Cambridge, MA: Harvard University Press, 1996), 34.
21. See Lewis Gordon's "Fanon's Tragic Revolutionary Violence," in *Fanon: A Critical Reader*, ed. Lewis Gordon, T. Denean Sharpley-Whiting, and Renée T. White, (Oxford, UK: Blackwell, 1996), 297-308.
22. Sekyi-Otu, 214.
23. This is a reference to a line in Robert Hayden's great poem "Runagate Runagate." See *Robert Hayden: Collected Poems*, ed. Frederick Glaysher (New York: Liveright Publishing Corporation, 1985), 59.
24. These citations come from an unpublished talk, "Translating the Old Greek Bible (The Septuagint): An Inconvenient Witness to Biblical History," that Melvin Peters, professor of religion at Duke University, delivered as a Kennedy Center lecture, at Brigham Young University, on April 2 in 2009.
25. James Francis Darsey, *The Prophetic Tradition and Radical Rhetoric in America* (New York: NYU Press, 1997), 27–28.
26. See volume I of Max Weber, *Economy and Society*, ed. Claus Wittich and Guenther Roth (Berkeley: University of California Press, 1978), where he analyzes the sociology of religion.
27. I refer to chapter 3 of Michael Walzer, *Interpretation and Social Criticism* (Cambridge, MA: Harvard University Press, 1987).
28. Walzer, 70–71.
29. Walzer, 71.
30. Walzer, 75.
31. Walzer, 89.
32. Walzer, 89–90, 93.
33. Yvonne Chireau, *Black Magic: Religion and the African American Conjuring Tradition* (Berkeley: University of California Press, 2003), 21.
34. Chireau, 74.
35. Chireau, 103.
36. Chireau, 15–17.

37. I presented a highly condensed version of these narratives in the introduction to *Black Religion* (2008).

2 Three Narratives of Black Religion

1. Omni-American is Albert Murray's term. According to Murray, "for all their traditional antagonisms and obvious differences, the so-called black and so-called white people of the United States resemble nobody else in the world so much as they resemble each other. And what is more, even their most extreme and violent polarities represent nothing so much as the natural history of pluralism in an open society" (Murray 1970, 22).
2. See Orlando Patterson, *Slavery and Social Death: A Comparative Study* (Cambridge, MA: Harvard University Press, 1985).
3. This argument is indebted to Clarence E. Walker, *We Can't Go Home Again: An Argument About Afrocentrism* (New York: Oxford University Press, 2001).
4. Cornel West, *Prophetic Fragments: Illuminations of the Crisis in American Religion and Culture* (Grand Rapids, MI: Eerdmans, 1988), 5–6.
5. W. E. B. DuBois, *The Souls of Black Folk*, ed. Henry Louis Gates, Jr. (New York: W. W. Norton, 1999), 123–29.
6. Kwame Anthony Appiah, *In My Father's House: Africa in the Philosophy of Culture* (New York: Oxford University Press, 1992), 31, 50.
7. DuBois, 16, 162–63.
8. Richard King, *Orientalism and Religion: Postcolonial Theory, India and 'The Mystic East,'* (London: Routledge, 1999), 35–38.
9. DuBois, 160.
10. Howard Thurman, *Deep River* (Mills College, CA: The Eucalyptus Press, 1945), 2–5.
11. Thurman, 19, 23, 27, 32.
12. James Cone, *The Spirituals and the Blues: An Interpretation* (New York: Orbis Books, Maryknoll, 1991), 29.
13. Cone, 100, 110.
14. Benjamin E. Mays and Joseph W. Nicholson, *The Negro's Church* (New York: Russell & Russell, 1969), 278.
15. Mays and Nicholson, 279–92.
16. Ruby Funchess Johnston, *The Development of Negro Religion* (New York: The Philosophical Library, 1954), xvii.
17. E. Franklin Frazier and C. Eric Lincoln, *The Negro Church in America/The Black Church Since Frazier* (New York: Knopf Publishing Group, 1974), 86–90.
18. Frazier and Lincoln, 1974, 70–71.
19. Ida Rousseau Mukenge, *The Black Church in Urban America: A Case Study in Political Economy* (Lanham, MD: Rowman & Littlefield, 1983), 10.
20. Mukenge, 51–65.
21. C. Eric Lincoln and Lawrence Mamiya, *The Black Church in the African American Experience* (Durham, NC: Duke University Press, 1990).
22. Lincoln and Mamiya, 10–11.

23. Molefi Kete Asante, *The Afrocentric Idea* (Philadelphia: Temple University Press, 1987), 6.
24. Asante, 71, 74.
25. Molefi Kete Asante, *Afrocentricity* (Trenton, NJ: Africa World Press, 1988), 77.
26. Asante, 1987, 183–95.
27. Mary Lefkowitz, *Not Out of Africa: How Afrocentrism Became an Excuse to Teach Myth as History* (New York: Basic Books, 1996); Stephen Howe, *Afrocentrism: Mythical Pasts and Imagined Homes* (New York: Verso, 1998); Wilson J. Moses, *Afrotopia: The Roots of African American Popular History* (New York: Cambridge University Press, 1998); and Walker, 2001.
28. Walker, 4. Walker's rhetoric is hyperbolic. For a more nuanced treatment of Afrocentrism, see Wilson J. Moses, *Afrotopia.* Moses rejects, proleptically, Walker's claim that Afrocentrism and Eurocentrism are equivalent. Walker focuses single-mindedly on the "totalitarian" and quietist dangers that Afrocentrism poses to the political agency and independent judgment of black people. Moses' focus is dual. In addition to the dangers that Walker describes, he is also concerned by the dangers of dismissive critique, exemplified by Lefkowitz's *Not Out of Africa* that wittingly or not reproduces racialized, Eurocentric narratives. Her view excludes the Glenn Lourys of the world who regard themselves as descendants of the Greeks. According to Moses: "Lefkowitz's book has served only to obscure definitions further; it is ahistorical, presentist, synchronic, and absolutely devoid of any of the methods of serious cultural or intellectual history. Like most polemicists, its author finds methodology inconvenient and precise definitions intolerable. Thus she is hardly different from the various demagogues and polemicists who have gathered on the other side of the Afrocentrism debate. Much silliness and ill will has been spewed forth by the likes of Mary Lefkowitz and the black nationalist polemicist Maulana Karenga, who represent two sides of the same hateful coin. As a result, it has become almost impossible for most persons to engage in analytical, dispassionate discussion of the various expressions of those movements—both intellectual and emotional—that constitute what we today refer to as 'Afrocentrism.'" If this were not bad enough: "Lefkowitz frequently makes statements that would be challenged by any shrewd undergraduate. For example, speaking of George James, she asserts that 'many otherwise well-educated people believe that what he claims is true.' Who are these 'otherwise well-educated people' to whom she refers? She does not identify them nor does she provide any data as to their numbers." "She has thoughtlessly muddled ideas derived from nineteenth-century ethnography, popular mythology of the 1920s, and cult literature of the 1980s. She makes the generalization that all of these ideas constitute Afrocentrism, and then implies that this 'Afrocentrism' is being widely taught in college classrooms. Has it ever occurred to her that proponents of African American studies are divided into numerous categories, influenced by disciplinary affiliations, ideological backgrounds, and political affiliations? Conservative, feminist, deconstructionist, and Marxist scholars in

black studies programs and departments have long and vocally opposed romantic and sentimental Afrochauvinism—indeed, far longer than she has" (Moses, 6, 9–10, 226).

29. Walker, 41.
30. Walker, 59.
31. Walker, 91.
32. Walker, 92.
33. Again, I refer the reader to Moses' *Afrotopia*, which shows quite clearly that Afrocentrism cannot be reduced to Egyptocentrism and anti-Semitism. Such reductions, among other things, ignore the prominent role of "white Afrocentrist," especially Jewish scholars, such as Franz Boas and Melville Herskovits. These reductions, furthermore, exoticize Afrocentrism by implying that the "practice of creating a monumental past for one's race or nationality" is unique to African contributionist and vindicationist history. As Moses observes, Afrocentrism, which predates the word, owes more to enlightenment Christianity, biblical typology, "eighteenth-century progressivism, and black resistance to white supremacy" than to Egyptology. Finally, Afrocentrism has a folksy, harmless, inoffensive face and a totalitarian face. In his desire to fight the latter, Walker conflates it with the former. In his effort to fight dangers on two fronts, Moses is determined to maintain the distinctiveness of two forms of Afrocentrism in a multileveled, comprehensive critique (Moses, 10–12, 15).
34. Though I use the term, I am skeptical of the notion of memes.
35. Countee Cullen, *The Black Christ and Other Poems* (New York: Harper and Brothers, 1929), 83.
36. This is a paraphrasing of Elaine Marks' characterization of Jacques Derrida and Hélène Cixous' dissent from the "death of God" language of Nietzsche by accenting undecidability regarding the concept of god. See Lawrence D. Kirtzman, ed., *The Columbia History of Twentieth Century French Thought* (New York: Columbia University Press, 2006), 133.
37. Afro-*Eccentricity* is a species of what John Dewey called "natural piety."

3 Art and the Ancestor Narrative

1. J. Lorand Matory, *Black Atlantic Religion: Tradition, Transnationalism, and Matriarchy in the Afro-Brazilian Candomblé* (Princeton, NJ: Princeton University Press, 2005), 291.
2. Paule Marshall, *Praisesong for the Widow* (New York: Penguin Books USA, 1983), 106.
3. Marshall, 107.
4. Marshall, 23, 29, 43.
5. Marshall, 111.
6. E. Franklin Frazier, *Black Bourgeoisie: The Rise of a New Middle Class* (Glencoe, IL: The Free Press, 1957), 60, 71–72, 75, 78.
7. Franklin, 85.
8. Marshall, 115.

9. Marshall, 131–32.
10. Frazier, 128–29.
11. Marshall, 136.
12. Daniel Bell, *The Cultural Contradictions of Capitalism* (New York: Basic Books, 1996), 293.
13. Marshall, 139. For a different view see Dorothy Hamer Denniston, *The Fiction of Paule Marshall: Reconstructions of History, Culture, and Gender* (Knoxville: University of Tennessee Press, 1995), 127.
14. Frazier, 237–38.
15. Marshall, 49–52.
16. Marshall, 48–49.
17. Max Weber, *The Protestant Ethic and the Spirit of Capitalism* (trans. Talcott Parsons (Mineola, NY: Dover Publications, 2003), 166
18. Weber, 163.
19. Marshall, 135.
20. Weber, 180–81.
21. Weber, 181-82.
22. Weber, 182.
23. Marshall, 139.
24. See http://www.youtube.com/watch?v=Xpmr8Shy_UA.
25. Marshall, 209.
26. Gay Wilentz regards Avey's bath as an example of a healing ritual—curing socially constructed diseases—that women characters often perform in novels written by women. See Gay Wilentz, *Healing Narratives: Women Writers Curing Cultural Dis-ease* (New Brunswick, NJ: Rutgers University Press, 2000), 3, 64.
27. Mircea Eliade, *The Sacred and the Profane: The Nature of Religion* (New York: Harcourt Brace, 1959), 130.
28. Eliade, 130–32, 135–37, 145–46, 156–57.
29. Mechal Sobel, *Trabelin' On: The Slave Journey to an Afro-Baptist Faith* (Westport, CT: Greenwood Press, 1979), 214.
30. John Mbiti contends that we should refrain from using the terms "ancestors" and "ancestral spirits" because these terms "imply only those spirits who were once the ancestors of the living." He complains that these terms exclude those who did not have offspring. See John S. Mbiti, *African Religions and Philosophy* (New York: Praeger Publishers, 1969), 85. I think that Mbiti is too pernickety on this point.
31. Albert Raboteau, *Slave Religion: The "Invisible Institution" in the Antebellum South* (New York: Oxford University Press, 1978), 8–15.
32. Marshall, 66–70, 72, 75–76.
33. Marshall, 230.
34. Henry Louis Gates, *The Signifying Monkey: A Theory of African-American Literary Criticism* (New York: Oxford University Press, 1989), 6.
35. Marshall, 179, 232, 233, 243.
36. Lewis Hyde, *Trickster Makes This World: Mischief, Myth, and Art* (New York: Farrar, Strauss, and Giroux, 1998), 365. Joseph Murphy identifies

five New World Yoruba Traditions: Candomble (Brazil), Santeria (Cuba), Shango (Trinidad), Vodun (Haiti), and conjure (USA).

37. Robert Farris Thompson, *Flash of the Spirit: African and Afro-American Philosophy* (New York: Vintage Books, 1984), 33, 52, 57, 61, 72, 80, 84.
38. Hyde, 118.
39. Marshall, 127.
40. Joseph Murphy, *Santeria: African Spirits in America* (Boston: Beacon Press, 1993), 131.
41. Marshall, 165.
42. Marshall, 166.
43. Sobel, 228.
44. Aunt Cuney is the great aunt of Avey's father and thus Avey's great great aunt. Marshall sometimes refers to her simply as Avey's great aunt. To facilitate ease of reading, I will only use "great great" where necessary for clarity, to distinguish Cuney's respective relations with father and daughter.
45. Raboteau, 245.
46. See Raboteau, 70.
47. Raboteau, 70. Raboteau takes this quote from John A. Lomax and Alan Lomax, *Folk Song USA* (New York: Duell, Sloan, and Pearce, 1947), 335.
48. Sterling Stuckey, *Slave Culture: Nationalist Theory and the Foundation of Black America* (New York: Oxford University Press, 1987), 12. Referring to the Pinkster Festival in eighteenth-century New York, Stuckey remarks: "So powerful are the bonds that link circularity to Kongo beliefs concerning the sun's movement, which is counterclockwise for them, and the states of life from birth to death that circularity in almost any form might serve to remind a significant number of slaves of religious values that were proper to them." Sterling Stuckey, *Going Through the Storm: The Influence of African American Art in History* (New York: Oxford University Press, 1994), 54.
49. Marshall, 40. See Lean'tin Bracks, *Writings of Black Women in the Diaspora* (New York: Garland Publishing, 1998), 110–11.
50. Marshall, 42.
51. Marshall, 41–45.
52. Joyce Pettis, *Toward Wholeness in Paule Marshall's Fiction* (Charlottesville: University Press of Virginia, 1995), 121.
53. Robert Hayden, *Collected Poems,* ed. Frederick Glaysher (New York: Liveright Publishing Corporation, 1985), 59.
54. Marshall, 9.
55. Marshall, 148.
56. Randall Jarrell, *Selected Poems: Including the Woman at the Washington Zoo* (New York: Atheneum, 1980), 2.
57. Milo Rigaud, *Secrets of Voodoo,* trans. Robert B. Cross (San Francisco: City Lights Books, 1969), 166.
58. Susan Sontag, *Against Interpretation and Other Essays* (New York: Farrar, Strauss, and Giroux, 1966), 125. Quoted in Marshall, 212.
59. Marshall, 238.
60. Marshall, 240.
61. Marshall, 244–45.

62. Marshall, 248–49. Alma Jean Billingslea-Brown, in *Crossing Borders through Folklore: African American Women's Fiction and Art* (Columbia: University of Missouri Press, 1999), refers to the way Marshall creates a confraternity through language (96–97). This may be true. But if we look at the story itself, "a wide 'confraternity'" is engendered not so much through language as through embodied ceremonies such as the Big Dance.
63. Indeed, Avatara was a reincarnation. According to John Mbiti, "Belief in reincarnation is reported among many African societies." Features of the living-dead (ancestors) are reborn in some descendents. "Some societies mark this belief through naming their children after the particular living-dead who is thought to be 'reborn' in them." See Mbiti, 164. Peter Paris shares Mbiti's basic view but raises an important question—why are female ancestors neglected in the scholarly literature? See Peter Paris, *The Spirituality of African Peoples* (Minneapolis: Fortress Press, 1995), 56. The obvious answer is male dominance and patriarchal priorities. In contrast to the scholarly literature that Paris cites, the artistry of *Praisesong for the Widow* highlights this gendered deficiency through the character of Aunt Cuney.
64. See Joanne Morra and Marquard Smith, eds., *Visual Culture: Critical Concepts in Media and Culture Studies* (New York: Routledge, 2006), 204; Elizabeth Brown-Guillory, ed., *Middle Passages and the Healing Place of History: Migration and Identity in Black Women's Literature* (Columbus: Ohio State University Press, 2006), 5; Gilbert H. Muller, *New Strangers in Paradise: The Immigrant Experience and Contemporary American Fiction* (Lexington: University of Kentucky Press, 1999), 153; and Dorothy Hamer Denniston, *The Fiction of Paule Marshall*, xii.
65. Sontag, 125.
66. For an example, see Dorothy Hamer Denniston, 134.
67. Eugenia C. DeLamotte, *Places of Silence, Journeys of Freedom: The Fiction of Paule Marshall* (Philadelphia: University of Pennsylvania Press, 1998), 82.
68. DeLamotte, 86.
69. DeLamotte, 89.
70. Molefi Kete Asante, *Afrocentricity* (Trenton, NJ: Africa World Press, 1988), 77.

4 The Archaeologist

1. Charles H. Long, *Significations: Signs, Symbols, and Images in the Interpretation of Religion* (Aurora, CO: The Davies Group Publishers, 1999), 188; published originally in *History of Religions* 11, no. 1 (August 1971): 54–66.
2. Long, 189. The work of Michael Gomez among others has complicated if not undermined this contention. See Michael A. Gomez, *Exchanging Our Country Marks: The Transformation of African Identities in the Colonial*

and Antebellum South (Chapel Hill: University of North Carolina Press, 1998).

3. Long, 190.
4. Long, 190–91.
5. Long, 211.
6. Long, 191.
7. See Gomez (1998) for a highly informative account of the persistence of African ethnicities and nationalities among black people in the United States. Gomez builds on the earlier work of Stuckey (1987), Thompson (1983), and Herskovits (1941).
8. Long, 191.
9. Long, 191.
10. In a nuanced account, Genovese (1976, 6) undermines this standard Marxist argument that Christianity made slaves docile. However, his claim that the religious world of Africans began to "disintegrate as a coherent system of belief" the moment Africans arrived in America (1976, 184) is disputed by Butler (1992), Frey and Wood (1998), and Gomez (1998). As Gomez argues, the transition from African religions to Christianity was a two-way process; Africans converted to Christianity and converted Christianity according to their African perspectives. As late as 1830 this process of mutual transformation touched only a minority of Africans (Genovese 1976, 256). These arguments decrease the significance of Christianity among slaves and thus the urgency around the question of whether Christianity promoted accommodation or resistance, a perennial question in the historiography of slavery.
11. Long, 192.
12. Long, 193.
13. As Derrida suggests in his essay "Faith and Knowledge: The Two Sources of 'Religion' at the Limits of Reason," we know that we believe and believe that we know. See Derrida (2002), 76.
14. Jennifer I. M. Reid, ed., *Religion and Global Culture: New Terrain in the Study of Religion and the Work of Charles H. Long* (Lanham, MD: Lexington Books, 2003), 17.
15. Charles H. Long, "Mircea Eliade and the Imagination of Matter." http://www.jcrt.org/archives/01.2/long.shtml (Last accessed 12/13/10).
16. This claim is highly controversial and has been subjected to trenchant critique. See McCutcheon (2003).
17. Long, 193.
18. Long, 193–97.
19. Long, 153.
20. Long, 149.
21. Long, 152.
22. Long, 156. See David E. Stannard, *American Holocaust: The Conquest of the New World* (New York: Oxford University Press, 1993).
23. Long, 157.
24. Long, 156.

25. Long, 162. See Jon Butler, *Awash in a Sea of Faith: Christianizing the American People* (Cambridge, MA: Harvard University Press, 1992).
26. Long, 163.
27. Long, 163.
28. Long, 166.
29. Long, 80.
30. Cornel West, *Prophesy Deliverance! An Afro-American Revolutionary Christianity* (Louisville, KY: Westminster John Know1982), 60-61. Also see Nell Irvin Painter, *History of White People* (New York: W. W. Norton, 2010) for an extensive analysis of the aesthetics and science of race thinking.
31. Long, 4.
32. Long, 4.
33. Long, 4.
34. Long, 5. See Winthrop Jordan, *White over Black: American Attitudes toward the Negro, 1550–1812* (Chapel Hill: University of North Carolina Press, 1995); John Solomos, ed., *Theories of Race and Racism* (New York: Routledge, 2000).
35. For a powerful and controversial critique of this kind of methodology, see Daryl Michael Scott, *Contempt and Pity: Social Policy and the Image of the Damaged Black Psyche, 1880-1996* (Chapel Hill: University of North Carolina Press, 1997).
36. Long, 8–9.
37. Malcolm Diamond, *Contemporary Philosophy and Religious Thought* (New York: McGraw-Hill, 1974), 82.
38. See Marianna Torgovnick, *Gone Primitive: Savage Intellects, Modern Lives* (University of Chicago Press, 1991).
39. Here I quote Long, who is quoting Norbert Elias, *The Civilizing Process: The Development of Manners* (New York: Urizen Books, 1977). Long cites this passage on page 94 of *Significations*.
40. Long, 100.
41. See George Steiner, *Grammars of Creation* (New Haven: Yale University Press, 2001).
42. Steiner, 16, 38, 184, 187.
43. See Alfred North Whitehead, "Mathematics in the History of Thought," at http://www-history.mcs.st-and.ac.uk/history/Extras/Whitehead_maths_thought.html.
44. Edward W. Said, *Beginnings: Intention and Method* (New York: Columbia University Press, 1975), 13.
45. Said, 43, 50, 74.
46. Said, 76–78.
47. Long wrote before the use of gender-inclusive language became common.
48. Long, 18–19.
49. Steiner, 11–12.
50. Steiner, 39.
51. Long, 18.
52. Long, 29.

53. Steiner, 16.
54. James A. Noel, *Black Religion and the Imagination of Matter in the Atlantic World* (New York: Palgrave Macmillan, 2009), ix.
55. Noel, ix–x.
56. Noel, x.
57. Noel, 2.
58. Noel, 2–3.
59. Noel, 5, 7–8, 13–14. I am not sure that "eschatological" with its Christian connotation is the right term for this future orientation.
60. Charles H. Long, "Indigenous Peoples, Materialities, and Religion: Outline for a New Orientation to Religious Meaning," in *Religion and Global Culture: New Terrain in the Study of Religion and the Work of Charles H. Long*, ed. Jennifer I. M. Reid (New York: Lexington Books, 2003), 177. Quoted in Noel, 15.
61. Noel, 15.
62. "Abstract from the Preface of *A Contribution to the Critique of Political Economy*." http://www.marxists.org/archive/marx/works/1859/critique-pol-economy/preface-abs.htm.
63. Noel, 49–50.
64. See Oliver Cromwell Cox, *Class, Caste, and Race* (Garden City, NY: Doubleday & Company, 1948).
65. Noel, 58.
66. Noel (pages 63–64) supports his claim by citing Elaine Scarry's analysis of torture in *The Body in Pain: The Making and Unmaking of the World* (Oxford: Oxford University Press, 1985).
67. Noel, 64.
68. On pages 62–63, Noel quotes extensively from Olaudah Equiano, *The Interesting Narrative of the Life of Olaudah Equiano, or Gustavus Vassa The African. Written by Himself.* (New York: Dover, 1999).
69. Gillian Rose, *Mourning Becomes the Law: Philosophy and Representation* (Cambridge: Cambridge University Press, 1996), 41, 43.
70. Noel, 60.
71. J. S. McGrath, *Heidegger: A (Very) Critical Introduction* (Grand Rapids, MI: William B. Erdmans, 2008), 62–63, 68–69.
72. Noel, 96.
73. Robert Gooding-Williams, *"Look, a Negro!": Philosophical Essays on Race, Culture and Politics* (New York: Routledge, 2006), 95.
74. Carter wrongly claims that Long's notions of oppugnancy and opacity violate Charles Sanders Peirce's claim that consciousness is mediated by otherness. See J. Kameron Carter, *Race: A Theological Account* (New York: Oxford University Press, 2008), 225.
75. Carter, 223.
76. Long, 195.
77. Victor Anderson, *Beyond Ontological Blackness: An Essay on African American Religious and Cultural Criticism* (New York: Continuum, 1995), 13.

78. Long, 208.
79. Long, 209–10.
80. See Karl Barth, "The Revelation of God as the Abolition of Religion," in *Church Dogmatics* Vol. 1, Part 2 (New York: T&T Clark Ltd., 1956).
81. Carter, 224.
82. Carter, 226.

5 The Renegade

1. Jones wrote in the early 1970s, when it was still politically fashionable to speak unselfconsciously and unproblematically in nationalistic and ethnocentric terms.
2. William R. Jones, *Is God a White Racist? A Preamble to Black Theology* (Boston: Beacon Press, 1974 rpt.1998), xvii.
3. Jones, xxvii, 68, 71. This point cannot be overemphasized. Jones provides a negative critique of black theology from the perspective not of a hostile critic but of one who wishes to make the enterprise more effective.
4. Jones, 3–4, 6–8, 10.
5. Jones, 11–14.
6. Jones, 18.
7. Jones, 116–18.
8. Jones, 19.
9. Jones, 18–19, 21–22.
10. Jones, 22.
11. Jones, 40, 43–44.
12. Jones, 44–45.
13. There are different kinds of evidence. Here the reference is to historical evidence.
14. Jones, 47–51.
15. Kenneth Surin, *Theology and the Problem of Evil* (New York: Basil Blackwell, 1986), 27. For a critique of Surin's account of theodicy, see Michael J. Quirk's review in *Theology Today* at http://theologytoday.ptsem.edu/oct1987/v44-3-bookreview13.htm. Surin is a former, highly regarded theologian. He now writes as a Marxist theorist. See Kenneth Surin, *Freedom Not Yet: Liberation and the Next World Order* (Durham, NC: Duke University Press, 2009).
16. Here I follow Althusser's use of this term. See Mikko Lahtinen, *Politics and Philosophy: Niccolò Machiavelli and Louis Althusser's Aleatory Materialism*, trans. Gareth Griffiths and Kristina Kohli (Leiden, The Netherlands: Brill, 2009), 34.
17. Surin, 50.
18. Surin, 67.
19. This is my language, not Surin's.
20. Surin, 102–3.
21. Surin, 103.
22. Jones, 8.

23. Surin, 103.
24. Surin, 104.
25. Even though he does not use the language of the multievidentiality of suffering and, no doubt, would object to Jones' line of argument, Quirk's (1987) critique of Surin appears to be motivated precisely by the kind of undecidability that Jones accents.
26. Jones, 76.
27. Jones, 64–65, 67.
28. Jones, 61.
29. Antti Kauppinen, "Reason, Recognition, and Internal Critique," Inquiry, 45 (2002), 482.
30. Kauppinen, 480-81, 85.
31. Kauppinen, 484.
32. Kauppinen, 484.
33. Kauppinen, 484-85.
34. See Edward Said, "Michael Walzer's 'Exodus and Revolution': A Canaanite Reading," *Grand Street* 5, no. 2 (1986): 86–106. I address this controversy and its relevance for black theology in chapter 7.
35. Jones, 90.
36. Jones, 131.
37. Jones, 103.
38. This is a reprise of my account in *Black Religion* (Hart, 2008), 43. For the original account, see Alex Haley, *The Autobiography of Malcolm X* (New York: Ballantine Books, 1992), 190–92.
39. James H. Cone, *God of the Oppressed* (New York: The Seabury Press, 1975), 267–68 n. 23.
40. Cone, 192.
41. Cone, 268 n. 23.
42. Cone, 176.
43. See Pinn's discussion of Cone's response to Jones' critique (93–94).
44. Jones, 119.
45. James Cone, *Black Theology and Black Power* (New York: The Seabury Press, 1969), 139–40. This passage is quoted in Anthony Pinn, ed., *By These Hands: A Documentary History of African Americanism* (New York: New York University Press, 2001), 50. Pinn notes the compatibility between Cone's position, as expressed in this passage, and black humanism. In any event, it is quite different from the conventional Jesus Christ that we get in *God of the Oppressed*. I contend that this resort to convention has everything to do with the power of Jones' critique.
46. Cone, 38.
47. Cone, 110.
48. My view is largely compatible with Anthony Pinn's claim that Cone's view of suffering is essentially unchanged from his earlier texts. See Pinn, 87.
49. Cone, 27.
50. Cone, 58.
51. Major Jones, *Black Awareness: A Theology of Hope* (New York: Abington Press, 1971), 123–28.

52. Major Jones, *The Color of God: The Concept of God in Afro-American Thought* (Macon, GA: Mercer University Press, 1987), 72–73.
53. Major Jones, *The Color of God*, 73.
54. William R. Jones, 156.
55. J. Deotis Roberts, *Black Theology Today: Liberation and Contextualization* (New York and Toronto: The Edwin Mellen Press, 1983), 37.
56. Roberts, 50.
57. Roberts, 49.
58. Roberts, 50.
59. Normative blackness may be conceived as the critical object of Afro-*Eccentricity*. It is similar to what Victor Anderson means by "ontological blackness."
60. Jones, 185.
61. Jones, 186.
62. Jones, 186.
63. Jones, 195.
64. Anthony Pinn, *Why, Lord? Suffering and Evil in Black Theology* (New York: Continuum, 1995), 96–100.
65. Pinn remarks: "It turns out, then, that even the two thinkers—Jones and Williams—who question traditional theological assumptions in actuality maintain them: the activity and responsibilities of God are given new packaging" (111). While her Christology is certainly innovative in relation to black theology, the rest of Williams' theology is quite traditional. But my primary point is the following: Pinn illegitimately lumps together the theist Delores Williams and the humanist Jones. Pinn thus positions himself as more radical in his secular humanism than Jones is. I do not accept this implicit self-appraisal. Pinn's claim ignores the argumentative role of humanocentric theism in Jones' analysis. Pinn leads the reader to believe that Jones endorses humanocentric theism as his preferred position. He does not. As I remarked in the body of the text, it is an olive branch to theists. On the other hand, Pinn is certainly right that Jones' act of generosity opens him up to precisely the critique that Pinn makes.
66. Terrance W. Klein, *How Things Are in the World: Metaphysics and Theology in Wittgenstein and Rahner* (Milwaukee, WI: Marquette University Press, 2000), 49, 58.
67. Ludwig Wittgenstein, *Philosophical Investigations*, trans. G. E. M. Anscrombe (New York: Macmillan, 1989), 6e.
68. Kai Nielsen, "Wittgensteinian Fideism," *Philosophy* 42 (1967): 191–209.
69. James H. Evans, *We Have Been Believers: An African American Systematic Theology* (Minneapolis: Fortress Press, 1992), 65. Evan claims incorrectly that Jones views "evil and suffering as synonymous" (65). This reading is so obviously erroneous that one is shocked that Evans would make it. In fact, this is the same mistake that Jackson (2009) makes regarding Islam. Contrary to Evans' claim, Jones spends a lot of time distinguishing negative suffering from positive suffering—suffering that is redemptive or deserved. He does not regard these forms of suffering as evil. (However, he does discuss the empirical

difficulty in distinguishing just from unjust and pedagogical from nonpedagogical suffering.) If such misreadings were not enough to sustain his critique of Jones, Evans pulls the racial authenticity card: we can ignore the force of Jones' argument, he claims, because he is not authentically black. Though raised in the "traditional black church," he is not "ensconced in the African American religious experience" (65)—in short, he is Afro-*Eccentric*.

70. Fergus Kerr, *Theology after Wittgenstein* (New York: Basil Blackwell, 1986), 147–48.
71. I express some reservations about this claim in chapter 6.
72. I recognize the politics and sensitivities regarding the use of this term.
73. Sherman A. Jackson, *Islam and the Problem of Black Suffering* (New York: Oxford University Press, 2009), 91–92.
74. Jackson, 148–49.
75. Jackson, 65–66.
76. Jackson, 65.
77. Jackson, 68–69.
78. Jones, 15.
79. Jackson, 67–68.
80. Jackson, 92.
81. Jones, 30.
82. This is a revision of my argument in the penultimate draft where sloppily I mischaracterized Jackson's claim.
83. Jones, 213.
84. Jackson, 95.
85. Jackson, 151–52.
86. Jackson, 155.
87. Jackson, 155–56.
88. Jones, 23.
89. Jones, xiii, xv–xvi, xxv–xxviii.
90. Jackson, 125.
91. Jackson, 93.
92. Jackson, 94.
93. Jackson, 98.
94. Jackson, 71.
95. Jackson, 69–70.
96. Elijah Muhammad, *Message to the Blackman in America* (Chicago: Muhammad Mosque of Islam No. 2, 1965), 51.
97. Mattias Gardell, In *the Name of Elijah Muhammad: Louis Farrakhan and the Nation of Islam* (Durham, NC: Duke University Press, 1996), 149.

6 The Prophet

1. My first published essay was an attempt to see where West's thinking ended and mine began. See William Hart, "Cornel West: Between Rorty's Rock and Hauerwas' Hard Place," *American Journal of Theology and Philosophy* 19, no. 2 (1998): 151–72.

2. Friedrich Nietzsche, *Thus Spoke Zarathustra*, trans. R. J. Hollingdale (London: Harmondsworth Penguin, 1969), 103.
3. Cornel West, *Prophesy Deliverance! An Afro-American Revolutionary Christianity* (Philadelphia: Westminster Press, 1982), 131.
4. West, 111–16.
5. West, 117.
6. West, 85.
7. Cf. George Yancy, Ed. *Cornel West: A Critical Reader* (Malden, MA: Blackwell, 2001), In his essay, "Religion and the Mirror of God: Historicism, Truth, and Religious Pluralism," Yancy describes West as a Kierkegaardian-Wittgensteinian crypto-fideist (135).
8. Yancy makes a similar argument when he queries the relationship between West's historicist philosophy of religion and his ontological commitments to a Christian metanarrative. There is a contradiction here that needs resolution. Yancy quotes Mason Olds, who describes perspectives such as the one attributed to West as a case of "bad faith," since the subject pretends that god is an ontic reality when he knows that god is merely a character within a language-game. Yancy,132.
9. See Cornel West, *The Cornel West Reader* (New York: Basic *Civitas* Books, 1999), xv. In an interview with George Yancy, there is the following exchange:

   Yancy: And how did reading Kierkegaard at such an early age impact your later philosophical development?

   West: I think that it was decisive. It gave me a profoundly Kierkegaardian sensibility that required then that philosophizing be linked to existentially concrete situations, wrestling with decision, commitment, actualized possibility and realized potential.... How do you really struggle against the suffering in a loving way, to leave a legacy in which people would be able to accent their own loving possibility in the midst of so much evil? So in that sense I think that the black church and its profound stress on the concrete and the particular—wrestling with limit situations, with death, dread, despair, disappointment, disease, and so on—has been influential on my Kierkegaardian outlook (page 20).
10. West, *Prophesy Deliverance!*, 95.
11. West, 95–96.
12. Despite West's claim that during "low moments" he entertains the possibility that his Christian faith may be false, Yancy questions whether West's faith claims regarding god and human destiny are falsifiable. This dovetails with his claim that West is a fideist. Yancy, 133.
13. Rosemary Cowan, in *Cornel West and the Politics of Redemption* (Cambridge, UK: Polity Press, 2003, 71–78) provides a good account of the triangular relationship between Rauschenbusch, Niebuhr, and King in West's prophetic Christian thought.
14. West, 99.
15. Though he does not specifically address this imbalance, Victor Anderson's "Is Cornel West Also among the Theologians? The Shadow of the Divine in

the Religious Thought of Cornel West" (Yancy, 2001) provides an account that helps us understand how that imbalance might arise.

16. Mark David Wood, *Cornel West and the Politics of Prophetic Pragmatism* (Champaign, IL: University of Illinois, 2000).
17. For a critique of West's historicist construction of Marx, see John P. Pittman, "Radical Historicism, Antiphilosophy, and Marxism" in Yancy (2001).
18. Wood, 34-5.
19. Wood, 34.
20. Wood, 34.
21. Wood, 38.
22. Readers might wish to compare Wood, who criticizes West, one might say, from his "right-wing" Marxist flank, with Clarence Sholé Johnson, who in *Cornel West and Philosophy* (New York: Routledge, 2003) criticizes West from his liberal, pro-capitalist flank. Contra West, Johnson claims that the well-being of blacks is attainable within a liberal capitalist regime.
23. A version of this account appears in Hart (2008, 97–101). For a thorough historical account of this myth, see David M. Goldenberg, *The Curse of Ham: Race and Slavery in Early Judaism, Christianity, and Islam* (Princeton, NJ: Princeton University Press, 2005).
24. William R. Jones, *Is God a White Racist? A Preamble to Black Theology* (Boston: Beacon Press, 1973), 4.
25. For a charitable account of King as a theologian, see Noel Erskine, *King among the Theologians* (Cleveland, OH: The Pilgrim Press, 1994).
26. See Cone's warm and generous assessment of West "Let Suffering Speak: The Vocation of a Black Intellectual" in Yancy (2001).
27. West, 106.
28. For a thorough account of Kierkegaard's anthropology, see Kresten Nordentoft, *Kierkegaard's Psychology* (Pittsburgh: Duquesne University Press, 1972).
29. West's views of existential anxiety are influenced by Ernest Becker's (1973) quasi-Kierkegaardian existential anthropology.
30. West, 105.
31. West, 121–22.
32. For an insightful notion of "minimal theology," see Hent de Vries, *Minimal Theologies: Critiques of Secular Reason in Adorno and Levinas,* trans. Geoffrey Hale (Baltimore: Johns Hopkins University Press, 2005).
33. I say this despite what is, perhaps, a more persuasive version of the argument in "Religion and the Left," which is included in the volume *Prophetic Fragment* (Grand Rapids, MI: Eerdmans, 1998) and was originally published in *Monthly Review,* July-August 1984.
34. George S. Hendry, "Review": *Dogmatics* by Hermann Diem, *Theology Today* 18, no. 2 (July 1961). Available at http://theologytoday.ptsem.edu/jul1961/v18-2-bookreview17.htm.
35. West, 136.
36. West, 136–37.
37. West, 137.
38. West, 137.

39. West, 137.
40. Lewis Gordon questions the coherence of Marxist politics in the absence of a viable communist party. See Lewis Gordon, "The Unacknowledged Fourth Tradition: Nihilism Decadence, and the Black Intellectual Tradition in the Existential Pragmatic Thought of Cornel West," (Yancy, 47).
41. Cornel West, *Prophetic Fragments* (Trenton, NJ: Africa World Press, 1990), 5–6.
42. Cornel West, *Democracy Matters: Winning the Fight Against Imperialism* (New York: Penguin, 2004), 192.
43. Anderson, 145-46.
44. Anderson, 146.
45. Anderson, 147–51. There is a conflict here between Anderson's account of West as a Deweyan theological liberal and Yancy's claim that he is a Kierkegaardian-Wittgensteinian fideist. The conflict, however, may be more apparent than real when we recall West's vacillation between minimalist and maximalist views of transcendence, which are compatible, respectively, with his Deweyan theological liberalism and his Kierkegaardian-Wittgensteinian fideism.
46. West, *Prophesy Deliverance!,* 29.
47. West, 31.
48. West, 44.
49. West, 48–49.
50. West, 53–55.
51. West, 57–59, 65.
52. West, 70, 77.
53. West, 71, 80.
54. West, 71, 85.
55. West, 70,
56. Gordon, 46–47.
57. Gordon, 49.
58. See Hortense J. Spillers—"*The Crisis of the Negro Intellectual:* A Postdate," in *Black, White, and in Color: Essays on American Literature and Culture* (Chicago: University of Chicago Press, 2003)—where she makes a similar point (442).
59. Gordon contends that West posits an impossible, if not perverse, set of criteria for black intellectuals, namely, validation by white institutions in a context where there are no strong black institutions that can do the work of validation. West rejects Gordon's characterization of his views in Yancy, 349–50.
60. Theodor Wiesengrund Adorno, *The Jargon of Authenticity*, trans. Knut Tarnowsky and Frederic Will (Evanston, IL: Northwestern University Press, 1973), 21–22.
61. I am quite aware of the distinction between Kierkegaard's named and pseudonymous authorship. It does not affect the claims and attributions with respect to West that I wish to make.
62. Guy B. Hammond, "Tillich, Adorno, and the Debate about Existentialism," *Laval théologique etphilosophique* 47, no. 3 (1991): 352.

63. For an analysis along these lines, see Mark David Wood, *Cornel West and the Politics of Prophetic Pragmatism* (Urbana: University of Illinois Press, 2000).
64. Jones, xvii.

7 The Conjuror

1. Theophus Smith, *Conjuring Culture: Biblical Formations of Black America* (New York: Oxford University Press, 1994), ix.
2. Smith, 4. Smith rejects the claim that magic (conjure) is merely irrationality or superstition; it is a proto- or pre-scientific attempt to cope with the world through the use of various signs and ritualized forms of speech and action. Like most forms of magic, conjuring is mimetic. It attempts to transform reality by imitating (performing) what it wants to occur (4–6).
3. Smith, 4, 6.
4. Smith, 6.
5. Smith, 7.
6. Smith, 55.
7. Smith, 6–7, 18.
8. Smith, 33.
9. Smith, 49.
10. Smith, 35.
11. Smith, 7.
12. Smith, 55, 63–64, 69.
13. Smith, 55.
14. See Nell Irvin Painter, *Exodusters: Black Migration to Kansas after Reconstruction* (New York: W. W. Norton, 1992).
15. Aaron Wildavsky, *The Nursing Father: Moses as a Political Leader* (Tuscaloosa: The University of Alabama Press, 1984), 192–95.
16. Wayne G. Boulton and Thomas D. Kennedy, *From Christ to the World: Introductory Reading in Christian Ethics* (Grand Rapids, MI: W. B. Eerdmans, 1994), 416. For an interesting interpretation of *Moses in Red*, see Wright (2003).
17. Wildavsky, 212.
18. Smith, 58.
19. Smith, 59. Smith quotes *David Walker's Appeal (1829)*, ed. Charles M. Wiltse (New York: Hill & Wang, 1965), xiv.
20. Smith, 60.
21. Smith, 58–61. Smith's remarks regarding a "stolen legacy" and the "destruction of black civilization" are obvious references to a couple of Afrocentric texts of dubious quality, namely, George G. M. James' *Stolen Legacy* (1976) and Chancellor Williams' *The Destruction of Black Civilization: Great Issues of a Race from 4500 B.C. to 2000 A.D.* (1974).
22. Delores S. Williams, *Sisters in the Wilderness: The Challenge of Womanist God-Talk* (New York: Orbis Books, Maryknoll, 1993), 150.

23. D. Williams, 150–51. For responses to Williams' claims, see Demetrius K. Williams, *An End to This Strife: The Politics of Gender in African American Churches* (Minneapolis: Augsburg Fortress, 2004), 141–44; Laurel Dykstra, *Set Them Free: The Other Side of Exodus* (New York: Orbis Books, Maryknoll, 2002), 44–46, 138–39.
24. D. Williams, 159–61.
25. I am citing the version of Warrior's essay that appears in R. S. Sugirtharajah, ed., *Voices from the Margins: Interpreting the Bible in the Third World* (Minneapolis: Orbis Books, Maryknoll, 1991).
26. Robert Allen Warrior, "A Native American Perspective: Canaanites, Cowboys, and Indians," in *Voices from the Margins: Interpreting the Bible in the Third World*, ed. R. S. Sugirtharajah (Minneapolis: Orbis Books, Maryknoll, 1991), 288.
27. Warrior, 289.
28. Warrior, 293.
29. Warrior, 292–93.
30. Warrior, 294.
31. Edward Said and Michael Walzer, "An Exchange: Michael Walzer and Edward Said," *Grand Street* 5, no. 4 (1986): 246-59.
32. William D. Hart, *Edward Said and the Religious Effects of Culture* (Cambridge: Cambridge University Press, 2000), 1.
33. Michael Walzer, *Exodus and Revolution* (New York: Basic Books, 1985), 149.
34. Walzer, 23.
35. Hart, 2000, 3.
36. Hart, (2000), 3.
37. Edward Said, "Michael Walzer's 'Exodus and Revolution': A Canaanite Reading," *Grand Street* 5, no. 2 (1985-6), 87.
38. Said, 92.
39. See Carol Meyers, *Exodus* (Cambridge: Cambridge University Press, 2005), 6–7.
40. Smith, 81.
41. Smith, 82, 95–100.
42. I am using Turner's concept somewhat against the grain of his usage. For a detailed account of *communitas,* see Victor Turner, *The Ritual Process: Structure and Anti-Structure* (New York: Aldine De Gruyter, 1969).
43. Smith, 100.
44. See Michele Wallace, *Dark Designs and Visual Culture* (Durham, NC: Duke University Press, 2004).
45. Smith, 111–12, 118–20, 149–51.
46. Smith, 121–25, 129.
47. Smith, 143, 145–47.
48. Smith, 144.
49. See Rufus Burrow, *God and Human Responsibility: David Walker and Ethical Prophecy* (Macon, GA: Mercer University Press, 2003) for an assessment of Walker's antitypical relation to the eighth-century Hebrew prophets.

50. Smith, 183, 195–96, 201–2.
51. Smith, 208–12.
52. Smith, 223–24, 239.
53. Smith, 243.
54. Smith, 254.
55. Jones, 79–80.
56. Smith, 211–12.
57. Smith, 213.
58. Jones, 95–96.
59. Jones, 80.
60. Smith, 199.
61. Martin Luther King, Jr., *Stride toward Freedom* (New York: Harper and Row, 1958), 103.
62. King, 105.
63. King, 105.

Selected Bibliography

Agamben, Giorgio. *What Is An Apparatus? And Other Essays*. Stanford: Stanford University Press, 2009.

Anderson, Victor. *Beyond Ontological Blackness: An Essay on African American Religious and Cultural Criticism*. New York: Continuum, 1995.

Appiah, Kwame Anthony. *In My Father's House: Africa in the Philosophy of Culture*. New York: Oxford University Press, 1992.

Asante, Molefi Kete. *Afrocentricity: The Theory of Social Change*. Buffalo, NY: Amulefi, 1980.

———. *The Afrocentric Idea*. Philadelphia: Temple University Press, 1987.

———. *Afrocentricity*. Trenton, NJ: Africa World Press, 1988.

———. *Kemet, Afrocentricity, Knowledge*. Trenton, NJ: Africa World Press, 1990.

———. *The Painful Demise of Eurocentrism*. Trenton, NJ: Africa World Press, 2000.

Barth, Karl. "The Revelation of God as the Abolition of Religion," in *Church Dogmatics* Vol. 2. New York: T&T Clark Ltd., 1956.

Bell, Daniel. *The Cultural Contradictions of Capitalism*. New York: Basic Books, 1996.

Billingslea-Brown, Alma Jean. *Crossing Borders through Folklore: African American Women's Fiction and Art*. Columbia: University of Missouri Press, 1999.

Bracks, Lean'tin. *Writings of Black Women in the Diaspora*. New York: Garland Publishing, 1998.

Brandom, Robert B. *Making It Explicit: Reasoning, Representing and Discursive Commitment*. Cambridge, MA: Harvard University Press, 1994.

Brown-Guillory, Elizabeth, ed. *Middle Passages and the Healing Place of History: Migration and Identity in Black Women's Literature*. Columbus: Ohio State University Press, 2006.

Burrow, Rufus. *God and Human Responsibility: David Walker and Ethical Prophecy*. Macon, GA: Mercer University Press, 2003.

Butler, Jon. *Awash in a Sea of Faith: Christianizing the American People*. Cambridge, MA: Harvard University Press, 1992.

Carter, J. Kameron. *Race: A Theological Account*. New York: Oxford University Press, 2008.

Cone, James. *Black Theology and Black Power.* New York: The Seabury Press, 1969.

———. *God of the Oppressed.* New York: The Seabury Press, 1975.

———. *The Spirituals and the Blues: An Interpretation.* New York: Orbis Books, Maryknoll, 1991.

Cullen, Countee. *The Black Christ and Other Poems.* New York: Harper & Brothers, 1929.

DeLamotte, Eugenia C. *Places of Silence, Journeys of Freedom: The Fiction of Paule Marshall.* Philadelphia: University of Pennsylvania Press, 1998.

Denniston, Dorothy Hamer. *The Fiction of Paule Marshall: Reconstructions of History, Culture, and Gender.* Knoxville: University of Tennessee Press, 1995.

Derrida, Jacques. *Acts of Religion.* Ed. Gil Anidjar. New York: Routledge, 2002.

DuBois, W. E. B. *The Souls of Black Folk.* Ed. Henry Louis Gates, Jr. New York: W. W. Norton, 1999.

Eliade, Mircea. *The Sacred and the Profane: The Nature of Religion.* New York: Harcourt Brace, 1959.

Elias, Norbert. *The Civilizing Process: The Development of Manners.* New York: Urizen Books, 1977.

Equiano, Olaudah. *The Interesting Narrative of the Life of Olaudah Equiano, or Gustavus Vassa, the African. Written by Himself.* New York: Dover, 1999.

Erskine, Noel. *King among the Theologians.* Cleveland, OH: The Pilgrim Press, 1994.

Evans, James H. *We Have Been Believers: An African American Systematic Theology.* Minneapolis: Fortress Press, 1992.

Frazier, E. Franklin. *Black Bourgeoisie.* Detroit: Free Press, 1997.

———. *The Negro Church in America.* New York: Schocken Books, 1974.

Frey, Sylvia R., and Betty Wood. *Come Shouting to Zion: African American Protestantism in the American South and British Caribbean to 1830.* Chapel Hill: University of North Carolina Press, 1998.

Gates, Henry Louis. *The Signifying Monkey: A Theory of African-American Literary Criticism.* New York: Oxford University Press, 1989.

Genovese, Eugene. *Roll, Jordan, Roll: The World the Slaves Made.* New York: Vintage Books, 1976.

Gomez, Michael A. *Exchanging Our Country Marks: The Transformation of African Identities in the Colonial and Antebellum South.* Chapel Hill: University of North Carolina Press, 1998.

Gooding-Williams, Robert. *"Look, a Negro!": Philosophical Essays on Race, Culture and Politics.* New York: Routledge, 2006.

Gordon, Lewis, T. Denean Sharpley-Whiting, and Renée T. White Eds. *Fanon: A Critical Reader.* Oxford, UK: Blackwell, 1996

Hart, William David. *Black Religion: Malcolm X, Julius Lester, and Jan Willis.* New York: Palgrave Macmillan, 2008.

Hayden, Robert. *Collected Poems.* Ed. Frederick Glaysher. New York: Liveright, 1985.

Hendry, George S. "Review": *Dogmatics* by Hermann Diem. *Theology Today* 18, no. 2 (July 1961).

Herskovits, Melville. *The Myth of the Negro Past.* New York: Harper and Brothers, 1941.

Howe, Stephen. *Afrocentrism: Mythical Pasts and Imagined Homes.* New York: Verso, 1999.

Hyde, Lewis. *Trickster Makes This World: Mischief, Myth, and Art.* New York: Farrar, Strauss, and Giroux, 1998.

Jackson, Sherman A. *Islam and the Problem of Black Suffering.* New York: Oxford University Press, 2009.

James, George G. M. *Stolen Legacy.* San Francisco: Julian Richardson & Associates, 1976.

Jarrell, Randall. *Selected Poems: Including the Woman at the Washington Zoo.* New York: Atheneum, 1980.

Johnston, Ruby Funchess. *The Development of Negro Religion.* New York: The Philosophical Library, 1954.

Jones, Major. *Black Awareness: A Theology of Hope.* New York: Abington Press, 1971.

———. *The Color of God: The Concept of God in Afro-American Thought.* Macon, GA: Mercer University Press, 1987.

Jones, William R. *Is God a White Racist? A Preamble to Black Theology.* Boston: Beacon Press, 1973.

Jordan, Winthrop D. *White over Black: American Attitudes toward the Negro, 1550–1812.* Chapel Hill: University of North Carolina Press, 1995.

Kauppinen, Antti. "Reason, Recognition, and Internal Critique," *Inquiry* 45 (2002): 479–98.

Kerr, Fergus. *Theology after Wittgenstein.* New York: Basil Blackwell, 1986.

King, Jr., Martin Luther. *Stride toward Freedom.* New York: Harper and Row, 1958.

King, Richard. *Orientalism and Religion: Postcolonial Theory, India and 'The Mystic East.'* London: Routledge, 1999.

Kirtzman, Lawrence D., ed. *The Columbia History of Twentieth Century French Thought.* New York: Columbia University Press, 2006.

Klein, Terrance W. *How Things Are in the World: Metaphysics and Theology in Wittgenstein and Rahner.* Milwaukee, WI: Marquette University Press, 2000.

Lahtinen, Mikko. *Politics and Philosophy: Niccolò Machiavelli and Louis Althusser's Aleatory Materialism.* Trans. Gareth Griffiths and Kristina Kohli. Leiden, The Netherlands: Brill, 2009.

Lefkowitz, Mary R. *Not Out of Africa: How Afrocentrism Became an Excuse to Teach Myth as History.* New York: Basic Books, 1996.

Lester, Julius. *All is Well.* New York: William Morrow, 1976.

Lincoln, C. Eric. *The Black Church since Frazier.* New York: Schocken Books, 1974.

Lincoln, C. Eric, and Lawrence H. Mamiya. *The Black Church in the African American Experience.* Durham, NC: Duke University Press, 1990.

Lomax, John A., and Alan Lomax. *Folk Song USA*. New York: Duell, Sloan, and Pearce, 1947.

Long, Charles H. "Perspectives for a Study of Afro-American Religion in the United States." *History of Religions* 11, no. 1 (August 1971): 54–66.

———. *Significations: Signs, Symbols, and Images in the Interpretation of Religion*. Aurora, CO: The Davies Group Publishers, 1999.

———. "Mircea Eliade and the Imagination of Matter" in Studia Universitatis Babes Bolyai (Studia 1/2006).

Marshall, Paule. *Praisesong for the Widow*. New York: Penguin Books USA, 1983.

Matory, J. Lorand. *Black Atlantic Religion: Tradition, Transnationalism, and Materiarchy in the Afro-Brazilian Candomblé*. Princeton, NJ: Princeton University Press, 2005.

Mbiti, John S. *African Religions and Philosophy*. New York: Praeger Publishers, 1969.

McCutcheon, Russell T. *Manufacturing Religion: The Discourse on Sui Generis Religion and the Politics of Nostalgia*. New York: Oxford University Press, 2003.

McGrath, J. S. *Heidegger: A (Very) Critical Introduction*. Grand Rapids, MI: William B. Erdmans, 2008.

Morra, Joanne, and Marquard Smith, eds. *Visual Culture: Critical Concepts in Media and Culture Studies*. New York: Routledge, 2006.

Moses, Wilson J. *Afrotopia: The Roots of African American Popular History*. New York: Cambridge University Press, 1998.

Muhammad, Elijah. *Message to the Blackman in America*. Chicago: Muhammad Mosque of Islam, No. 2, 1965.

Muller, Gilbert H. *New Strangers in Paradise: The Immigrant Experience and Contemporary American Fiction*. Lexington: University of Kentucky Press, 1999.

Murphy, Joseph. *Santeria: African Spirits in America*. Boston: Beacon Press, 1993.

Murray, Albert. *The Omni-Americans: Some Alternatives to the Folklore of White Supremacy*. New York: Outerbridge & Dienstfrey, 1970.

Nielsen, Kai. "Wittgensteinian Fideism." *Philosophy* 42 (1967): 191–209.

Noel, James A. *Black Religion and the Imagination of Matter in the Atlantic World*. New York: Palgrave Macmillan, 2009.

Nordentoft, Kresten. *Kierkegaard's Psychology*. Pittsburgh: Duquesne University Press, 1972.

Painter, Nell Irvin. *Exodusters: Black Migration to Kansas after Reconstruction*. New York: W. W. Norton, 1992.

Paris, Peter. *The Spirituality of African Peoples*. Minneapolis: Fortress Press, 1995.

Pettis, Joyce. *Toward Wholeness in Paule Marshall's Fiction*. Charlottesville: University Press of Virginia, 1995.

Pinn, Anthony, ed. *By These Hands: A Documentary History of African Americanism*. New York: New York University Press, 2001.

———. *Why, Lord? Suffering and Evil in Black Theology.* New York: Continuum, 1995.

Quirk, Michael J. Review of *Theology and the Problem of Evil,* by Kenneth Surin. *Theology Today* 44, no. 3 (1987): 405–8.

Reid, Jennifer I. M., ed. *Religion and Global Culture: New Terrain in the Study of Religion and the Work of Charles H. Long.* Lanham, MD: Lexington Books, 2003.

Rigaud, Milo. *Secrets of Voodoo.* Trans. Robert B. Cross. San Francisco: City Lights Books, 1969.

Roberts, J. Deotis. *Black Theology Today: Liberation and Contextualization.* New York and Toronto: The Edwin Mellen Press, 1983.

Rose, Gillian. *Mourning Becomes the Law: Philosophy and Representation.* Cambridge: Cambridge University Press, 1996.

Said, Edward W. *Beginnings: Intention and Method.* New York: Columbia University Press, 1975.

———. "Michael Walzer's 'Exodus and Revolution': A Canaanite Reading." *Grand Street* 5, no. 2 (1986): 86–106.

Scarry, Elaine. *The Body in Pain: The Making and Unmaking of the World.* Oxford: Oxford University Press, 1985.

Scott, Daryl Michael. *Contempt and Pity: Social Policy and the Image of the Damaged Black Psyche, 1880–1996.* Chapel Hill: University of North Carolina Press, 1997.

Smith, Theophus H. *Conjuring Culture: Biblical Formations of Black America.* New York: Oxford University Press, 1994.

Sobel, Mechal. *Trabelin' On: The Slave Journey to an Afro-Baptist Faith.* Westport, CT: Greenwood Press, 1979.

Solomos, John, ed. *Theories of Race and Racism.* New York: Routledge, 2000.

Sontag, Susan. *Against Interpretation and Other Essays.* New York: Farrar, Strauss and Giroux, 1966.

Stannard, David E. *American Holocaust: The Conquest of the New World.* New York: Oxford University Press, 1993.

Steiner, George. *Grammars of Creation.* New Haven: Yale University Press, 2001.

Stuckey, Sterling. *Slave Culture: Nationalist Theory and the Foundation of Black America.* New York: Oxford University Press, 1987.

———. *Going Through the Storm: The Influence of African American Art in History.* New York: Oxford University Press, 1994.

Surin, Kenneth. *Theology and the Problem of Evil.* New York: Basil Blackwell, 1986.

———. *Freedom Not Yet: Liberation and the Next World Order.* Durham, NC: Duke University Press, 2009.

Thompson, Robert Farris. *Flash of the Spirit: African and Afro-American Philosophy.* New York: Vintage Books, 1984.

Thurman, Howard. *Deep River: Reflections on the Religious Insight of Certain of the Negro Spirituals.* Mills College, CA: The Eucalyptus Press, 1945.

Torgovnick, Marianna. *Gone Primitive: Savage Intellects, Modern Lives.* University of Chicago Press, 1991.

Turner, Victor. *The Ritual Process: Structure and Anti-Structure*. New York: Aldine De Gruyter, 1969.
Walker, Clarence E. *We Can't Go Home Again: An Argument about Afrocentrism*. New York: Oxford University Press, 2001.
Walker, David. *David Walker's Appeal (1829)*. Ed. Charles M. Wiltse. New York: Hill & Wang, 1965.
Wallace, Michele. *Dark Designs and Visual Culture*. Durham, NC: Duke University Press, 2004.
Weber, Max. *Economy and Society*. Ed. Claus Wittich and Guenther Roth. Berkeley: University of California Press, 1978.
———. *The Protestant Ethic and the Spirit of Capitalism*. Trans. Talcott Parsons. Mineola, NY: Dover Publications, 2003.
West, Cornel. *Prophesy Deliverance! An Afro-American Revolutionary Christianity*. Philadelphia: Westminster Press, 1982.
———. *Prophetic Fragments*. Grand Rapids, MI: William B. Erdmans, 1988.
———. *American Evasion of Philosophy: A Genealogy of American Pragmatism*. Madison: University of Wisconsin Press, 1989.
———. *The Cornel West Reader*. New York: Basic *Civitas* Books, 1999.
Democracy Matters: Winning the Fight Against Imperialism. New York: Penguin Press, 2004.
Whitehead, Alfred North. *Mathematics in the History of Thought*. http://www-history.mcs.st-and.ac.uk/history/Extras/Whitehead_maths_thought.html.
Wilentz, Gay. *Healing Narratives: Women Writers Curing Cultural Dis-ease*. New Brunswick, NJ: Rutgers University Press, 2000.
Williams, Chancellor. *The Destruction of Black Civilization: Great Issues of a Race from 4500 B.C. to 2000 A.D*. Chicago: Third World Press, 1974.
Wittgenstein, Ludwig. trans. G. E. M. Anscrombe. *Philosophical Investigations*. New York: Macmillan, 1989.
Wood, Mark David. *Cornel West and the Politics of Prophetic Pragmatism*. Champaign, IL: University of Illinois, 2000.
Wright, Melanie J. *Moses in America: The Cultural Uses of Biblical Narrative*. New York: Oxford University Press, 2003.
Yancy, George, ed. *African-American Cornel West: A Critical Reader*. Malden, MA: Blackwell, 2001.

Index